Supporting children's learning in the early years

Second edition

Supporting Children's Learning in the Early Years is aimed at early years practitioners who are developing their knowledge and understanding of professional practice through studying at undergraduate level. The book encourages readers to consider their professional development as reflective practitioners, building on and supporting the government agenda to provide quality provision for young children and their families.

Combining theory and practice, and bringing together current research and thinking in a broad range of areas, the book covers:

- Learning environments: young children as learners, assessment of learning, well-being and children's rights, diversity and inclusion.
- Learning and development: children's development including social and emotional development, literacy and mathematical development, the potential of ICT, fostering creativity, musical development and knowledge and understanding of the world.
- Reflective practice: the learning environment, safeguarding and wellbeing and the reflective practitioner.

Throughout, the contributions in this book encourage the reader to consider the diverse range of experiences which young children bring to early years and early primary settings and suggest ways in which they can be supported. The book will also be a valuable and unique resource for training providers of a range of courses at further and higher education level that prepare people to work with, and lead in, early years settings in the UK.

Linda Miller is Emeritus Professor of Early Years at The Open University.

Carrie Cable is a Senior Lecturer in Education at The Open University and Director of a DCSF funded research project into language learning in primary schools.

Gill Goodliff is a Senior Lecturer and Head of Awards for Early Years at The Open University.

This Reader, along with the companion volume *Working with Children in the Early Years*, 2nd edition (edited by Linda Miller, Carrie Cable and Gill Goodliff), forms part of the Open University course *The Early Years: Developing practice* (E100). This is a 60 point, level 1 course for anyone working with young children in public, private, voluntary and independent childcare and education settings.

Details of this and other Open University courses can be obtained from the Student Registration and Enquiry Service, The Open University, PO Box 197, Milton Keynes MK7 6BJ, United Kingdom: Telephone +44 (0) 845 300 6090, e-mail general-enquiries@open.ac.uk.

Alternatively, you may wish to visit the Open University website at http://www.open.ac.uk, where you can learn more about the wide range of courses and packs offered at all levels by The Open University.

Supporting children's learning in the early years

Second edition

Edited by Linda Miller, Carrie Cable and Gill Goodliff

The Open University

Routledge
Taylor & Francis Group
LONDON AND NEW YORK

First edition published 2004 by David Fulton Publishers

This edition published 2010
by Routledge
2 Park Square, Milton Park, Abingdon, Oxon OX14 4RN

Simultaneously published in the USA and Canada
by Routledge
270 Madison Ave, New York, NY 10016

Routledge is an imprint of the Taylor & Francis Group, an informa business

Published in association with The Open University, Walton Hall, Milton Keynes, MK7 6AA, United Kingdom.

Typeset in ITC Garamond by
RefineCatch Limited, Bungay, Suffolk
Printed and bound in Great Britain by
MPG Books in the UK

British Library Cataloguing in Publication Data
A catalogue record for this book is available from the British Library

Library of Congress Cataloging-in-Publication Data
Supporting children's learning in the early years / edited by Linda Miller, Carrie Cable and Gill Goodliff.—2nd ed.
　　p. cm.
　　1. Education, Preschool—Great Britain.　2. Preschool children—Services for—Great Britain.　I. Miller, Linda, 1946–　II. Cable, Carrie.　III. Goodliff, Gill.
　　LB1140.25.G7S87 2009
　　372.210941—dc22　　　　　　　　　　　　　　　　　　　　　　　　　　2009004255

ISBN 10: 0–415–49696–9 (hbk)
ISBN 10: 0–415–49697–7 (pbk)

ISBN 13: 978–0–415–49696–4 (hbk)
ISBN 13: 978–0–415–49697–1 (pbk)

Contents

Acknowledgements

We wish to thank those who have written chapters for this Reader of who have given permission for us to edit and reprint writing from other publications. Special thanks to Caroline Davies (Course Manager), Liz Santucci (Course Assistant) and Gill Gowans (Copublishing Executive) for their help in preparing the manuscript.

Grateful acknowledgement is made to the following sources for permission to reproduce material in this book:

Chapter 1: Anning, A. and Edwards, A. (2006) 'Young children as learners', *Promoting Children's Learning from Birth to Five: Developing the new early years professional* (2nd edn), ed. A. Anning and A. Edwards; Maidenhead: McGraw-Hill Open University Press. Copyright © 2006 A. Anning and A. Edwards, reprinted with the kind permission of Open University Press. All rights reserved. Edited for this edition.

Chapter 2: Landsdown, G. 'Promoting children's welfare by respecting their rights', updated version of Landsdown, G. and Lancaster, P. (2001) 'Promoting children's welfare by respecting their rights' *Contemporary Issues in Early Years: Working collaboratively with children* (3rd edn), ed. G. Pugh; London: Paul Chapman Publishers/ Sage Publications. Copyright © 2001 G. Landsdown and P. Lancaster, reprinted with the kind permission of Sage Publications.

Chapter 3: Siraj-Blatchford, I. and Clarke, P. (2000) 'Identity, self-esteem and learning', *Supporting Identity, Diversity and Language in the Early Years*; Maidenhead: McGraw-Hill Open University Press. Copyright © 2000 I. Siraj-Blatchford and P. Clarke, reprinted with the kind permission of Open University Press. All rights reserved.

Chapter 4: Paige-Smith, A. (2002) 'Parent partnership and inclusion in the early years', updated version of this chapter from *Exploring Early Years Education and Care*, ed. L. Miller, R. Drury and R. Campbell; London: David Fulton Publishers.

Chapter 5: Young, C. (2004) 'Living and learning', *Primary Teaching Assistants: Learners and learning*, ed. R. Hancock and J. Collins; London: David Fulton Publishers. Copyright © The Open University. Edited for this edition.

Chapter 6: Carr, M. (2001) 'A folk model of assessment – and an alternative', *Assessment in Early Childhood Settings Learning Stories*; London: Paul Chapman Publishers/Sage Publications. Copyright © 2001 M. Carr, reprinted with the kind permission of Sage Publications. Edited for this edition.

Chapter 7: Clark, A. (2004) 'Listening to children', *Supporting Children's Learning in the Early Years*, ed. L. Miller and J. Devereux; London: David Fulton Publishers. Copyright © The Open University.

Chapter 8: Devereux, J. 'Observing children', updated version of Devereux, J. (1996) 'What we see depends on what we look for: observation as a part of teaching and learning in the early years' *Education in Early Childhood: First things first*, ed. S. Robson and S. Smedley; London: David Fulton Publishers in association with The Roehampton Institute.

Chapter 9: Browne, N. (2008) 'Children's social and emotional development', *Developing Reflective Practice in the Early Years*, ed. A. Paige-Smith and A. Craft; Maidenhead: McGraw-Hill Open University Press. Copyright © 2008 A. Paige-Smith and A. Craft, reprinted with the kind permission of Open University Press. All rights reserved. Edited for this edition.

Chapter 10: Manning-Morton, J. and Thorp, M. (2003) 'Children from birth to three playing, growing, and learning through moving and doing', *Key Times for Play: The first three years*; Maidenhead: McGraw-Hill Open University Press. Copyright © 2003 J. Manning-Morton and M. Thorp, reprinted with the kind permission of Open University Press. All rights reserved. Edited for this edition.

Chapter 11: Campbell, R. 'Young children becoming literate', updated version of Campbell, R. (2002) 'Exploring key literacy learning: own name and alphabet', *Exploring Issues in Early Years Education and Care*, ed. L. Miller, R. Drury and R. Campbell; London: David Fulton Publishers.

Chapter 12: Feasey, R. and Still, M. (2006) 'Science and ICT', *ICT in the Early Years: Learning and teaching with information and communication technology*, ed. M. Hayes and D. Whitebread; Maidenhead: McGraw-Hill Open University Press. Copyright © 2006 R. Feasey and M. Still, reprinted with the kind permission of Open University Press. All rights reserved. Edited for this edition.

Chapter 13: Craft, A. and Jeffrey, B. (2004) 'Creative practice and practice which fosters creativity' updated version of this chapter from, *Supporting Children's Learning in the Early Years*, ed. L. Miller and J. Devereux; London: David Fulton Publishers. Copyright © The Open University.

Chapter 14: Whitehead, M. (1999) 'Great communicators', *Supporting Language and Literacy Development in the Early Years*; Maidenhead: Open University Press. Copyright © 1999 M. Whitehead, reprinted with the kind permission of Open University Press. All rights reserved. Edited for this edition.

Chapter 15: Pound, L. (2004) 'Born Mathematical?', updated version of this chapter from *Supporting Children's Learning in the Early Years*, ed. L. Miller and J. Devereux; London: David Fulton Publishers. Copyright © The Open University.

Chapter 16: Gifford, S. (2005) 'Problem solving', *Teaching Mathematics 3–5: Developing learning in the foundation stage*; Maidenhead: McGraw-Hill Open University Press. Copyright © 2005 S. Gifford, reprinted with the kind permission of Open University Press. All rights reserved.

Chapter 17: Devereux, J. and Bridges, A. (2004) 'Knowledge and understanding of the world developed through a garden project', updated version of this chapter from *Supporting Children's Learning in the Early Years*, ed. L. Miller and J. Devereux; London: David Fulton Publishers. Copyright © The Open University.

Chapter 18: Moss, P. (2008) 'The democratic and reflective professional: rethinking and reforming the early years workforce', *Professionalism in the Early Years*, ed. L. Miller and C. Cable; London: Hodder Arnold.

Chapter 19: Paige-Smith, A. and Craft, A. (2008) 'Reflection and developing a community of practice', *Developing Reflective Practice in Early Years*, ed. A. Paige-Smith and A. Craft; Maidenhead: McGraw-Hill Open University Press. Copyright © 2008 A. Paige-Smith and A. Craft, reprinted with the kind permission of Open University Press. All rights reserved. Edited for this edition.

Chapter 20: Elfer, P. (2006) 'Exploring children's expressions of attachment in nursery', *European Childhood Education Research Journal* 14(2): 81–96. Reprinted with the kind permission of Taylor and Francis. Edited for this edition.

Chapter 21: Dowling M. (2005) 'Emotional wellbeing', updated version of this chapter from *Young Children's Personal, Social and Emotional Development*; London: Paul Chapman Publishers/Sage Publications. Copyright © 2005 M. Dowling, reprinted with the kind permission of Sage Publications.

Chapter 22: Robson, S. (1996) 'The physical environment', updated version of this chapter from *Education in Early Childhood: First things first*, ed. S. Robson and S. Smedley; London: David Fulton Publishers.

Chapter 23: Lindon, J. (1999) 'The future of childhood', *'Coordinate': The Journal of the National Early Years Network*. Sept. 1999 Reprinted by kind permission of The National Early Years Network.

Chapter 24: Anning, A. and Edwards, A. (2006) 'Creating contexts for professional development', *Promoting Children's Learning from Birth to Five* (2nd edn); Maidenhead: McGraw-Hill Open University Press. Copyright © 2006 A. Anning and A. Edwards, reprinted with the kind permission of Open University Press. All rights reserved. Edited for this edition.

General introduction

Carrie Cable, Linda Miller and Gill Goodliff

> A critical difference between contemporary and traditional views of childhood is that the former recognises the differing contexts of children's lives, children's agency and the significance of children's involvement in co-constructing their own childhood through participation in family, community and culture.
>
> (Waller 2005: 95)

Views of children and childhood are changing as Waller notes above. This has implications for the ways in which practitioners interact with children, with one another and with parents and carers. The rights of children, as conceptualised in the UN Convention on the Rights of the Child (UNCRC), have had a major influence on the development of policy, research and practice in the UK and elsewhere in recent years. Seeing childhood as a series of stages to be passed through on the way to adulthood, a view that owes much to Piagetian theories of learning and development, dominated policy and practice in the last century and is still influential today. These views see learning and development as largely biologically determined and likely to follow a fairly predictable and measurable pattern. However, this perspective on learning and development does not sit well with a rights-based approach.

An alternative position, outlined by Waller, is underpinned by an understanding of children as 'beings' as well as 'becomings' (Uprichard 2008, cited in Woodhead 2008). The work of Vygotsky has been influential in shaping thinking and ideas around the significance of children's participation in decision making about their own lives and the ways in which adults work with children to support and extend their learning. This socio-cultural view of childhood draws attention to the importance of children's experiences and relationships and how they are enabled to interact with their environment and others; that is, how their social and cultural experiences support their learning. The articulation of these understandings is evident in the work of the nurseries in Reggio Emilia in Italy as Malaguzzi suggests:

> Our image of children no longer considers them as isolated and egocentric . . . does not belittle feelings or what is not logical . . . Instead our image of the child is rich in potential, strong, powerful, and competent and most of all connected to adults and other children.
>
> (Malaguzzi 1993: 10)

Many policy documents in the UK reflect both contemporary and traditional views of childhood. They also reflect dominant and country specific discourses and agendas which are influenced by political, economic and social priorities. The end of the last century saw an increasing emphasis on safeguarding the welfare of children and the need to protect them from harm and possible abuse. *Every Child Matters* (DfES 2003) and the associated legislation, frameworks and guidance documents were strongly influenced by the desire to safeguard children while meeting their 'needs' and improving outcomes for all. In Scotland, Wales and Northern Ireland there have been similar developments with each country identifying its own priorities. The concept of quality in terms of services, provision and practice has been a key driver behind much of the reform agenda with an increase in regulation and inspection designed to ensure that prescribed standards are being met and adhered to. The expansion in early years provision is also designed to meet government priorities in terms of reducing levels of child poverty and social inequalities while enabling women to return to the paid work-force in all UK countries. Strong arguments have also been made at individual and societal levels about the importance of investing in children's services as a means of investing in the future economic and social wellbeing of the country and the importance of providing sound foundations for children so that their chances in later schooling and life will be enhanced.

Practitioners in all early years settings, whether they are home based or working in nurseries, nursery schools, children's centres, schools, playgroups or extended day provision in both the maintained and private, voluntary and independent sectors, all need to be enabled to face the challenges of new and developing agendas. Many of the chapters in this book include a focus on children's learning and the importance of listening to children; some may challenge you to consider your own assumptions and beliefs. One of the key challenges is for you to critically examine new curriculum and policy initiatives, allowing time to consider what they mean for practice and for children's learning and wellbeing, rather than simply responding to and implementing requirements without question. As you explore the chapters in this book, questions you might like to consider include:

- What views of the child underpin policy and curriculum guidance?
- How do these accord with your own views, values and beliefs and those of colleagues you work with?
- What opportunities are there to draw on what children already know, understand and can do?
- How are you going to ensure parents and carers are involved in and enabled to contribute to their child's learning?
- How will you draw on children's views and perspectives and ensure their active participation?
- How do we ensure that children understand different perspectives and what it means to grow up in a diverse, multilingual society?
- What are the implications for the environment you provide for children's learning?
- What does this mean for your relationships with those you work with inside and outside your place of work?

Reading and studying are important features of on-going learning and further professional development. We hope that the chapters in this book will support you in reviewing and reflecting on your own learning and development and support you in developing a critical and questioning approach to policy and practice.

References

Department for Education and Skills (DfES) (2003) *Every Child Matters*. Nottingham, DfES.

Malaguzzi, L. (1993) 'History, ideas and basic philosophy', in C. Edwards, L. Gandini and G. Forman (eds) *The Hundred Languages of Children*. Norwood, NJ: Ablex.

Uprichard, E. (2008) 'Children as "Being and Becomings": Children, Childhood and Temporality', *Children & Society*, 22.

Waller, T. (2005) *An Introduction to Early Childhood: A multidisciplinary approach*. London: Paul Chapman.

Woodhead, M. (2008) 'Promoting young children's development: implications of the UN Convention on the Rights of the Child', in L. Miller and C. Cable. (eds) *Professionalism in the Early Years*, London: Hodder Education.

Part 1
Supporting learning

Linda Miller

Introduction

At the heart of all that practitioners in the early years do on a daily basis is children's development, learning and wellbeing. However, in order to successfully plan for children's learning, practitioners need to be prepared to reflect on why they do things and whether they are truly considering the needs, backgrounds and aspirations of all the children and parents with whom they work. The chapters in this part represent a holistic view of learning, teaching and assessment. Themes which run through the chapters include: developing an understanding of children's rights and promoting the welfare of children; the importance of developing practice underpinned by an understanding of diversity and equal opportunities; the significant part that listening to children and watching them engaged in experiences and activities plays in assessing and planning for their learning, and especially in supporting them in developing the disposition to learn; and the role of responsive relationships between children and adults and between practitioners and parents and carers in supporting learning.

Recent thinking about learning suggests that the 'what, who and how' of learning are crucially interlinked. In Chapter 1 Angela Anning and Anne Edwards explore the importance of relationships in enabling children to develop the disposition to learn. They set out four key features of a socio-cultural approach to understanding learning, illustrated by case studies, which exemplify these features and in which the role of responsive relationships between adults and children is seen as crucial to successful learning.

Promoting children's welfare and wellbeing is a fundamental aspect of early learning and is the responsibility of all those who work in the early years. In Chapter 2 Gerison Lansdown reviews the history, and considers the limitations, of an approach that has focused on the views of adults rather than children and the consequences of this for children. She argues that we need to reconsider our current understanding and how this relates to children's rights, how we enable children's voices to be heard and how we take these voices into account in decisions that affect them. In Chapter 3 Iram Siraj-Blatchford and Priscilla Clarke explore the complexities of identity formation, the factors that influence the way children see and feel about themselves and the implications for their learning and achievement. The authors explore differences in practice and provide useful suggestions as to how practitioners and settings may move forward in developing effective practice to promote children's self-esteem and wellbeing through an approach which foregrounds diversity, equality and learning.

Early years practitioners know the important role that parents and carers play in children's learning and development and how important it is to work in partnership Working closely with families of children with learning difficulties or disabilities is especially important but can be challenging for both practitioners and the families concerned. In Chapter 4 Alice Paige-Smith considers this experience from the perspective of parents and how the rights of parents to be fully involved in decisions relating to and provision for their children, are interpreted. Chapter 5 focuses on one particular parent, Claire Young, who has home-educated her three sons. In the chapter she draws on her diary entries over some eight years to reflect on what she and her three children have learned together. She provides important insights into the process of learning, and particularly the importance of tuning in to children's interests and motivation, which as a parent she is in a unique position to do.

In Chapter 6 Margaret Carr explores the transformation of her personal and professional thinking about models for assessment of children's development and learning. She discusses how she moved from a 'deficit' model to an alternative 'credit' model of assessment which values children's participation in the process and enhances their disposition to learn. Children's participation in their own learning is the focus of Chapter 7, where Alison Clark draws on a study which explored ways of listening to the views of young children. The Mosaic approach utilises a range of methods: observation, child-conferencing, cameras, tours and mapping to gain perspectives on children's daily lives in a setting. The author suggests that this approach can be used as a tool to help children reflect on their own lives and enable them to develop new skills and competencies and increase their ability to communicate with adults. She suggests it can also provide a context for communication between the adults involved in the children's lives. In the final chapter in this part of the book, Chapter 8, Jane Devereux provides a rationale for observing children and offers suggestions as to ways of observing that have direct implications for practice. She discusses how information gathered by watching children at play or involved in other activities, provides insight into their current interests and ways of learning, their next steps and also possible concerns.

Chapter 1

Young children as learners

Angela Anning and Anne Edwards

Recent thinking about learning suggests that the 'what, who and how' of learning are crucially interlinked. In this chapter Angela Anning and Anne Edwards set out four key features of a socio-cultural approach to understanding learning, illustrated by case studies which exemplify these features and in which the role of responsive relationships between adults and children is seen as crucial to successful learning.

The what, who and how of learning

Decisions about curricula for young children are often gambles. We simply can't predict exactly what knowledge and kinds of expertise will be needed 20 years from now. However, we can be pretty certain that the very young children of today need to become adults who are able to adapt to work practices that will change throughout their working lives and able to cope with the changing demands coming from families and communities. Those of us who are involved in the education of young children therefore need to focus on helping children to become resilient learners, to enjoy learning and to feel that they are people who are able to learn. This is no small challenge but it is a safe bet that investment in children's dispositions to learn will pay dividends.

This point is made clearly by Schweinhart and Weikart (1993: 4) when they discuss the lasting change that occurred as a result of High Scope interventions with disadvantaged children in the USA in the 1970s:

> The essential process connecting early childhood experience to patterns of improved success in school and community seemed to be the development of habits, traits and dispositions that allowed the child to interact positively with other people and with tasks. This process was based neither on permanently improved intellectual performance nor on academic knowledge.

Schweinhart and Weikart are pointing to dispositions. We can see dispositions as orientations towards the world around us. We therefore need to support children's orientations or dispositions so that they approach activities in ways that allow them to be open to the learning opportunities to be found in them. Schweinhart and Weikart's emphasis is on helping children to see themselves as people who can learn. Their focus is on creating learners. An emphasis on disposition was also central to New Zealand early years curriculum (MoE 1993) where they referred to dispositions as 'habits of mind' and 'patterns of learning' which provide the foundation for future independent learning.

We know that these habits of mind are shaped in young children's interactions with others and in the opportunities for being a learner that are available to them, particularly in their families and in early childhood settings. We can think about dispositions as learnt competences and within-person characteristics that orient behaviour. It seems that is the view taken by Schweinhart and Weikart. However, seeing disposition as only within the child does not explain how a child may be oriented to think and act as a competent mathematical thinker in one setting but not in another. Therefore it may help to think about dispositions as within person propensities which are brought into play when they are supported by the situation. These pathways, the opportunities for participation or action, and dispositions to engage may vary between settings.

One advantage of that view is that it allows us to see how important it is to strive for some alignment between the support children receive in early childhood education and the other settings in which they are able to learn. This is an argument for multi-professional collaboration and for strong reciprocal links between home and early education settings. These collaborations can help children to be seen as learners in all settings so that dispositions to engage are supported across settings.

Focusing on pathways of participation does not mean that we can overlook *what* is being learnt. Participation is not only about behaviour. It involves developing an increasingly rich set of concepts to be used when we try to make sense of the world, and it highlights children's use of the concepts that they encounter in these socially sustained pathways. Early educators therefore have a difficult task. They need to attend to *what* children are learning, how they become people *who* are learners and *how* children learn and *how* that learning is supported.

Traditionally, early education has been based on a developmental view of how children learn. Important as this is, recent thinking about learning suggests that the *what, who* and *hows* of learning are crucially interlinked. For example, a disposition to seek out the patterns in a striped shirt is nurtured by previous success as a mathematical thinker. This success is, in turn, connected to a developing capacity to deal with mathematical concepts and the ways that the setting is oriented to mathematical actions, through the resources available and the actions of adults and other learners.
[. . .]

A sociocultural view of learning: learning and context

There has been a lot written about sociocultural approaches to learning which focuses on participation as behaviour and underplays Vygotsky's original emphasis on learning as a change in how a child understands and acts. One of the major contributions of Vygotsky, the forefather of sociocultural approaches, was to help us see that how we think is revealed in how we use material and conceptual tools. He was interested in behaviour, but only to the extent that it revealed how we think so that he could then work on enhancing that thinking.

A quick example. If a 4-year-old is doing a jigsaw puzzle she may approach it randomly, or she may look at the picture on the box and start to sort pieces by colour, or she may identify the flat-sided pieces and start to build the frame. What she does reveals the concepts she is bringing into play as she completes the puzzle. She will, of course, have learnt those concepts while doing puzzles with others who know how to approach them and who shared that knowledge with her in their actions and language. She will have learnt a lot in those interactions. As well as how to set about doing a puzzle she will have learnt persistence, the care of resources, that puzzles are a worthwhile activity and that working with others involves sensitivity and turn-taking.

Because they are concerned, at least in part, with thinking and the use of knowledge, sociocultural approaches do have aspects in common with Piagetian ideas about learning. They acknowledge that learning occurs as a result of active involvement with the environment; and that children construct, that is build up, increasingly complex understandings over time. So it is likely that very young children will operate, at times, with misconceptions about the world. However, sociocultural approaches are more clearly rooted in analyses of culture and context. They tell us that children learn what is important in their culture through interactions in and with that culture. They focus on how language carries the meanings and values of a particular culture. Also they remind us how opportunities for learning can vary from setting to setting.

Let us, therefore, look at four of the key features of a sociocultural approach to understanding learning: [. . .]

1. the impact of cultural expectations (i.e. we learn to do what we think the context demands of us);
2. the relationship between our sense of who we are and what we do (i.e. between our identities, dispositions and our actions);
3. an understanding that learning occurs through interaction with others (i.e. through language and imitation);
4. an understanding that learning occurs through and in the use of resources that are valued in our cultures (i.e. through using resources in the same way as others do).

Cultural expectations

Sociocultural psychology tells us that learning is a process of being able to participate increasingly effectively in the world in which we find ourselves. At birth, that world is fairly straightforward, albeit heavily emotionally charged, consisting of the presence or absence of sources of food and comfort. It soon becomes more complicated so that, for example, young children learn that although rowdy behaviour might be fine in the garden it is not appropriate in the supermarket.

By the time children are ready to enter compulsory schooling it is usually expected that they know how to participate as pupils, rather than members of a family, when at school. There is also the expectation that they have begun to acquire particular ways of thinking, such as how to be someone who can solve a puzzle or handle a book. These expectations are, of course, more likely to be fulfilled by children from some backgrounds than from others, simply because different families will provide different pathways of participation with different resources and opportunities for sense-making, with the result that different cultural expectations will have started to shape children's thinking.

These are important ideas for early educators. They help us understand two important issues. First, children who arrive at early education settings from different cultural backgrounds are likely to bring different ways of making sense and engaging. It is therefore necessary to try to understand what these are and to value them as important and valued prior learning. Second, they remind practitioners of how complex, yet crucial, the learning environment is and how it is worth investing time in thinking about and constructing it. The environment is an intricate interaction of spaces, resources, values, patterns of expected behaviour and interactions. These are under the control of early educators and can be shaped and sustained by them.

In summary, sense-making and action are heavily dependent on what is possible and expected. Learners look for cues in contexts for guidance on how to interpret what is going on and how to respond to those interpretations. Educators who can move between thinking about learners and thinking about how their learning experiences are shaped have a powerful approach to pedagogy. They need, of course, to identify first the kinds of thinking they want to develop. Siraj-Blatchford and Sylva (2004) describe this kind of analyses done by practitioners as 'pedagogical framing'. That is 'the behind the scenes aspects of pedagogy which include planning, resources and establishment of routines'. They suggest the settings that are most effective at enhancing children's development offer both pedagogical framing and interactions oriented to developing children's thinking and learning.

The way that Alison shaped the construction area in her pre-school centre is a nice example of pedagogical framing.

Alison wanted to provide 3- and 4-year-old children with opportunities to think and act as young designers and mathematicians with construction materials. Having resourced the area with books about boats, small- and medium-size wooden blocks, yellow 'engineers' helmets, tape measures, paper and pencils, staff encouraged children to work in pairs to build boats. Once finished, the boats were measured and the measurements recorded by the children. The children were encouraged to operate as designers and mathematicians and to participate in a sequence of actions from planning to recording. The children tackled the activities in ways that reflected their own physical development and grasp of concepts and achieved a sense of success through completing the activities. They therefore left the construction area with memories of an experience in which thinking and acting as designers and mathematicians was associated with their own effectiveness.
[. . .]

Identities and dispositions

One way of looking at disposition so that we can become clearer about how adults can support children's dispositions to respond positively and appropriately, is to connect disposition to children's developing sense of who they are and what they can do. To make the connection we need to look briefly at the idea of 'personal identity' – that is, the *who* of learning. Rom Harré, for example, uses the words 'self' and 'identity' interchangeably and talks of both as organizing principles for action (Harré 1983).

Harré's definition helps us to see that our sense of who we are – which will include what we are capable of doing – guides our orientation to the world around us and ultimately how we participate in it. For example, if a child's identity includes a belief that she is good with numbers, she will find herself attracted to number activities. At a more detailed level, if that identity includes a capacity to see mathematics as sets of patterns then the child will seek out the patterns in the learning opportunities provided. In other words, she will have a disposition to engage with aspects of the mathematics available in the experience provided for her. [. . .]

Dispositions are rooted in our sense of our likely effectiveness. The challenge for educators is to assist the development of a sense of effectiveness through careful and sensitive support while children acquire the capabilities and understandings which will underpin their effectiveness. Here we connect the *how* and the *what* to the *who* of learning and need to examine the relationships that support early learning. Claxton and Carr (2004) offer some guidelines for thinking about how adults can enhance children's dispositions in early education settings. Reminding us that a disposition is not acquired, rather that we are disposed towards certain ways of acting, they look at how dispositions are supported by the environments created by practitioners. They suggest that adults should at the very least create environments that are 'affording' i.e. provide opportunities for children's active engagement. Better still is an 'inviting' environment which highlights clearly what is valued and gives some guidance to the child. Best of all is what they call a 'potentiating' context, which stretches and develops young children. They argue that potentiating environments involve frequent participation in shared activity.

Learning often occurs in interaction with others

The learning trajectory followed by most children from birth to 5 can be summarized as a gradual and parallel shift from interdependence to a capacity for independence and from a focus on personal sense-making to a focus on public meanings. Hence, the role of carers of young children is to support them as they acquire the capacity to participate in their social worlds.

Their responsibilities shift from the close and often symbiotic relationships of key caregivers with infants immediately after birth and through much of the first year of life, to supporting children as they begin to experience and act upon a world that is external to their relationship with their caregivers. Finally the role becomes one of assisting children to understand the external world in the way that it is understood by other members of society.

Let us look at these three stages in turn and consider their implications for supporting children as learners. Although we are presenting them as a set of stages we are not proposing a simple continuum. [. . .]

The intersubjective phase

Initially children experience the world, and participate in it, through their relationships with their main caregivers who bring them into involvement with some of the basic features of social life by highlighting particular behaviours. The most important of these behaviours is the turn-taking that underpins, for example, language development. Young babies are not, however, entirely passive participants in these relationships.

Colwyn Trevarthen's detailed analyses of videotaped interactions between mothers and babies in their first few months of life has drawn attention to the finely tuned patterns of interaction that occur. It has shown the extent to which these interactions can be mutual and not simply a matter of infants responding to their mothers. [. . .]

The close relationship between infant and caregiver which Trevarthen observed and which enables an infant to experience the world in the physical and emotional safety provided by the relationship is characterized by *intersubjectivity*. [. . .]

Intersubjectivity demands considerable attention to the emotional state of infants and a capacity to slow down and tune into young children's ways of experiencing the world so that children are brought into interaction with the world. One of the most important elements of intersubjective relationships is how they help infants to develop as members of society with their own intentions and capabilities. A key feature of the adult role in an intersubjective relationship, in the Western world, appears to be to act *as if* the infant has intentions and is able to make evaluations. We see this behaviour in the conversations that mothers have with infants about feeding – for example, 'You want your bottle now don't you, I can tell'. This *as if* behaviour appears to prepare children for their later intentional and purposeful interactions with the world.

What we know of intersubjectivity is reason enough for ensuring that key worker systems are safeguarded, particularly for infants. If education is to be a feature of provision from birth we need to attend carefully to the subtle and demanding nature of work with babies. [. . .]

Millie and Amy in their inner-city nursery worked cautiously and carefully in this area through the use of 'action songs'. They collected songs from the nursery workers and the parents involved in the nursery. They then produced a song book with, alongside each song, suggestions for ways of holding the babies and for actions associated with the lyrics. The songs were sung both at home and at the nursery. In both settings the infants were held in similar ways and were involved in consistent sets of patterns and responses with both sets of caregivers.

[. . .]

Learning to look outwards

Once infants have gained some sense of their own intentionality through knowing that adults will respond to them and they are familiar with turn-taking, they are ready to look beyond the familiar patterns of sense-making found in their intersubjective relationships. This is an important stage in the move towards being able to deal with the social world and the public meanings found in it.

The key concept here is a *joint involvement episode* (JIE) (Schaffer 1992). In a JIE an adult and a child pay joint attention to, and act together on, an object. An object may be a toy, part of the environment or a task such as making a 'pie'. As children get older the object may be a play on words or a joke. The important point is that JIEs direct children's attention to objects and events outside their relationships with their caregivers while giving them opportunities to act on these objects within the security and fund of expertise available in their caregiver relationships.

Schaffer therefore emphasizes that adults in JIEs should be sensitive to children's needs and abilities so that children are able to try out their ability to communicate with others while receiving the kind of support that assists them to develop as communicators. There is now considerable evidence to connect experience of JIEs with language development (Wells 1987). [. . .]

The Effective Provision of Pre-school Education (EPPE) study (Sylva *et al.* 2004) has more recently highlighted the importance of what they call 'sustained shared thinking' for children from 3 to 5. One element of the study examined in detail the practice of 28 practitioners from 12 pre-school settings identified as effective in relation to child development outcomes. They found that child-initiated interactions between children and adults, which were extended by adults who increased the challenge for the child and 'lifted the level of thinking', were more likely to be found in settings where children made the most developmental progress (Siraj-Blatchford and Sylva 2004). [. . .]

Working independently (with just a little help)

This phase marks a shift to children's independent action and use of public meanings when they communicate with others in the pre-school years. It is frequently the most difficult for adults to manage as it requires them to maintain sensitivity to children's need for support together with an ability to intervene without inhibiting children's sense-making in context. In the previous two stages, adults have provided a supporting structure for children's thinking and actions as part of their close relationships with children. Now the support has increasingly to occur outside relationships that have dependency at their core. We therefore need to look carefully at how adults provide support, or *scaffolding*, at this stage of children's development as learners.

Scaffolding has been defined as 'the contingent control of learning' by an adult with a child (Wood 1986). [. . .] Wood's definition is important because the word 'contingent' reminds us that scaffolding as a form of support needs to be sensitively responsive to (that is, contingent upon) the learner's need for assistance. The responsive nature of support is particularly relevant when working with very young learners who are gaining confidence as effective participants in the world and are developing dispositions to engage with the learning opportunities provided. [. . .]

Scaffolding learning is an interactive process and demands close observation and continuous assessment of children as they participate in the learning contexts provided for them. Scaffolding can be seen as a form of *guided participation*. Guided participation is not simply based on interactions between adults and children. Children's participation in an activity is also, in part, shaped by the resources available and the expectations for the use of the resources in a particular setting. [. . .]

Learning occurs through the manipulation of the tools of a culture

This feature of a sociocultural approach to understanding learners and learning provides a useful framework for looking at resource-based preschool provision. Cultural tools (Cole 1996; Wertsch 1991) include the meanings carried in the language we use – for example, referring to children as 'little' allows them to get away with breaking rules and is a reason for their being sent to bed before their older brothers and sisters.

Tools can be intellectual and include the way we think about activities – for example, the children in Alison's centre were encouraged to plan and evaluate. Also, cultural tools are the objects or artefacts with which we surround ourselves and with which we interact in culturally specific ways. For example, although pieces of wooden puzzles make good missiles, we offer them to children as puzzles and expect them to use them as such. Similarly, children are guided into participation in preschool settings by learning the accepted way of using familiar materials, such as sand or water, while they are there. A focus on how language and artefacts are used can help practitioners identify how they can promote learning.

[. . .]

In order for children to understand how material resources are used and learn the ways of thinking associated with them, they need to experience those resources in conversation with those who do have some understanding. So when first given a wooden puzzle children need to work on it with someone who will use it as a puzzle and not a missile store. While jointly assembling the puzzle, through trial and error or the sorting of pieces, children learn how members of their knowledge communities tackle such tasks. They learn not only the meanings of words 'here is another blue piece', but also how to approach the task by sorting, planning, testing and completing. They do this, as Bruner (1996: 57) suggests, through 'discourse, collaboration and negotiation', a set of ideas which is echoed in the Effective Provision of Pre-school Education (EPPE)'s 'sustained shared thinking' (Sylva, Melhuish *et al.* 2003).

The role of adults in guiding children into being competent users of the cultural tools of their society is therefore crucial (Edwards 2004). [. . .]

How children develop as thinkers

What goes on in children's minds is a fascinating field of study but we are probably still only at the 'best bet' stage of creating a complete framework for understanding children's thinking. We found that the insights into children as thinkers and learners offered by constructivism (a view that we construct our understandings of the world over time) and by sociocultural psychology (which focuses on how the cultural is incorporated into thinking and action), resonated with the experiences which were being recorded in the pre-school settings. We therefore worked selectively within these frameworks as we made sense of the children's experiences.

In this section we look at some of the features of the sense-making process. We focus on children as individual and as social thinkers.

Children as individual thinkers

The frameworks offered by Piaget for understanding how children process the information they glean from their experiences are 'best bets' and underpin most constructivist perspectives on children as learners (Wood 1988). The key words are *schema, assimilation, accommodation, equilibration* and *development*. These key concepts help us understand the processes of constructing understandings.

Schema are the mental structures into which we organize the knowledge we hold about the world. For example, 3-year-old Naomi playing in the water area might think that big things sink and small things float. She will have a sinking/floating schema, which although not in tune with expert knowledge, does work. The schema will change once she experiences enough counter evidence and needs another way of organizing that knowledge to make sense of the world. [. . .]

Assimilation occurs when we take in information which does not demand that we alter our existing schema. For example, if another large object sinks Naomi won't need to adjust her schema. Assimilation can also occur when we experience something that is so beyond our capacity to understand it that we cannot engage with its meaning and therefore there is no impact on our schema.

Young children frequently find themselves in situations where they simply don't have the knowledge that allows them to make sense of an object or experience. We see this when children make 'music' with a keyboard, or mark-make when recording orders in the 'cafe'. We also see it when they turn an object to their own purposes and hand out leaves as 'cakes'. Much of children's play is assimilation and it is through this kind of imaginative play that children become familiar with the rituals and objects that are part of their worlds. [. . .] Children need a great deal of assimilation-oriented play, as the familiarization with objects and how they might be acted upon is an essential part of sense-making.

Accommodation is what happens when we adjust our existing schema to take in new information. This is often simply a case of refining existing schema. For example, a child might eventually show by his language and behaviour that there is a schema that both he and adults call 'hat' and that his shorts do not now belong to it. Sometimes the adjustment is quite radical, demanding new schema, such as when Naomi recognizes that some large objects float and some small objects sink. A strictly Piagetian interpretation might argue that Naomi would manage the reorganization of her schema without adult help. A more educationally oriented interpretation, and one we would advocate, would suggest that the adults' role is to provide the language support that helps children to recognize and label their new understandings. [. . .]

Importantly, accommodation only occurs when the difference between existing schema and the new information is not too great. (Hence the importance of the opportunity for familiarization through imaginative play.) Problem-solving play is particularly valuable for encouraging accommodation of new information, as during this kind of play children are able to work using their existing schema on materials that have been selected to give them the opportunity to refine those schema. One should not, therefore, see assimilation and accommodation as distinct phases in a learning cycle that can be planned for. Rather they occur together when a child uses existing understandings and has to adjust them to be able to cope with new information. The sense-making process can, in this way, be seen as a search for a balance between what is understood and what is experienced.

Equilibration is the term used by Piaget to explain the constant adjustments made to schema by learners as they encounter events that disturb their current understandings and lead them to new explanations and a reorganization of the relevant schema. [. . .]

Learning and resilience

Learning is a process of increasingly informed participation in specific cultures and adults can do a great deal to promote children's learning through creating challenging environments and through sensitive attention to how children are interpreting and acting on their worlds. At the core of successful learning lie sound, responsive relationships between young children and adults.

[. . .]

References

Bruner, J.S. (1996) *The Culture of Education*. Cambridge, MA: Harvard University Press.

Claxton, G. and Carr, M. (2004) A framework for teaching learning: the dynamics of disposition, *Early Years*, 24 (1): 87–97.

Cole, M. (1996) *Cultural Psychology*. Cambridge, MA: Harvard University Press.

Edwards, A. (2004) Understanding context, understanding practice in early education, *European Early Childhood Education Research Journal*, 12 (1): 85–101.

Harré, R. (1983) *Personal Being*. Oxford: Blackwell.

MoE (Ministry of Education, New Zealand) (1993–96) *Te Whariki, He Whaariki Matauranga: Early Childhood Curriculum*. Wellington: New Zealand Learning Media.

Schaffer, H.R. (1992) Joint involvement episodes as contexts for cognitive development, in H. McGurk (ed.) *Childhood and Social Development: Contemporary Perspectives*. Hove: Lawrence Erlbaum.

Schweinhart, L. and Weikart, D. (1993) *A Summary of Significant Benefits: The High Scope Perry Pre-School Study Through Age 27*. Ypsilanti, MI: The High Scope Press.

Siraj-Blatchford, I. and Sylva, K. (2004) Researching pedagogy in English pre-schools, *British Educational Research Journal*, 30 (5): 713–30.

Sylva, K., Melhuish, E., Sammons, P., Siraj-Blatchford, I., Taggart, B. and Elliott, K. (2003) *The Effective Provision of Pre-school Education (EPPE) Project: Findings from the Pre-School Period. Research Brief No. RBX15–03*. London: Department of Education and Skills.

Sylva, K., Melhuish, E., Sammons, P., Siraj-Blatchford, I. and Taggart, B. (2004) *The Effective Provision of Pre-school Education (EPPE) Project: Final Report*. Nottingham: DfES Publications.

Trevarthen, C. (1993) The functions of emotions in early infant communication and development, in J. Nadel and L. Camaiori (eds) *New Perspectives on Early Communicative Development*. London: Routledge.

Wells, G. (1987) *The Meaning Makers: Children Learning Language and Using Language to Learn*. London: Heinemann Educational.

Wertsch, J. (1991) A sociocultural approach to socially shared cognition, in L. Resnick, J. Levine and S. Teasley (eds) *Perspectives on Socially Shared Cognition*. Washington: APA.

Wood, D. (1986) Aspects of teaching and learning, in M. Richards and P. Light (eds) *Children of Social Worlds*. Cambridge: Polity Press.

Wood, D. (1988) *How Children Think and Learn*. Oxford: Blackwell.

Chapter 2

Promoting children's welfare by respecting their rights

Gerison Lansdown

Promoting children's welfare is a fundamental aspect of the responsibilities of all those who work in the early years. In this chapter Gerison Lansdown reviews the history and limitations of an approach that has focused on the views of adults rather than children and the consequences for children. She argues that we need to reconsider our current understanding and how this relates to children's rights, how we enable children's voices to be heard and how we take these into account in decisions that affect them.

Children are defined as minors in law. They do not have autonomy, or the right to make choices or decisions on their own behalf. Instead, responsibility for decisions, which affect them, has traditionally been vested with those adults who care for them. It has always been presumed not only that adults are better placed than children, particularly when they are young, to exercise responsibility for decision-making, but also that in so doing, they will act in children's best interests. And this presumption has been established as a legal obligation on the courts, which are required to give paramountcy to the welfare of the child in making decisions concerning their day-to-day lives (DoH 1989, *The Children Act*, Section 1). This welfare model of adult/child relationships constructs the child as a passive recipient of adult protection and goodwill, lacking the competence to exercise responsibility for his or her own life.

In recent years, we have begun to question the adequacy of this approach and re-examine the assumptions on which it is based:

- that adults can be relied on to act in children's best interests;
- that children lack the competence to act as agents in their own lives;
- that adults have the monopoly of expertise in determining outcomes in children's lives.

The limitations of a welfare approach

Adults can abuse their power over children

Adults in positions of power over children can exploit and abuse that power to the detriment of children's wellbeing. The 1970s witnessed a growing awareness of the extent to which children are vulnerable to physical abuse within their own families. The extent and scale of violence perpetrated by parents on their own children emerged through the work of Henry Kempe in the US and was brought home forcefully in this country with the case of Maria Colwell, an eight-year-old girl who was returned from care to live with her parents who subsequently beat her to death (Howells 1974). No opportunity then existed for her views and concerns to be taken seriously by those responsible for the decision. During the 1980s, the phenomenon of sexual abuse within families, as a day-to-day reality for many thousands of children, hit the public consciousness in this country with the Cleveland scandal into sexual abuse of children (Butler-Sloss Inquiry 1988). There was, and probably still is, considerable resistance to the recognition that parents and other adult relatives could and do rape and assault their children. Particularly shocking has been the realisation that even babies and toddlers are not exempt from such abuse. It challenges the very notion of family life that we wish to believe exists for all children – the view that children are safest within their families. It also challenges the legitimacy of the powerful cultural desire for protecting the privacy of family life because it undermines the comfortable assumption that parents can always be relied on to promote the welfare of their children.

It took until the1990s to uncover the next scandal in the catalogue of failure on the part of responsible adults to protect and promote the welfare of children. In a series of public inquiries it became apparent, not only that children in public care in a number of local authorities had been subjected to systematic physical and sexual abuse by staff in children's homes, but that these practices had been surrounded by a culture of collusion, neglect, indifference and silence on the part of the officers and elected members within those authorities. It is now acknowledged that this experience of abuse was not simply the consequence of a few paedophiles entering the public care system (Utting 1997). Rather it is an endemic problem, affecting children in authorities across the country and symptomatic of a fundamental failure to provide effective protective care towards vulnerable children. One of the most forceful lessons to emerge from the series of public inquiries into abuse of children in public care has been the extent to which the children involved were denied any opportunity to challenge what was happening to them (Levy and Kahan 1991; Kirkwood 1993; Waterhouse 2000). They were systematically disbelieved in favour of adult accounts. They were denied access to any advocacy to help them articulate their concerns. Indeed, if and when they did complain they risked further abuse. In other words, the adults involved could, with impunity, behave in ways entirely contrary to the children's welfare.

We can, then, no longer disregard the fact that children can be and are both physically and sexually abused by the very adults who are responsible for their care, both within families and in state institutions. Accordingly, it becomes necessary to move beyond the assumption that simple reliance on adults to promote the wellbeing of children, because of their biological or professional relationship with the child, is an adequate approach to caring for children.

Adults do not always act in children's best interests

Actions detrimental to the wellbeing of children do not merely occur when adults deliberately abuse or neglect children. During the course of this century, adults with responsibility for children across the professional spectrum have been responsible for decisions, policies and actions that have been inappropriate, if not actively harmful to children, whilst claiming to be acting to promote their welfare. One does not have to look far for the evidence – the separation of young children from parents in the war evacuations, the exclusion of mothers from hospital when their small children were sick, in pain and frightened, the failure to recognise that babies experience pain and consequent denial of analgesics, the pressure on unmarried mothers to have their babies adopted with no possibility of future contact, the placement of children in care in large, unloving institutions which stigmatised them and denied them opportunities for emotional and psychological wellbeing. In all these examples, there is now public recognition that children were more harmed than helped by these practices.

And the existence of public policy, which serves to act against the best interests of children, is not simply a matter of history. We continue to place disabled children in special schools on grounds of the 'efficient use of resources', rather than the promotion of the child's best interests (DfEE, 1996, *Education Act*, Section 316). The UK stands out from almost all its European partners in both the age of criminal responsibility being as low as 10 years (8 in Scotland), and in the disproportionately high number of children in custody (Joint Committee on Human Rights, 2003). This, despite a considerable body of evidence as to both its ineffectiveness and the potential harm it causes to children. Children in the UK are tested in schools significantly more frequently than in most other OECD countries, with detrimental impact on levels of stress and anxiety, and little evidence of its efficacy (Tymms and Merrell 2007).

Parents' rights are protected over those of children

Public policy often supports the rights and interests of parents ahead of those of children, even when the consequences of so doing are detrimental to the welfare of children. In 2004, the government supported legislation which allows parents to justify common assault on their children as 'reasonable punishment'. It refused to acknowledge a campaign by an alliance of over 400 organisations, including all the major children's organisations, to allow Labour MPs a free vote on an alternative proposal removing the defence of reasonable punishment completely in order to give children the same protection as adults enjoy from being hit. This proposal would have satisfied the UK's human rights obligations, and complied with the findings of the UN Committee on the Rights of the Child in both 1995 and 2002 in which they expressed 'deep regret' that the UK 'persists in retaining the defense of "reasonable chastisement" and has taken no significant action towards prohibiting all corporal punishment of children in the family'. The Committee emphasised then that UK proposals to limit rather than remove the defence do not comply with the principles and provisions of the Convention, constitute a serious violation of the dignity of the child, and imply that some forms of corporal punishment are acceptable, thereby undermining educational measures to promote positive and non-violent parenting. It recommended a total prohibition on the use of corporal punishment. A similar recommendation has been made by the Committee on Economic, Social and Cultural Rights. Since then, in 2005, the European Committee of Social Rights has also told the UK that it is not in compliance with the European Social Charter because it has not prohibited all corporal punishment in the family. The Committee on the Rights of the Child, in September 2008, recommended yet again that a prohibition is introduced.

There is considerable evidence that physical punishment of children is not an effective form of discipline, that it can and does cause harm and that as a form of punishment it can and does escalate (Gerschoff 2002). And almost every professional body working with children is unanimous that we should change the law to protect children better and give parents a positive message that hitting children is both wrong and unnecessary (see Barnardos 1998). A consultation exercise conducted by Willow and Hyder with 70 children aged 5–7 provides graphic evidence of the humiliation, pain and rejection they experience when their parents hit them. When asked what they understood by a 'smack', they all described it as a hit. Comments such as 'it feels like someone banged you with a hammer', 'it's like breaking your bones', 'it's like you're bleeding' and 'it hurts, it's hard and it makes you sore' were amongst those used to describe how it felt. Their eloquent accounts contrast starkly with the widely promulgated view from parents that such punishment is delivered with love, does not cause real hurt and is only applied *in extremis* (Willow and Hyder 1998). The UN Study on Violence against Children provides a devastating critique on the prevalence, frequency and severity of violence faced by children throughout the world at the hands of the very people who are responsible for their protection (WHO/UNICEF/OHCHR 2005).

It can also be seen from the experience of the 23 countries that have introduced a total ban on corporal punishment in all settings, that it does not lead to a rise in prosecutions of parents, it does change parental behaviour in favour of more positive forms of discipline and it does not lead to worse behaved or ill-disciplined children (see Durrant 1999). Indeed, overall, it can be seen that it is not the welfare of children which informs the law and its proposed reform, but the need to assuage adult public opinion.

Children's interests are often disregarded in public policy

Children's interests are frequently disregarded in the public policy sphere in favour of more powerful interest groups. It is not necessarily the case that children's welfare is deliberately disregarded, but rather that children, and the impact of public policy on their lives, are not visible in decision-making forums and accordingly never reach the top of the political agenda. Just consider, for example, the impact of public policy on children during the 1980s and 1990s. In 1979, one in ten children were living in poverty. By 1991, the proportion had increased to one in three (DWP 1991). That alone is sufficient indictment of our neglect of children. But even more significantly, it is children who bore the disproportionate burden of the increase in poverty during that period. No other group in society experienced a growth in poverty on a comparable scale. And the consequences of that poverty on children's life chances are profound – it impacts on educational attainment, physical and mental health, emotional wellbeing, and employment opportunities. At a collective level, then, our society failed to promote and protect the welfare of children over two decades. Even now with a government commitment to ending child poverty, official figures show that 3.8 million children (33%) still live in poverty in the UK (DWP 2007).

There is little analysis of public expenditure to assess whether the proportion spent on children and their wellbeing reflects either their levels of need or their representation within the community. What little we do know indicates that the lack of data is likely to cover very significant inadequacies in spending on children, indicating their weak position in the lobbies that influence public agendas and expenditure. For example, we know that in the later 1990s, health authorities spent 5% of their mental health budgets on children and adolescent mental health services, even though that age group represents 25% of the population (Audit Commission 1999). Of course, it is likely that services for older people will necessitate a disproportionate claim on these budgets, but no systematic assessment has been made as to whether the current balance in any way reflects comparative levels of assessed needs. And as long as children lack powerful advocates in the field of health, such discrepancies will not be effectively challenged. In a completely different arena, but providing even more dramatic evidence of low priority given to children, a report by the National Playing Fields Association in 1993 estimated that the then Department of National Heritage spent 3p of its budget on children for every £100 spent on adults (NPFA 1993).

Similarly, in the field of housing, countless estates have been built in which the needs of children have been completely disregarded – no play spaces or facilities, dangerous balconies and lifts with controls out of the reach of small children (Freeman *et al*. 1999). And we have grown increasingly intolerant of children in the public arena. Far from developing towns and cities which are designed with children in mind, which are child-friendly as befits a society which has the welfare of children at its heart, we now tend to view children as undesirable in streets and shops, particularly when they are in groups. A new form of "dispersal" of teenagers is now being widely employed. The mosquito anti-social device "repels" them from public places by emitting a high-pitched noise only heard by the under-25s. The human rights organisation Liberty has found the device is being used in every region of England except the north-east. When asked about the effect of the ultrasonic device, the Home Office said the Health and Safety Executive had determined there to be no long-term risks and did not set out any government protective action. The mosquito device obviously affects babies and young children as well as young people. Children who do not talk may be distressed by the noise but be unable to move out of the zone because they are with an adult who cannot detect the noise.

In 2002, the UN Committee urged the government to review the "child safety" powers included in the Crime and Disorder Act 1998, including the use of curfews for vulnerable children. Although these powers were not, in fact used by local authorities, the government has since introduced wider powers that allow the police and local councils to designate an area a "dispersal zone" simply because any member of the public has been alarmed, harassed or distressed by a "group" of two or more people. It also gave the police a new blanket power to take home under-16s between the hours of 9pm and 6am.

Research by the Home office shows that 42 police forces designated 809 areas as dispersal zones in the 12 months to June 2005. In 18 police authority areas, an estimated 520 under-16s were escorted home from 236 areas. These powers are all testimony to a perception of children as threatening, hostile and outside the legitimate bounds of society. Too little attention has been paid to developments such as safe routes to school and home zones, which allow opportunities for younger children to play and move within their local communities. Public spaces are seen to be 'owned' by adults, with young people's presence in those spaces representing an unwanted intrusion. Yet these are the adults on whom children rely to promote their best interests. These are the adults who are responsible for protecting children's welfare.

Moving beyond a welfare perspective

Once it is acknowledged, not only that adults are capable of abuse of children, but also that children's welfare can be undermined by conflicting interests, neglect, indifference and even hostility on the part of adults, then it becomes clear that it is not sufficient to rely exclusively on adults to define children's needs and be responsible for meeting them. Indeed, the welfare model has failed children. Rather, there is a need to recognise children as subjects of rights, a concept that developed gradually during the course of the twentieth century, culminating in the adoption by the UN General Assembly in 1990 of the UN Convention on the Rights of the Child (UNCRC 1989). The Convention, which now has almost universal acceptance, having been ratified by every country in the world, except the US and Somalia, is a comprehensive human rights treaty, which encompasses social, economic, and cultural as well as civil and political rights. Acknowledgement of children as rights-bearers rather than merely recipients of adult protective care introduces a new dimension in adult relationships towards children. It does not negate the fact that children have needs but argues that, accordingly, children have rights to have those needs met.

Implications of respecting children's human rights

One of the underlying principles of the Convention is that the best interests of the child must be a primary consideration in all actions concerning the child (see UNCRC 1989, Article 3). But this principle does not merely take us back to a welfare approach. A commitment to respecting the human rights of children requires an acceptance that promoting children's welfare or best interests requires more than the goodwill or professional judgement of adults. It injects two fundamental challenges to traditional practices in respect of children.

First, the means by which the best interests of children are assessed must be the extent to which all their human rights are respected in any particular policy, action or legislation. In other words, the rights embodied in the Convention must provide a framework through which to analyse the extent to which proposals promote the best interests of children (see Hodgkin and Newell 2007). And this approach extends both to matters affecting the rights of an individual child and children as a body. For example, in providing child protection services, do interventions which seek to protect the child from abuse also respect the child's right to privacy, to respect for the child's views and evolving capacities, to continuity in family life, to contact with immediate and extended family? In a proposed local housing development, have the rights of children to adequate play facilities and to safe road crossings been fully considered? Likewise one can apply a comparable analysis to decisions taken within families. Many parents currently drive their children to school and justify so doing in terms of the potential dangers of both traffic and abduction or assault to which children might otherwise be exposed. A rights-based approach would necessitate a broader analysis of the rights of children. What impact does driving children to school have on their right to the best possible health, to freedom of association, to play, to growing respect for their emerging competence?

In all these examples, it can be argued that unless a comprehensive rights-based approach is taken, there is a risk that a decision or intervention is made which responds to one aspect of the child's life and in so doing fails to acknowledge other rights or needs. Indeed, it may inadvertently impact adversely on the child.

Secondly, if children are subjects of rights, then they themselves must have the opportunity to exercise those rights and be afforded means of seeking redress when rights are violated. In other words, they must have opportunities to be heard. Article 12 of the Convention (UNCRC 1989) embodies the principle that children have the right to express their views on matters of concern to them and to have those views taken seriously in accordance with their age and maturity. It is a procedural right, which has increasingly been recognised as necessary if children are to move beyond their traditional status as recipients of adult care and protection and become social actors entitled to influence decisions that affect their lives (see for example Lansdown 1996; Willow 1997). And it applies to all children capable of expressing their views however young. Children are entitled to be actively involved in those decisions that affect them as individuals – in the family, in schools, in public care, in the courts, and as a body in the development, delivery, monitoring and evaluation of public policy at both local and national levels.

The welfare model of childcare has perpetuated the view that children lack the capacity to contribute to their own wellbeing, and that their involvement may place them at risk, with adverse effects on family and school life. Yet failure to involve children in decisions that affect their own lives is the common thread, which underpins many of the mistakes and poor judgements exercised by adults when acting on children's behalf. Furthermore, the experience of child participation around the world provides a growing body of evidence not only that these concerns are unfounded, but that participation has a widespread positive impact. Indeed, the Committee on the Rights of the Child considers that recognising the right of the child to express views and to participate in various activities, according to her or his evolving capacities, is beneficial for the child, for the family, for the community, the school, the State and for democracy (Committee on the Rights of the Child 2006).

Participation contributes to personal development

The realisation of the right to be heard and have views given due weight serves to promote the capacities of children. Through participation, children acquire skills, build competencies, extend aspirations, and gain confidence. A virtuous circle is created. The more children participate, the more effective their contributions and the greater the impact on their development. Children acquire competence in direct relation to the scope available to them to exercise agency over their own lives. The most effective preparation for building self-confidence is to achieve a goal for oneself and not merely to observe someone else achieving that goal.

Participation leads to better decision-making and outcomes

Adults do not always have sufficient insight into children's lives to be able to make informed and effective decisions on the legislation, policies and programmes designed for children. Children have a unique body of knowledge about their lives, needs and concerns, together with ideas and views which derive from their direct experiences. This knowledge and experience spans both matters affecting them as individuals and matters of wider concern to children as a group. It needs to inform all decision-making processes affecting children's lives. Decisions which are fully informed by children's own perspectives will be more relevant, more effective and more sustainable.

Participation serves to protect children

The right to express views and have them taken seriously is a powerful tool through which to challenge situations of violence, abuse, threat, injustice or discrimination. Children have, traditionally, been denied both the knowledge that they are entitled to protection from violence, and the mechanisms through which to challenge it. The consequent silencing of children and the abuse they experience has had the impact of protecting abusers rather than children. However, if they are encouraged to voice what is happening to them, and provided with the necessary mechanisms through which they can raise concerns, violations of rights are far more easily exposed. The self-esteem and confidence acquired through participation also empowers children to challenge abuses of their rights. Furthermore, adults can only act to protect children if they are informed about what is happening in children's lives – and often, it is only children who can provide that information. Violence against children in families, schools, prisons, and institutions, or exploitative child labour can only be tackled effectively if children themselves are enabled to tell their stories to those people with the authority to take appropriate action.

Participation promotes civic engagement, democracy, tolerance and respect for others

Respecting children and providing them with opportunities to participate in matters of concern to them is one of the most effective ways of encouraging them to believe in themselves, to gain confidence, and to learn how to negotiate decision-making with other people. Children's involvement in groups, clubs, committees, NGOs, boards, unions and other forms of organisation offers opportunities for strengthening civil society, learning how to contribute towards community development, and recognising that it is possible to make a positive difference. Participation also offers opportunities for children from diverse backgrounds to build a sense of belonging, solidarity, justice, responsibility, caring and sensitivity. Democracy requires a citizenry with the understanding, skills, and commitment to building and supporting its institutions. It is through participation that children can develop those capacities – starting with negotiations over decision-making within the family, through to resolving conflicts in school, and contributing to policy developments at the local or national level. Such engagement provides children with a sense of citizenship, and enables them to develop understanding of the consequences of their actions, their responsibilities to others, and their capacity to make a difference. One of the most effective routes to becoming a responsible adult is to be granted respect as a child and to learn that one's opinions and feelings are taken seriously and have value. Supporting a child's right to be heard in the early years is integral to nurturing citizenship over the long term. In this way, the values of democracy are embedded in the child's approach to life – a far more effective grounding for democracy than a sudden transfer of power at the age of 18 years.

The Rights Respecting Schools programme

UNICEF-UK's Rights Respecting Schools programme teaches about children's and human rights but most importantly, supports schools to model rights and respect in all its relationships: teacher/adults–pupils; pupils–teacher/adults; pupils–pupils. In an independent evaluation comparing schools in which the Rights Respecting School (RRR) approach was fully incorporated with those in which it was less fully incorporated, the following outcomes were found (Covell and Howe 2008). Among pupils of all age groups were improvements in social relationships, behaviour, and achievement. Pupils:

- were more respectful and helpful to others, and less aggressive and disruptive;
- showed greater respect for the school environment;
- were more careful with books, desks, and school equipment;
- participated more in the classroom and in extra-curricular activities such as clubs and school councils;
- showed enhanced academic engagement and achievement (this was reflected in improved critical thinking skills, confidence in tackling new tasks, and increased test scores);
- demonstrated increased self-regulatory capacity, accepting the responsibilities they have learned are the concomitants of their rights.

In addition:

- Teachers reported an overall positive effect of RRR on their teaching and relationships within the school.
- Teachers in the fully implemented schools reported fewer feelings of exhaustion as a direct result of their work, felt more energised when dealing with students, experienced less frustration with teaching, and reported an increase in a sense of personal achievement.

Implementation was most sustained and progressive where head teachers were fully supportive of RRR, were strategic in its implementation, and were able to use RRR as an overarching integrative framework into which all other initiatives were fit. Some head teachers reported a number of challenges to implementation, including pressures to improve pupil achievement, reluctance from individual teachers to adopt the RRR, and initiative overload. However, the data from those schools in which RRR has become fully embedded indicate that over time, the implementation of the RRR becomes self-perpetuating through its positive outcomes on pupils and teachers.

Conclusion

There is a continuing resistance to the concept of rights in this country, particularly when applied to children. It is a resistance shared by many parents, politicians, policy makers and the media. It derives, at least in part, from a fear that children represent a threat to stability and order if not kept under control. Further, it reflects the strong cultural tradition that children are 'owned' by their parents and the state should play as minimal a role as possible in their care. Attempts by the state to act to protect children are viewed with suspicion and hostility. But promoting the rights of children is not about giving a licence to children to take complete control of their lives irrespective of their levels of competence. It is not about allowing children to ride roughshod over the rights of others, any more than adult rights permit such abuses. It is, rather, about moving away from the discredited assumption that adults alone can determine what happens in children's lives without regard for children's own views, experiences and aspirations. It means accepting that children, even very small children, are entitled to be listened to and taken seriously. It means acknowledging that as children grow older they can take greater responsibility for exercising their own rights. It involves recognising that the state has explicit obligations towards children, for which it should be held accountable. A commitment to respecting children's rights does not mean abandoning their welfare. It means promoting their welfare by adherence to the human rights standards defined by international law.

References

Audit Commission (1999) *Children in Mind*. London: Audit Commission.

Barnardos (1998) *Children are Unbeatable*. London: Barnardos.

Butler-Sloss, E. (1988) Report of Inquiry into Child Abuse in Cleveland 1987. London: HMSO.

Committee on the Rights of the Child, Forty-third session, 11–29 September 2006, Geneva.

Covell, K. and Howe, R. B. (2008) *Rights, Respect and Responsibility, Report on the Hampshire County Initiative, September 2007*. Cape Breton University, Children's Rights Centre, available from http://discovery.cbu.ca/psych/index.php?/children/journal_list/

Department for Education and Employment (DfEE) (1996) *Education Act*. London: DfEE publications.

Department of Health (DoH) (1989) *The Children Act*. London: HMSO.

Department for Work and Pensions (DWP) (1991) *Households Below Average Income An analysis of the income distribution 1979–1990/91*.

Department for Work and Pensions (DWP) (2007) *Nineteenth report of the HBAI, Households Below Average Income: An analysis of the income distribution 1994/5–2005/6*. London: HMSO Available from www.dwp.gov.uk/asd/hbai.asp

Durrant, J. E. (1999) 'Evaluating the success of Sweden's corporal punishment ban', *Child Abuse – Neglect*, Vol. 23, No. 5, pp. 435–448.

Freeman, C., Henderson, P. and Kettle, J. (1999) *Planning with Children for Better Communities*. Bristol: The Policy Press.

Gerschoff, E. T. (2002) 'Corporal Punishment by Parents and Associated Child Behaviors and Experiences: A Meta-Analytic and Theoretical Review', *Columbia University, Psychological Bulletin by the American Psychological Association*, Vol. 128, No. 4, pp 539–579.

Hodgkin, R. and Newell, P. (2007) *Implementation Handbook on the Convention on the Rights of the Child*. New York: UNICEF.

Howells, J. H. (1974) *Remember Maria*. London: Butterworths.

Joint Committee on Human Rights (2003) *Points and Recommendations Relating to Youth Justice*. London: HMSO.

Kirkwood, A. (1993) *The Leicestershire Inquiry*, Leicester: Leicestershire County Council.

Lansdown, G. (1996) *Taking Part*. London: Institute for Public Policy Research.

Levy, A. and Kahan, B. (1991) *The Pindown Experience and the Protection of Children: The Report of the Staffordshire Child Care Inquiry*, Stafford: Staffordshire County Council.

Report of the National Playing Fields Association (NPFA) (1993). London: National Playing Fields Association.

Tymms, P. and Merrell, C. (2007) *Standards and Quality in English Primary Schools over Time: The National Evidence*. Cambridge: Primary Review, University of Cambridge.

UNCRC (1989) *United Nations Convention on the Rights of the Child*. Geneva: Office of the United Nations High Commissioner for Human Rights.

Utting, W. (1997) *People Like Us : The Report of the Review of the Safeguards for Children Living Away from Home*. London: The Stationery Office.

Waterhouse, R. (2000) *Lost in Care: Report of the Tribunal of Inquiry into the abuse of children in care in the former county council areas of Gwynedd and Clwyd since 1974*. London: The Stationery Office.

WHO/UNICEF/OHCHR (2005) *World Report on Violence against Children*. New York: WHO/UNICEF/OHCHR.

Willow, C. (1997) *Hear! Hear! Promoting Children and Young People's Democratic Participation*. London: Local Government Information Unit.

Willow, C. and Hyder, T. (1998) *It Hurts You Inside*. London: Save the Children/National Children's Bureau.

Chapter 3

Identity, self-esteem and learning

Iram Siraj-Blatchford and Priscilla Clarke

In this chapter Iram Siraj-Blatchford and Priscilla Clarke explore the complexities of identity formation, the factors that influence the way children see and feel about themselves and the implications for their learning and achievement. They explore differences in practice and provide useful suggestions as to how practitioners and settings may move forward in developing effective practice to promote children's self-esteem and wellbeing through an approach which foregrounds diversity, equality and learning.

In all of our modern multicultural societies, it is essential that children learn to respect other groups and individuals, regardless of difference. This learning must begin in the very earliest years of a child's education. In this chapter we identify the groups that are often disadvantaged owing to the poor understanding many early years staff have of them. We argue that there is a need to challenge the hidden oppression that is often imposed upon particular individuals and groups. While most early childhood settings appear to be calm and friendly places on the surface, we argue that there may be a great deal of underlying inequality. This may occur through differential policies, interactions, displays, or through variations in the curriculum or programme that the staff offer to some individuals or groups. These are important issues to be considered because they concern the early socialisation of all of our children. In the early years children are very vulnerable and every adult, and other children as well, has the power to affect each child's behaviour actions, intentions and beliefs.

Children can be disadvantaged on the grounds of diversity in ethnic background, language, gender and socio-economic class in both intentional and in unintentional ways. The structures through which inequity can be perpetuated or measured are related to societal aspects such as employment, housing or education. For instance, we know that women earn less than men, as a group, and that working-class people live in poorer homes. We are concerned with the structural inequalities that create and support an over-representation of some groups in disadvantaged conditions. However, we do caution against the assumption that all members of a structurally oppressed group, for example, *all girls*, are necessarily oppressed by those members of a structurally dominant group, for example, all boys. Because of the interplay between social class, gender, ethnicity and disability, identities are multifaceted. We therefore argue that children can hold contradictory individual positions with respect to the structural position that their 'group' holds in society. Interactional contexts are also often highly significant.

We will end the chapter by identifying the salient features of effective and ineffective practice in challenging oppression and in promoting respect for children, for parents and for staff in early child care and education settings (Siraj-Blatchford 1996).

The complexity of identity

A number of authors have written about the origins of inequality, about the implications for practice, and the need for a truly inclusive pedagogy and curriculum in the early years (see Davies 1989; Lloyd and Duveen 1992; Siraj-Blatchford 1992, 1994; Clarke 1993; Siraj-Blatchford and Siraj-Blatchford 1995). We argue here that children can only learn to be tolerant, challenge unfair generalisations and learn inclusiveness and positive regard for diversity if they see the adults around them doing the same. Children will often imitate adult behaviour whether it is positive or negative, but they need to learn to discuss what they already know, just as we do (Brown 1998).

The way children feel about themselves is not innate or inherited, it is learned. A number of researchers (Lawrence 1988; Siraj-Blatchford 1994) have shown that positive self-esteem depends upon whether children feel that others accept them and see them as competent and worthwhile. Researchers have also shown the connection between academic achievement and self-esteem. Purkey (1970) correlates high self-esteem with high academic performance. Positive action to promote self-esteem should form an integral part of work with children and ought to be incorporated into the everyday curriculum. Roberts (1998) argues that the process by which all children develop their self-esteem and identity rests heavily upon the type of interactions and relationships people form with young children.

Identity formation is a complex process that is never completed. The effects of gender, class and other formative categories overlap, in often very complicated ways, to shape an individual's identity. While we do not attempt to discuss this complexity in detail, it is important for practitioners to be aware of the nature of shifting and changing identities. No group of children or any individual should be essentialised (in other words, defined and bound within this definition as if it were impossible for any individual to escape this) and treated as having a homogeneous experience with others of their 'type'.

It is important to highlight the complexity of identity formation in children. To ignore it is to ignore the child's individuality. It illustrates why each minority ethnic child and every girl or child with disabilities does not perceive themselves in the same way. In fact, children from structurally disadvantaged groups often hold contradictory positions, which is why we might find in our classrooms black and other minority ethnic children who are very confident and academically successful in spite of the structural, cultural and interpersonal racism in society. Similarly, we will find working-class boys who do not conform to a stereotype and are caring and unaggressive and African-Caribbean boys who are capable and well behaved. We should not be surprised at any of this (Siraj-Blatchford 1996).

The sexism, racism and other inequalities in our society can explain why at a structural level certain groups of people have less power while others have more. But at the level of interaction and agency we should be critically aware of the danger of stereotyping and should focus on individual people. This is not to suggest that we should ignore structure, far from it, we need to engage in developing the awareness of children and staff through policies and practices that explain and counter group inequalities. We will turn to the point of practice later. What we are suggesting is that educators need to work from a number of standpoints to fully empower the children in their care. Children need to be educated to deal confidently and fairly with each other and with others in an unjust society (Siraj-Blatchford 1992, 1994, 1996).

Recent research has focused on the under-sevens. Many educators have begun to ask how it is that young children who are in our care learn about and experience class bias, sexism and racism. We know that children pick up stereotypical knowledge and understanding from their environment and try to make their own meanings from this experience. Outside experiences can come from parental views, media images and the child's own perceptions of the way people in their own image are seen and treated. In the absence of strong and positive role models children may be left with a negative or a positive perception of people like themselves.

Many parents and staff conclude from children's behaviour that they are naturally different, without considering their own contribution to the children's socialisation. Difference, therefore, is also a matter of social learning, as well as physiology. This has implications for practice and the kinds of activities to which we should make sure all children have access, regardless of their gendered or other previous experiences.

Identity and achievement

Cultural identity should be seen as a significant area of concern for curriculum development (Siraj-Blatchford 1996). All children and adults identify with classed, gendered and racialised groups (as well as other groups), but what is especially significant is that some cultural identities are seen as less 'academic' than others (often by the staff and children). We know that children can hold views about their 'masterful' or 'helpless' attributes as learners (Dweck and Legett 1988). Dweck and Leggett (1988) therefore emphasise the importance of developing 'mastery' learning dispositions in children. There is evidence that children who experience education through taking some responsibility for their actions and learning become more effective learners. They are learning not only the content of the curriculum but the processes by which learning takes place (Siraj Blatchford 1998). Roberts (1998) argues that the important area of personal and social education should be treated as a curriculum area worthy of separate activities, planning and assessment.

The 'helpless' views' adopted by some children can be related to particular areas of learning and can lead to underachievement in a particular area of the curriculum. Children construct their identities in association with their perceived cultural heritage (Siraj-Blatchford 1996). Recently we have heard a good deal in the British press about (working-class) boys' underachievement. The results from the school league tables suggest that some boys do underachieve in terms of basic literacy, but it is important to note that this is only certain groups of boys and not all boys. In the UK working-class white boys and African-Caribbean boys are particularly vulnerable. Similarly, children from some minority ethnic groups perform poorly in significant areas of the curriculum while other minority ethnic groups achieve particularly highly (Gillborn and Gipps 1997).

It is apparent that certain confounding identities, for instance, white/working-class/male, can lead to lower outcomes because of expectations held by the children and adults. In asserting their masculinity, white working-class boys might choose gross-motor construction activities over reading or pre-reading activities. Similarly, some girls may identify more strongly with home-corner play and favour nurturing activities over construction choices. Class, gender and ethnicity are all complicit here and the permutations are not simple, but they do exist and do lead to underachievement. The answer is to avoid essentialising children's identities, but it also requires educators to take an active role in planning for, supporting and developing individual children's identities as masterful learners of a broad and balanced curriculum (Siraj-Blatchford 1998).

Diversity, equality and learning

Four main conditions need to be satisfied for learning to take place; we want to argue here that we need an understanding of the first two to lay the foundations for learning:

- the child needs to be in a state of emotional wellbeing and secure;
- the child needs a positive self-identity and self-esteem;
- the curriculum must be social/interactional and instructive;
- the child needs to be cognitively engaged.

It is widely recognised that an integrated, holistic and developmental approach is needed to learning, teaching and care with children from birth to 7. Many adults believe children remain innocent, but even the very youngest children are constantly learning from what and who is around them. They learn not only from what we intend to teach but from all of their experiences. For example, if girls and boys or children from traveller families are treated differently or in a particular manner from other people then children will learn about the difference as part of their world-view. To deny this effect is to deny that children are influenced by their socialisation. The need for emotional, social, physical, moral, aesthetic and mental wellbeing all go hand in hand.

The early years curriculum should therefore incorporate work on children's awareness of similarities and differences, and to help them to see this as 'normal'. For instance, research evidence produced by David Milner (1983) has shown that children have learned positive and negative feelings about racial groups from an early age. Milner suggests that children as young as three demonstrate an awareness of a racial hierarchy in line with current adult prejudices (1983: 122) Some children can be limited in their development by their view that there are people around them who do not value them because of who they are. This would suggest that early years staff need to offer *all* children guidance and support in developing positive attitudes towards all people.

A focus on similarities is as important as dealing with human differences (see Siraj-Blatchford and Macleod-Brudenell 1999). The early years is an appropriate time to develop this work with young children.

How do young children who are in our care experience and learn about social class or linguistic prejudice, sexism or racism? How does this affect their learning more generally? These are questions that staff need to address. We know that children adopt biased (both good and bad) knowledge and understanding from their environment. This can be from parental views, media images, and the child's own perceptions of the way people are seen and treated. The most common form of prejudice young children experience is through name-calling or through negative references by other children (or adults) to their gender, dress, appearance, skin colour, language or culture. Educators may hear some of these remarks and it is vital that these are dealt with appropriately as they arise. The following childlike remarks have deep consequences for the children who utter them, and for those receiving them:

'You're brown so you're dirty.'
'Girls can't play football.'
'Don't be a sissy.'
'Boys can't skip.'
'She's got dirty clothes.'

Early years educators are often worried about their lack of experience and their lack of knowledge and understanding in dealing with these matters. They often display a profound sense of inadequacy when faced with prejudice from children. They may also doubt whether name-calling is wrong and they might even see it as 'natural behaviour' (Siraj-Blatchford 1994).

Students, teachers, childminders and playgroup workers have often asked how they can deal with class, gender and ethnic prejudice. The first step is to recognise that the problem exists. As Davey (1983) has argued, we have to accept that a system of racial categorisation and classification exists and that, until it is finally rejected by everyone, it will continue to provide an irresistible tool by which children can simplify and make meaning of their social world. It would be a great mistake to assume that this is only a 'problem' in largely multi-ethnic settings. Strategies which allow children to discuss, understand and deal with oppressive behaviour aimed at particular groups such as minority ethnic children, girls, the disabled and younger children are essential in all settings. We suggest that educators should always make opportunities for stressing similarities as well as differences.

Promoting positive self-esteem

Early childhood educators have an instrumental role to play in this development. Staff need to help children learn to guide their own behaviour in a way that shows respect and caring for themselves, other children and adults, and their immediate and the outside environment. Values education goes hand-in-hand with good behaviour management practices. The way that adults and children relate to each other in any setting is an indication of the ethos of that setting. To create a positive ethos for equity practices, staff in every setting will need to explore what the ethos in their setting feels like to the users, such as parents, children and staff. Staff need to explore what behaviours, procedures and structures create the ethos, what aspects of the existing provision are positive and which are negative, and who is responsible for change.

Children need help from the adults around them in learning how to care for each other and to share things. To help the children in this respect, the educator must have the trust of the children and their parents: Young children's capacity to reflect and see things from another person's point of view is not fully developed. Most small children find it difficult to see another person's view as equally important. Children need a lot of adult guidance to appreciate the views and feelings of others. This can be learnt from a very early age. In her research on the relationship between mothers and their babies, and relationships between very young siblings, Judy Dunn (1987) suggests that mothers who talk to their children about 'feeling states' have children who themselves 'become particularly articulate about and interested in feeling states' (1987: 38). Consideration for others has to be learnt.

We believe that children need educators who will consciously:

- encourage positive interactions;
- encourage discussion about how they and others feel;
- encourage attention to other points of view;
- encourage communication with others;
- try to ensure that they learn constructive ways to resolve differences;
- promote co-operation, not competition.

(Adapted from Stonehouse 1991: 78)

Of course educators cannot expect children to behave in this way if they do not practise the same behaviour themselves. If children see us showing kindness, patience, love, empathy, respect and care for others, they are more likely to want to emulate such behaviour. For many educators the experience of working actively with children in this way may be underdeveloped, especially when it comes to dealing with incidents of sexism or racism. Each setting, as part of their equity policy, will need to discuss the issue of harassment and devise procedures for dealing with it. According to Siraj-Blatchford (1994) staff can take some of the following actions in dealing with incidents of name-calling:

Short-term action

- If you hear sexist, racist or other remarks against other people because of their ethnicity, class or disability, you should not ignore them or you will be condoning the behaviour and therefore complying with the remarks.
- As a 'significant other' in the children's lives, they are likely to learn from your value position. Explain clearly why the remarks made were wrong and hurtful or offensive, and ask the abused children and the abusers how they felt so that the children can begin to think actively about the incident.
- Do not attack the children who have made the offending remarks in a personal manner or imply that the children are wrong, only that what was said is wrong.
- Explain in appropriate terms to the abusers why the comment was wrong and give all the children the correct information.

- Support and physically comfort the abused children, making sure that they know that you support their identity and that of their group and spend some time working with them on their activity.
- At some point during the same day, work with the children who made the offending remarks to ensure that they know that you continue to value them as people.

Long-term action

- Target the parents of children who make offensive discriminatory comments to ensure that they understand your policy for equality, and that you will not accept abuse against any child. Point out how this damages their child.
- Develop topics and read stories which raise issues of similarities and differences in language, gender and ethnicity and encourage the children to talk about their understandings and feelings.
- Create the kind of ethos that promotes and values diverse images and contributions to society.
- Involve parents and children (depending on the age of the children) in decision-making processes, particularly during the development of a policy on equality.
- Talk through your equality policy with all parents as and when children enter the setting, along with the other information parents need.
- Develop appropriate teaching and learning strategies for children who are acquiring English so that they do not get bored, frustrated and driven to poor behaviour patterns.

(Adapted from Siraj-Blatchford 1994)

Working towards effective practice

The identity (or ethos) of the early childhood setting is very important (Suschitzky and Chapman 1998). We identify six stages of equity oriented practice, stage one being the least desirable and least developed practice in the area. These are based on our own and other colleagues' experiences within and observations of a very wide range of early years settings. The six stages are not meant to be prescriptive or definitive, but they are intended to stimulate discussion and thought among early years staff and parents. Different kinds of beliefs and practices are identified that promote or hinder the implementation of equity practices that allow children, parents and staff to feel either valued or devalued.

Stage 1

Discriminatory practice – where diversity according to gender, class, ability or cultural and racial background is seen as a disadvantage and a problem, and no effort has been made to explore positive strategies for change. There is a separatist, or overtly racist, sexist and/or classist environment. We may observe some of the following:

- Staff believe that all children are 'the same' and that sameness of treatment is sufficient regardless of a child's gender, social class, special needs or ethnicity.

- Parents are blamed for children not 'fitting in' to the way the setting functions and that if parents are dissatisfied with the service they should take their children elsewhere.
- Inflexible curriculum and assessment procedures which do not reflect a recognition for the need for positive minority ethnic or gender role models, multilingualism in society or sufficient observations that detect special needs.
- There is no policy statement of intent, or policy documents relating to equal opportunities. British culture, child rearing patterns, etc., are universalised.

Stage 2

Inadequate practice – where children's special needs are recognised according to disability but generally a deficit model exists. If children who perform poorly also happen to be from a minority ethnic group this is seen as contributory. Gendered reasons may be given for poor achievement. Alternatively the parents are blamed for being inadequate at parenting. We may observe some of the following.

- There is a general acceptance that staff are doing their best without actually undertaking staff development for equality issues except for special needs.
- It is recognised that extra resources should be provided for children with English as an additional language, but it is felt that this is a special need which should be met by an English as an Additional Language (EAL) teacher or assistant, and that 'these' children will find it difficult to learn until they have acquired a basic grasp of English.
- Staff encourage children to play with a range of resources but no special effort is being made to encourage girls to construct or boys to play in the home corner.
- Staff do not know how to, or do not want to, challenge discriminatory remarks because they feel the children pick these up from home, and they do not feel they can raise these issues with parents.

Stage 3

Well meaning but poorly informed practice – where staff are keen to meet individual children's needs and are receptive to valuing diversity. We may observe some of the following:

- Token measures at valuing diversity can be observed, for example, multilingual posters, black dolls and puzzles and books with positive black and gender role models may be found but are rarely the focus of attention.
- There is an equal opportunities policy statement but this does not permeate other documents related to parent guides, curriculum or assessment.
- Staff respond positively to all parents and children and appreciate diversity as richness but are not well informed about their cultures or about anti-racist, sexist or classist practice.
- Bilingual staff are employed as extra 'aides' or 'assistants'.

Stage 4

Practice that values diversity generally where some attempts are made to provide an anti-discriminatory curriculum and environment. We may observe some of the following:

- There is a centre policy on equal opportunities which includes promoting gender, race and other equality issues.
- Staff are inhibited through worries about parents raising objections to anti-racist or anti-sexist practice.
- Resources are applied which promote anti-discriminatory work and special activities to promote racial harmony and gender and race equality are practised. All children are observed carefully to detect any special learning needs.
- Children's home languages are valued and attempts are made to encourage parents to support bilingualism at home.

Stage 5

Practice that values diversity and challenges discrimination, where equal opportunities is firmly on the agenda. We may observe some of the following:

- The centre staff have made a conscious effort to learn about inequality through staff development and someone is allocated with responsibility for promoting good practice in the area.
- There is a policy statement on equal opportunities and a document which applies the statement of intent to everyday practice, curriculum evaluation and assessment and to the positive encouragement of anti-discriminatory activities.
- Staff observe the children's learning and interactions with equality in mind and develop short- and long-term plans to promote self-image, self-esteem, language and cultural awareness.
- Staff are keen to challenge stereotypes and confident to raise issues with parents and support them through their learning if they hold negative stereotypes.
- Bilingual staff are employed as mainstream staff.

Stage 6

Challenging inequality and promoting equity, where staff actively try to change the structures and power relations which inhibit equal opportunities. We may observe some of the following:

- Staff value the community they work in and encourage parents to be involved in decision making. Bi/multi-lingualism is actively supported.
- The management take full responsibility for promoting equal opportunities and try positively to promote their service to all sections of the community.
- Management actively seek to recruit more male and minority ethnic staff.
- The equal opportunities policy is monitored and evaluated regularly and staff are confident in their anti-discriminatory practice.

- Equality issues are reflected across curriculum, resources, assessment and record keeping and the general ethos of the centre.
- Parents and children are supported against discrimination in the local community.
- Staff know how to use the UK Sex Discrimination Act, Race Relations Act, the Warnock Report, Code of Practice, the Children Act and the United Nations Convention on the Rights of Children to achieve equality assurance

(Adapted from Siraj-Blatchford 1996)

A positive self concept is necessary for healthy development and learning and includes feelings about gender, race, ability, culture and language. Positive self-esteem depends on whether children feel that others accept them and see them as competent and worthwhile. Young children develop attitudes about themselves and others from a very early age and need to be exposed to positive images of diversity in the early years setting. Children need to feel secure and to learn to trust the staff that care for them in order to learn effectively.

References

Brown, B. (1998) *Unlearning Discrimination in the Early Years*. Stoke-on-Trent: Trentham Books.

Clarke, P. (1993) 'Multicultural perspectives in early childhood services in Australia', *Multicultural Teaching*, Stoke-on-Trent: Trentham Books.

Davey, A. (1983) *Learning to be Prejudiced*. London: Edward Arnold.

Davies, B. (1989) *Frogs and Snails and Feminist Tales*. St Leonards, NSW: Allen & Unwin.

Dunn, J. (1987) 'Understanding feelings: the early stages', in J. Bruner and H. Haste (eds) *Making Sense: the child's construction of the world*, 26–40. London: Routledge.

Dweck, C. S. and Leggett, E. (1988) 'A social-cognitive approach to motivation and personality', *Psychological Review* 95 (2): 256–73.

Gillborn, D. and Gipps, C. (1997) *Recent Research on the Achievements of Minority Ethnic Pupils*. London: HMSO.

Lawrence, D. (1998) *Enhancing Self-esteem in the Classroom*. London: Paul Chapman.

Lloyd, B. and Duveen, G. (1992) *Gender Identities and Education*. London: Harvester Wheatsheaf.

Milner, D. (1983) *Children and Race: Ten Years On*. London: Ward Lock Educational.

Purkey, W. (1970) *Self-concept and School Achievement*. London: Paul Chapman.

Roberts, R. (1998) 'Thinking about me and them: personal and social development', in I. Siraj-Blatchford (ed.) *A Curriculum Development Handbook for Early Childhood Educators*, 155–74. Stoke-on-Trent: Trentham Books.

Siraj-Blatchford, I. (1992) 'Why understanding cultural differences is not enough', in G. Pugh (ed.) *Contemporary Issues in the Early Years*. London: Paul Chapman.

Siraj-Blatchford, I. (1994) *The Early Years: Laying the Foundations for Racial Equality*. Stoke-on-Trent: Trentham Books.

Siraj-Blatchford, I. (1996) 'Language, culture and difference', in C. Nutbrown *Children's Rights and Early Education*, 23–33. London: Paul Chapman.

Siraj-Blatchford, I. (1998) (ed.) *A Curriculum Development Handbook for Early Childhood Educators*. Stoke-on-Trent: Trentham Books.

Siraj-Blatchford, J. and Siraj-Blatchford, I. (eds) (1995) *Educating the Whole Child: Cross-curricular Skills, Themes and Dimensions in the Primary Schools*. Buckingham: Open University Press.

Siraj-Blatchford, J. and MacLeod-Brudenell, I. (1999) *Supporting Science, Design and Technology in the Early Years*. Buckingham: Open University Press.

Stonehouse, A. (1991) *Opening the Doors: Childcare in a Multicultural Society*. Melbourne, Victoria: Australian Early Childhood Association Inc.

Suschitzky, W. and Chapman, J. (1998) *Valued Children, Informed Teaching*. Buckingham: Open University Press.

Chapter 4

Parent partnership and inclusion in the early years

Alice Paige-Smith

> Early years practitioners know the important role parents play in children's learning and development and how important it is to work in partnership with parents. Working closely with parents of children with learning difficulties or disabilities is especially important but can be challenging for both practitioners and parents. In this chapter Alice Paige-Smith considers this experience from the perspective of parents and how the rights of parents to be fully involved in decisions relating to and provision for their children are interpreted.

Introduction

In this chapter I consider different perspectives towards parents of children with learning difficulties and disabilities and how the concept of parent partnership has developed. An analysis of policy documents which describe parent partnership indicates that there has been a shift in perspective from a 'supportive' model in the 1970s towards a 'rights' model represented in the *Special Educational Needs Code of Practice* (DfES 2001a). Parents are considered to have the right to participate in their child's education and to indicate their choices in their child's schooling. Local Education Authorities are instructed in the Code to provide parents with independent advisors to support them in making these choices. This shift will be outlined in this chapter by considering the sometimes conflicting attitudes between parents and professionals and how one particular group of parents supported and became involved in the education of their children in the early years.

Parents and professionals

Since the 1981 Education Act there has been a repositioning of 'special educational needs' in the early years within an inclusive framework (Wolfendale 2000). Issues of inclusion in the early years were firstly recognised in the Green Paper 'Excellence for

All Children, Meeting Special Educational Needs' (DfEE 1997) and the subsequent Programme of Action (DfEE 1998) announced initiatives such as Sure Start (Wolfendale 2000). Alongside these developments there has been a growth in expertise for practitioners working in the early years with children who experience difficulties in learning or have disabilities (Wolfendale 2000). The notion of 'parent partnership' in the early years has also been recognised in the curriculum guidance for the Early Years Foundation Stage (DfES 2007a, 2007b). The Principles into Practice card 2.2 'Parents as partners' states:

> Parents are children's first and most enduring educators. When parents and practitioners work together in early years settings, the results have a positive impact on children's development and learning.

> (DfES 2007b)

The 1981 Education Act represented a major change in the education of children; the term 'special educational needs' replaced previous categories of learning difficulties that had been based on assessments by professionals. This term came out of discussions during the Warnock Committee in 1978 which recognised that 20% of all children would experience difficulties at some time during their school career. The Committee also acknowledged that input from parents was important during the assessment process. A statement of special educational needs was recommended by the Warnock Report (DES 1978) as a way of assessing a child's needs and provision, and in 1981 parents were given the legal right to participate in this process. In 2005 about 3% of children – 1.5 million children – had statements of special educational needs, with one third in special schools (House of Commons Education and Skills Committee 2006, p. 5).

However, while the 1978 Warnock Report had a chapter dedicated to parent partnership this could be considered to have a patronising attitude towards parents. Professionals are considered to be the people who know or are the 'experts' on the child. This theme recurs throughout the education of children with learning difficulties and disabilities and the notion of parent partnership has developed as a way of recognising the tensions which exist between parents and professionals. An example of the attitudes towards parents is in this extract from the Warnock Report (DES 1978):

> Parents must be assisted to understand their child's difficulties. They must also be helped to adopt attitudes to him most conducive to his feeling that he is accepted and has the same status in the family as any brothers or sisters.

> (Department of Education and Science 1978, Section 7.19)

Parents are considered to need help in order to understand and accept their child. Models of how parents 'parent' their child who has a disability or learning difficulty have been proposed by professionals (Mittler and Mittler 1982; Cunningham and Davis 1985). These may neglect the difference in the power relationship between parents and professionals and also the relationship with the child.

Professionals and prejudicial attitudes

Incidences of prejudicial attitudes towards disability and difficulties of learning abound in the literature on parents' experiences. Professional practice may fail to consider the best interests of the child where his or her opinions differ from those of the parents. Doctors have been criticised for the way they break the news to the parent that they have a disabled child because they pre-judge the child:

> When my son was two he was diagnosed at a London hospital. I [the father] saw the doctor. He just told me that my son was an imbecile, then closed the interview by ringing for the next patient.
>
> (Furneaux 1988, p. 9)

The parents of this child were told by a paediatrician to 'put him away and forget you ever had him' (Furneaux 1988). These parents found the doctors judgements painful to experience. They did not perceive their child in the same way as their doctor. Birth and the early years are considered to be hard for parents especially if they have a child with a learning difficulty or a disability. They are recognised to go through stages of shock through to acceptance during the diagnosis of their child's learning difficulty or disability (Cunningham 1982). Some parents have attempted to redefine what this period of time is like for them. They stress the negative attitudes of other people towards their child, including professionals (Goodey 1992). The lack of sensitivity which parents face at the time of the diagnosis of their child's learning difficulty or disability in the early years has been acknowledged by the guidelines 'Right from the Start' (Scope 2003) produced by Scope, a disability charity whose focus is cerebral palsy, a number of voluntary bodies and the Department of Health (DfES 2003). These guidelines support professionals in how to break the news of disability and the advice 'promotes a culture of respect for children and parents' (DFES 2003).

Parents – challenging ideologies

Challenging perceptions of disability or of difficulties of learning is an experience common to parents of children born with Trisomy 21 (so-called Down's Syndrome). Chris Goodey (1992) researched how parents' experiences clashed with the professionals' perceptions of parenting a child with Trisomy 21. Contrary to the myth that the child is automatically rejected by the parent who 'mourns the death of the normal child that didn't emerge', Goodey reports that parents feel the expectation of rejecting their child is imposed on them. Parents are subjected to ideologies of how disability is perceived, in the first instance, by professionals like doctors and nurses, and others, such as family members. He suggests in his research carried out with eighteen families, that parents challenge perceptions of disability and difficulties in learning held by professionals in the medical field. He claims that parents become 'includers' through their experiences and contact with members of the 'excluded' group, however, their power to change prevailing views is negated by the institutionalised power of professionals who define and dominate practice. Goodey, as a parent of a child with 'Trisomy 21', is advocating inclusion as a belief, or a philosophy. He suggests that an inclusive philosophy may be held by parents and others who have experienced a 'shift in human values'.

Parents' experiences and views – ensuring inclusion

What are parents' experiences if they have a child with learning difficulties or disabilities; what are their experiences in the early years; how do these relate to their involvement in education and their choice of inclusion? Robina Mallet set up a parents' group in the West of England to support parents and provide information for them. She has articulated what it is like to be a parent – she could be considered to be a 'professional parent' as she provides advice, information and support for other parents:

> The title a professional acquires gives status, recognition of the body of knowledge they have achieved and perhaps reinforces self-confidence. The social standing of a parent of a child with 'special needs' seems to depend, to an extent, on the disability experienced. This can range between 'super human' to 'ineffectual parent'. Wherever the judgement rests we may be perceived uncomfortably – other parents feeling sorry for us or suspecting we resent their 'better fortunes'. We are (accidentally one hopes) frequently called 'special needs parents'!
>
> (Mallett 1997, p. 29)

Other parents have set up parents' groups since the 1981 Education Act and I interviewed eight parents to find out what their experiences had been and why they had become involved in setting up parents' groups (Paige-Smith 1996). The experiences of these parents indicate that they had similar philosophies and attitudes towards their children, and that these influenced the choice of schooling for their children. Jane's experiences illustrate the barriers in ensuring inclusion and how some of these barriers were overcome.

Jane's experiences

Jane had set up a parents' campaign and support group with other mothers whose children attended a pre-school playgroup. They wanted their children to attend mainstream schools rather than a special school which was the practice of the local education authority. When Jane's son was a year old he was diagnosed as having cerebral palsy. Jane joined a local playgroup funded by social services and MENCAP. This playgroup had been established in her town for children referred by social services because their children experienced difficulties in learning or were disabled. When all the mothers from the playgroup met they realised they had a common concern:

> We all got together one day and the biggest thing we were concerned about was education. Talking together we all found that we had a common concern about our kids – that when they reach five, where are they going to go?
>
> Jane

This group of parents became concerned about the practice of sending all children with disabilities or learning difficulties to special schools. Jane was not satisfied with the prospect of this for her son:

> If a child had spina bifida, say, or cerebral palsy, or a physical disability they would be bussed or taxied to Coventry which is the nearest school. So, for young children, often as young as four, because they often liked them to go to nursery, they would be spending up to two hours travelling. We thought that was appalling, given all the problems our kids have anyway, you know, isolation, to spend all that time travelling – and it's very expensive.

The mothers from the playgroup arranged for a parents' group from Coventry to visit and talk to them. They were impressed with this group and decided to set up a campaign and support group in order to try to ensure the inclusion of their children into mainstream school. Jane described how the parents' group emerged out of a group of parents who shared similar views on what they wanted for their children. The group, which began with a group of mothers meeting informally, turned into a structured group with a set of aims. They gathered and disseminated information to support their campaign, they decided on a name and met every week. The parents were asking for support for their children to attend mainstream school, however the local authority wanted the children to attend special schools:

> They were saying 'I'm sorry but I have got no money'. I mean it always came down to resources. They said, 'look the special school, is there – there is separate funding for that and for mainstream'. They didn't have a policy, the authority didn't even have a written policy, they were just hoping that they could carry on as normal. They were saying, 'we've got the set up and that is it, basically'.
>
> Jane

The parents' group responded to the 'deadlock' situation with the local authority by providing individual support for parents by attending meetings with them to talk to education officers. The group also ensured that disabled people at open meetings provided information on disability awareness issues. As people came to talk at the meetings from different parts of England the parents recognised that inclusion varied according to location. This knowledge strengthened the aims of the group and reduced their sense of isolation.

Jane put her son's name down at the nursery at the local school where her eldest son attended. However, she found the head teacher hostile to her son attending her school, and she was very concerned about the prejudicial attitudes towards her son's disability:

> The head teacher said 'O.K. well, we'll see when the time comes'. Anyway when the time did come the letter that was sent out to welcome new parents to the nursery, I didn't have one. So I went to her and said; 'O.K. what's going on?' – she was quite frightened of us actually, and she avoided me for quite a long time, and I cornered her in the hall in the school and I got very upset about it and I drafted a letter to the governors and she wouldn't have him and I said 'Why won't you take Alexis?' I mean it's awful when you are actually saying 'Well he's quite a nice boy really' and all this kind of shit. You know, having to sort of persuade people to take your children to school, and she [the headteacher] said: 'Well he'd take up too much space, and maybe later, when he'll be walking by that time', because he had a rollator then, he wasn't walking at that time.
>
> Jane

The head teacher told Alexis' father that she feared she would get a flood of handicapped children in the school if she let Alexis and another disabled child in. Alexis' parents were told by an education officer that 'he wouldn't want his son in a classroom with a handicapped child in it'. These prejudicial attitudes meant that Alexis' parents were unable to trust professionals:

> They would say lots of things and then they would completely deny that they said that and so we had a policy that we would take a tape recorder in to meetings, or I would go along and

take notes, and they didn't like that at all, that really got up their nose. But of course, they would say things in one breath and then say they'd never said them. I mean you couldn't trust them at all.

Jane

The authority had an 'unwritten' policy of refusing full-time support in mainstream. Alexis was finally granted 10 hours support in mainstream because of his difficulties in reading and writing. Jane feels that his support benefited the whole class and the class teacher because she had an 'extra pair of hands'. The decision to make this support available to her son was made by an education officer. Jane thought that the authority had 'backstepped' on their decision not to provide support because of the cost of transporting her son to special school. Jane managed to ensure that her son was integrated into his local school, however three other parents from the group tried for three years to get their children into their local mainstream school. It proved harder for these parents because, Jane suggests, their children were categorised as having 'severe learning difficulties'. The appeal process experienced by these parents has been written about by Will Swann (1987). The barriers to their inclusion were the local authority's inability to provide support in mainstream for these pupils and the lack of flexibility of the special schools to provide support in mainstream for these pupils.

The parents from LINC continued to work through encouraging disability awareness in their local community. The LINC group were also involved in the national parents' group Network '81. The two groups found that they had a common aim for parents, children and young people.

Parental involvement

Robina Mallett (1997) has written about her involvement in setting up the parents' group in the West of England and the services and support that are provided for parents. Jane's experiences also illustrate how parents' collective experiences can lead to their empowerment and involvement in decision-making concerning their child's education. Major changes have occurred in the development of parents' rights since the 1981 Education Act, as the *Special Educational Needs and Disability Act* (DfES 2001b) has recognised children's rights to attend mainstream school and parents rights to assert this choice. The power of Local Education Authorities, and hence professionals, to segregate children in special schools has been reduced through the changes in education law which have been campaigned for by disabled people and parents' groups (Reiser 2001).

In the *Practice Guidance for the Early Years Foundation Stage* (DfES 2007a) section 1.11 on 'Partnership working' has recognised that early years practitioners should:

- have a key role in working with parents to support their young children
- identify learning needs and opportunities for children
- respond quickly to any difficulties
- liaise with other professionals
- provide regular information for parents about activities undertaken by the children.

(DfES 2007a p. 6)

The Principles into Practice card 2.2 'Parents as Partners' (DfES 2007b) that relates to the theme of Positive Relationships within the Early Years Foundation Stage outlines the importance of:

- Respecting diversity – all families should be welcomed and valued.
- Learning together – parents and practitioners have a lot to learn from each other.
- Communication – a two-way flow of information, knowledge and expertise between parents and practitioners.

The 'Reflecting on practice' section of the Principles into Practice card 2.2 (DfES 2007a) places an emphasis on the importance of listening and valuing what parents say, as well as ensuring that parents contribute to children's profiles. Robina Mallet, who set up the parents' group in the West of England suggested that:

> Parents often are the only people who know everything that has happened to the child. They actually carry a body of knowledge that the other professionals haven't shared in whether they are carrying messages from the medics about diagnosis and things which just haven't been shared. It is often as if the parent is the *key worker* in what is going on. Some will be able to cope with that, others can't. What they actually know should be respected. They know that their children need encouragement . . . they know when they get tired, they know their likes and dislikes and how much they like being teased or joked with.
>
> Robina

Conclusion

The *Special Educational Needs Code of Practice* (DfES 2001a) does recognise this perspective and parents are considered to hold 'key information' and to have a 'critical role to play in their children's education' (*ibid.*, p. 16). Effective communication with parents by professionals, according to this document, should draw on parental knowledge and expertise in relation to their child. However, in the section on key principles in communicating and working in partnership with parents, the role of parents as participants in supporting their children's learning is not emphasised. The section on the roles and responsibilities of schools, and in particular the Special Educational Needs Co-ordinator notes that parents should be encouraged to participate, but that they may need 'emotional support', indicating that there may be conflict experienced by parents (*ibid.*, p. 26). The role of Local Education Authorities and parent partnership has been outlined in the Code of Practice where LEAs are instructed to provide 'access to an independent Parental Supporter for all parents who want one' as well as 'accurate, neutral information on their rights, roles and responsibilities within the SEN process, and on the wide range of options that are available for their children's education' (DfES 2001, p. 21).

The Code of Practice (2001) does acknowledge the ways in which parents should be provided with information and support in order to understand their rights and roles in the education of their child with a learning difficulty or a disability. The 1978 Warnock Report suggested that parents should be 'helped' to adopt the right attitudes towards their child; the shift has been towards a 'rights' model of parent partnership. Perhaps this shift is due to the actions of parents and parent groups that have campaigned for changes in the attitudes and perspectives of professionals.

References

Cunningham, C. (1982) *Down's Syndrome; An Introduction for Parents*. London: Souvenir Press.

Cunningham, C. and Davis, H. (1985) *Working with Parents: Frameworks for Collaboration*. Milton Keynes: Open University Press.

Department for Education and Employment (1997) *Excellence for all Children, Meeting Special Educational Needs*. London: Stationery Office.

Department for Education and Employment (1998) *Meeting Special Educational Needs, A Programme of Action*. London: DfEE.

Department of Education and Science (1978) *The Warnock Report, Special Educational Needs*. London: HMSO.

Department of Education and Science (1981) *The Education Act, 1981*. London: HMSO.

Department for Education and Skills (2001a) *Special Educational Needs Code of Practice*. Nottinghamshire: DfES Publications.

Department for Education and Skills (2001b) *The Special Educational Needs and Disability Act*. London: HMSO.

Department for Education and Skills (2003) *Disabled children to get more support*, DfES Press Notice 2003/0078, info©dfes.gsi.gov.uk

Department for Education and Skills (2007a) *Practice Guidance for the Early Years Foundation Stage*. Nottingham: DfES Publication.

Department for Education and Skills (2007b) *Positive Relationships Principles into Practice Card, Parents as Partners*. Nottingham: DfES Publications.

Furneaux, B. (1988) *Special Parents*. Milton Keynes: Open University Press.

Goodey, C. (1992) 'Fools and heretics: parents' views of professionals', in Booth, T. *et al*. *Policies for Diversity in Education*, 165–176. London: Routledge.

House of Commons Education and Skills Committee (2006) *Special Educational Needs: Third report of Session 2006–6*, Volume 1. London: The Stationery Office.

Mallett, R. (1997) 'A parental perspective on partnership', in Wolfendale, S. (ed.) *Working with Parents of SEN Children After the Code of Practice*, 27–40. London: David Fulton Publishers.

Mittler, P. and Mittler, H. (1982) *Partnership with Parents*. Stratford-Upon-Avon: National Council for Special Education.

Paige-Smith, A. (1996) 'Choosing to campaign; a case study of parent choice, statementing and integration', *European Journal of Special Needs Education* 11 (3), 321–329.

Rieser, R. (2001) 'New Act a Turning Point: Disability, Special Educational Needs and the Law', *Inclusion Now* 2, 4–5.

Scope (2003) *Right from the Start – Template*, London: Scope.

Swann, W. (1987) 'Statements of intent: an assessment of reality', in Booth, T. and Swann, W. (eds) *Including Pupils with Disabilities*. Milton Keynes: Open University Press.

Wolfendale, S. (2000) 'Special needs in the early years; prospects for policy and practice', *Support for Learning* 15 (4), 147–151.

Chapter 5

Living and learning

Claire Young

Claire Young has home educated her three sons. In this chapter she draws on her diary entries over some eight years to reflect on what she and her three children have learned together. She provides important insights into the process of learning, and particularly the importance of tuning in to children's interests and motivation.

Our learning took place as we lived life to the full; we are a family who love reading and talking and being out of doors. That just about sums up how we home educated. I know families who played musical instruments for hours each day, and others who painted, sewed and trailed through charity shops. Each has produced well socialised children who are active learners. Success comes when adults actively engage with children in whatever way comes naturally to both parties.

Learning memories

Remembering incidents from when my children were younger, it amazes me that so much learning took place in and around ordinary living. Some was planned, but more often it happened as we did chores, met friends and even while having arguments. At the time it felt as if they never stopped learning, it was 24 hours a day education. Actually, I think everyone home educates, like it or not. It's just that some people also send their children to school.

In January 1993, Tony was 6 years old, Michael 4, and Paul 1. One Sunday after church we went to a country park, running, hiding and watching motorised model boats. On returning I wanted to make a phone call to my brother in Canada. We used the atlas to look for date lines and time zones and ended up discussing pie charts and colour keys. Tony asked for us to sew a Canadian flag; we discussed the relationship between the words 'Canada and Canadian' and 'Britain and British'.

In November 1994, Tony got a Lego container ship for his birthday. We read books about ships, looked up our junior encyclopedia on ports and container ships, and then visited a container ship base in Gourock. This was how a lot of learning happened, by picking up on something happening in the family, and seeing what else linked in via newspapers, library books, conversations with friends. I wanted them to see the range of options for following an interest. This would probably constitute a 'project' at school, but ours only ran as long as it sustained the child's interest, the learning being the aim, not project presentation.

Michael and Tony wanted to collect a cereal box special offer; this resulted in much counting of pocket money and they very swiftly became competent with pounds and pence. When Paul was 6, he was given 5 pounds per person for Christmas presents, and by having to work out prices in shops, swiftly came to a similar understanding. Decimals were never a problem in maths.

In December 1995, Paul, aged 3, was inclined to fall asleep if we travelled in the car after 4.00 pm – not a good idea as he then stayed up late. To keep his interest, we started counting Christmas trees in people's houses. This became the way Michael, then 6 years, learned to count past 10. By Christmas he could count to 90.

The concept of learning subjects or concepts in a particular sequence didn't seem to apply at home. There would be spurts of interest and then a lull with no apparent learning, only to have them bound forward a month or so later. I had made myself a 'mind map' of the maths concepts for primary-aged children and about every six months I'd glance at it to see if there were any yawning gaps. For instance, if we hadn't done graphs we'd do a survey of birds coming to the feeding table and draw a relevant graph.

Travelling down to Grand-da at Christmas we looked at maps to help pass time. Enjoying maps has become a feature of our family life. We have used a world map pinned on a dining room wall to talk about news items or understand history books, road maps to plan holidays, and town maps to plan cycling trips to friends. Talking about scales and keys of maps came up naturally.

By this stage Tony and Michael had a small 'desk-work' programme which I put together. This would take about an hour each day and was fitted around chores and trips to the park and long, daily sessions of reading together.

Normally children develop speech and walking without being taught. However, I don't believe it happens in the same way with writing, reading or written maths. (There are, however, home educators who have proved me absolutely wrong!) I used a variety of exercises found in books at the Teachers Resource Centre, local stationers and ideas from friends. Maths was as practical as possible, reading and writing little and often.

In June 1996, the toy library was threatened with closure. The boys asked 'Why?' This resulted in a discussion which covered councils, their functions, their funding, decision making and democracy. This conversation ran for about three days, and, as I have no particular political interest, involved asking many other people for the answers.

That year, with Tony 9, Michael 7 and Paul 5, they each had their own piece of garden and grew plants of their own choice. Gardening has always been a great source of learning opportunities, for example organic versus chemical, different types of soil, root formations, and the need for light and nutrients.

There was a General Election May 1997, and the boys, taking note of this, decided to run their own soft toy elections. The Tyrannosaurus Rex Party won, on the promise that they would set up burger bars for the carnivores and investigate DNA storage to prevent extinction. I always enjoy sharing interesting things I've been reading with them so the week before had read them a brief article on DNA and cloning.

A week did not go by without us doing something together in the kitchen. Cooking is a rich area of learning; making a cake, we would discuss what made it rise. When melting chocolate, we would discuss reversible reactions. Recipes require reading, measuring gets learnt naturally, and discussions about nutrition would arise from why it wasn't a great idea to make toffee shortbread every week.

As they got older I found we did about two or three six-week sessions of 'homework', as we termed it, per year and for the rest just read copiously, covering every subject under the sun, in fiction or non-fiction. Book work included a variety of maths and English work and I'd add in science, geography or history, depending on the child's interests or lack of. One child was physically a little lazy, so he had exercise on his list.

I set a weekly quota from textbooks and work books and put up the social diary for the week so they could decide when to work. If we got to Thursday and they wanted to play out but had done no homework, as agreed, the answer was 'after work'. I have always told the boys 'School is optional, education is not.' Having said that, home education can only be done by mutual consent, which I think is one of its strengths. We have talked together using Edward de Bono's 'six hat thinking' and Tony Buzan's 'mind maps' to get the children to take responsibility for their learning.

In November 1999 Paul, aged 7, continued to collect bones and interesting rocks, and noticed on a walk the clear layers of different rock in a freshly eroded river bank. He still has an abiding interest in the out of doors – fishing, Scouting, hawking lessons, reading adult-level books on survival and fishing.

Ways of learning

Answering questions as they came up was one way they learned.

As a 6-year-old Paul asked, 'What does "hotel" mean?' I replied, 'You know what it means.' 'Yes,' he said, 'but what does it really mean?' 'Do you mean where does it come from?' I asked. (Noise of possible agreement from him.) I said, 'Find me a dictionary.' (I was probably cooking dinner at the time.) Paul fetches me the big dictionary which he knows shows word origins, not just spelling, so I take it I have correctly guessed what his question meant. We look up 'hotel', read it out and he goes off with no further comment.

Aged 7, Paul came in holding a cardboard toilet roll with a mini rolling pin as the plunger and a plasticine 'cannon ball'. 'Look how far it can fire,' he said. I look. He says, 'Hmm not very far, but if I aim it higher.' He tries again with more success.

When 9 and cuddling up in bed in the early morning, Paul says, 'If we had a glass almost full of water, just air at the top. If we closed it and turned it over where would the air go?' After puzzling that through, he then moved on to ask 'What would happen if you had a metal box of air and you closed it and squashed it?' This led onto a discussion of how a pressure cooker works – there being a well known family story of when a pressure cooker blew beetroot all over the kitchen!

I have had to adapt to their ways of learning, otherwise it would have been just a waste of time. It took me till one child was four to realise he was scared of new things. I actually love new things and was making his life difficult by emphasising 'new' as we started anything, even swimming lessons. He needed to know he would be in the same pool and wearing the same costume and not that he had a *new* teacher and was in a *new* class. When I realised this tactic also worked academically I would approach a new step in learning saying it was a slightly different way of doing something that he already knew. So division was introduced as multiplication done backwards.

Our family has several of the learning types Howard Gardener has identified, and it's been a challenge to learn how to present the same thing differently. Tony learned to read easily with phonics. Michael wanted to be able to read at 5, but disliked being taught. I eventually gave up when he was 6, as it was causing such fights. A year later, I discovered he could read even complicated words like 'through'. Paul proved to be different again, much more a physical learner. So he has 'run' letter shapes out in the garden, laid rope out in their shapes and then written them on the patio in chalk. While learning to read he had to get up and run around the house between each few lines because his legs went 'funny'. He always came back to work, but found concentrating such hard work he needed to blow off steam. [. . .]

I often felt the tension between letting a child discover for himself and actively teaching. On one occasion, Michael, of his own accord, made a set of traffic lights. I made several comments on how to improve the design, and he ended up crying because I had confused him with too many ideas. If I believed in self-discovery, why did I still want to butt-in?

What did not come naturally with any of our boys was writing. I found getting the boys to write was like pulling teeth and early on decided I was going to use our time to learn, not fight over pages of writing. Most 'creative writing' was done orally. I would type out stories they told, or just listen to their endless imaginative accounts. Michael would, of his own accord, draw a detailed picture and then come and tell me about it. Tony and Paul would make complicated clay models of an island, or a mine, and then tell me the story behind it.

I never worked out whether it was better to present a new concept practically or via a book at first. It was easier to read a book about estuaries when we had followed a river to the sea; but we discussed racism in reading books like *Kim* by Rudyard Kipling, in a way we might not have done otherwise in our mainly white town.

We have often joined with other home educators for group events, numbers varying from eight to 28 children. These have included felt-making with a friend, a talk on Romans at a museum, a series of art lessons and a technology workshop. [. . .]

The drama workshops were taken by a home educating mother, who'd been a professional actor. She was brilliant in her ability to set a theme and then work in all the ideas the children came up with. With her interactive approach she totally hooked the children.

We found group learning benefited only a few in the group and seldom equalled one-to-one conversation, because the child tends to get talked at rather than with. However, the children remember the group events as happy times and so as socialising times they were useful.

The love of learning

I was pro-home not anti-school. I never wanted to teach, but I did want them to be hooked on learning. I home educated because I did not believe young children needed teachers. I think they need loving and enthusiastic companions in learning, and a normal environment. We eventually had to make a decision as to when, and if, to use the school system. I wanted them at home at least long enough for them to see learning as enabling and interesting, not 'boring' as I often hear children describe it around here.

Many home educators, in the USA and here in the UK, have continued right the way through to school-leaving age, not sitting exams, and found the children are actively welcomed into colleges and employment. Home education has been reported as producing mature, active learners who will give of their best.

We have chosen to put the boys into the last year of primary school, for a settling-in year, and then on to secondary in order to sit exams. I've been delighted, and relieved, to find our minimalist approach to written and formal work has, so far, resulted in two of the boys doing very well in all subjects. They found the first year in school a steep learning curve in terms of speed and quantity of writing expected, but did not struggle in any other way. With one son, I told the teacher, after the first month, he was very aware of how little he wrote compared with others. The teacher's reply was she'd rather have one paragraph of his writing than a page of the others because the quality of ideas and word use was so much better.

My third son, the one who takes book learning and writing like medicine, has struggled with his first year at school and has a long way to go before he realises his ability. He is bright, but I sense that school is never going to suit his interests and style of learning. He continues to have an enquiring mind with subjects he values; they just aren't in the school curriculum!

Watching children develop, mind, body and spirit, is a source of wonder for me. To be involved as an enabler and encourager, perhaps like a sports coach, has been hard work sometimes, but it's been great fun and so rewarding.

Chapter 6

A folk model of assessment – and an alternative

Margaret Carr

In this chapter Margaret Carr explores the transformation of her personal and professional thinking about models for assessment of children's development and learning. She discusses how she moved from a deficit model to an alternative 'credit' model of assessment which values children's participation in the process and enhances their disposition to learn.

When I was a beginning kindergarten teacher, twenty years ago, I believed that assessment was about checking to see whether the nearly-school-age children had acquired what I considered to be the requisite skills for school: the list included early writing (writing their name), self-help skills, early mathematics (counting), turn-taking scissor-cutting. I therefore looked out for the gaps in a school-readiness repertoire, keeping a checklist, and used some direct teaching strategies to do something about them in the months before school. I did not find the process interesting or helpful to me, but I certainly saw it as linked to my reputation as a competent early childhood teacher with the children's families and with the local schools.

There are a number of assumptions about assessment here, and twenty years later I don't hold any of them. My interest has been captured by children like four-year-old Emily, an articulate and confident child, who, when her friend Laura tells her that she has done a jigsaw 'wrong', shouts angrily 'No! Don't call me wrong. If you call me wrong I won't let you stroke my mouse.' I am intrigued by processes in the kindergarten whereby Jason changes the simple activity of 'marble-painting' into a complex and difficult process, teaches Nell (who normally avoids this kind of difficulty) and then Nell teaches Jinny and Nick. In one activity in one centre I frequently hear 'good girl' from the adults but I never hear 'good boy', although boys are participating too. I pursue Myra and Molly who are practising a language that I have called *girl-friend-speak*, a language that involves reciprocal and responsive dialogue but appears to exclude Lisa. I interview Danny about what he finds difficult, and he tells me that it is drawing the triangular back windows of cars. I read a story to two-year-old Moses and he puzzles about whether the ducks have feet under the water, and what kind of feet they are. I hear Trevor advising his friend that if he finds something difficult he should just leave it. I puzzle about whether there is learning going on both above and 'under the water', what kind of learning it is, how we might assess it, and whether, as early childhood educators, it is any of our business.

I have called those twenty-year-old ideas of mine about assessment my 'folk' model of assessment. David Olson and Jerome Bruner (1996) point out that these everyday intuitive theories and models reflect deeply ingrained cultural beliefs and assumptions. In the case of my folk model of assessment, the assumptions were about: the *purpose* for assessment (to check against a short list of skills that describe 'competence' for the next stage of education), *outcomes of interest* (fragmented and context-free school-oriented skills), *focus for intervention* or attention (the deficits), *validity* of assessment data (objective observations of skills, reflected in a checklist, are best), *progress* (hierarchies of skill, especially in literacy and numeracy), *procedures* (checklists) and *value* (surveillance of me as a teacher). I developed these assumptions as I grew up, from my own experience of teachers and assessment at school and university, from my perception of the experience of my own children in early childhood settings and in school, and from the views of my family and peers. Teacher education had done nothing to shift them.

Later, together with a group of practitioners who wanted to explore some alternative assessment practices, I had the opportunity to try to integrate our ideas about learning and teaching with a different set of assumptions about assessment. Table 6.1 lists the assumptions of my folk model about assessment, and sets alongside them the assumptions of an alternative model. These alternative assumptions are outlined in this chapter.

Table 6.1 Assumptions in two models of assessment: a folk model and an alternative

Assumptions about	My folk model about assessment	An alternative model
Purpose	To check against a short list of skills that describe 'competence' at school entry	To enhance learning
Outcomes of interest	Fragmented and context-free school-oriented skills	Learning dispositions
Focus for intervention	Deficit, gap-filling, is foregrounded	Credit, disposition enhancing, is foregrounded
Validity	Objective observation	Interpreted observations, discussions and agreements
Progress	Hierarchies of skills	Increasingly complex participation
Procedures	Checklists	Learning stories
Value to practitioners	Surveillance by external agencies	For communicating with four audiences: children, families, other staff and self (the practitioner)

Purpose

An assumption that I was making twenty years ago was that assessment sums up the child's knowledge or skill from a predetermined list. Harry Torrance and John Pryor (1998) have described this assumption as 'convergent' assessment. The alternative is 'divergent' assessment, which emphasises the learner's understanding and is jointly accomplished by the teacher and the learner. These ideas reflect not only views about assessment, but views about learning and teaching as well. I think I was holding a convergent and a divergent view of learning at the same time. In convergent mode I checked the children's achievement against a short list of skills that described 'competence' at school entry. When my checklist indicated a gap in the requisite skills, I devised ways of directly teaching them. In divergent mode I was implementing a play-based programme to enhance the learning I valued at this site, but I did not see a role for assessment or documentation in that.

I don't have any examples of those convergent assessments. However, I do have an example of my working in more divergent mode at that time. Some years after the event I wrote about the invention by one of the four-year-olds at the kindergarten of an accessible carpentry drill (Carr 1987). I had observed one of the children wielding a G-clamp upside down to 'drill' a dent in the carpentry table. Normally a G-clamp has a cap on the end of the thread so that it doesn't mark the inside of the table when it is clamped on, but this clamp had lost the cap, and the thread had a pointed end. He called out: 'Look, Margaret, I'm drilling a hole.' We discussed how he had transformed a G-clamp into a carpentry drill, and evaluated this invention as potentially providing an extremely helpful artefact for enhancing the children's carpentry. Our drills at that time were of the egg-beater variety, where children had to keep the drill upright while they both pressed down and rotated the handle in a vertical plane. In the new 'drill', the thread maintained the pressure while the child could use both hands to turn the horizontally aligned handle at the top to drill the hole. I later persuaded a parent to weld a threaded bit onto the G-clamp, and set it into a block of wood, and it did indeed enhance the children's problem-solving and planning processes in carpentry. I wrote the story of one of the boys making a boat by drilling two 5mm holes in a block of wood, sawing and hammering in short lengths of dowel (for masts), and then floating it in the water trough (it fell to the side; later modifications to the design to get it to float the right way up were not recorded); and of one of the girls drilling holes in 'wheels' cut from an old broom handle, attaching them with flat-headed nails to the side of a piece of wood, and pulling it along as a car or cart. I had taken photos for the families, but it did not occur to me to write up either the invention or the carpentry as part of an assessment procedure. I think now that documenting that learning at the time would have given the children and the families, and me, some new insights into the goals of our early childhood programme, and of how they might be recognised and developed in other activities.

I was therefore only documenting part of the curriculum, and I was documenting it for an external audience. This may be true for many early childhood educators, and as demands for external accountability press more insistently on the profession, surveillance begins to encroach on intuitive and responsive teaching. The alternative model tries to connect external accountability and responsive teaching together: it advocates the documenting of learner outcomes and it is embedded in episodes of responsive teaching. However, it defines learner outcomes rather differently from the convergent checklist that I employed twenty years ago.

Outcomes of interest

My folk model of documented assessment viewed learning as individual and independent of the context. Learner outcomes of interest were fragmented and context-free school-oriented skills. The alternative model says that learning always takes some of its context with it, and that, as James Wertsch (1991) has suggested, the learner is a 'learner-in-action'. This viewpoint derives mainly from Lev Vygotsky's (1978) notion of 'mediated action'. It takes a view of learning that focuses on the relationship between the learner and the environment, and seeks ways to define and document complex reciprocal and responsive relationships in that environment. Emphasising this view of learning, Barbara Rogoff (1997, 1998) has described development as the 'transformation of participation'.

A number of other writers have emphasised the context- and culture-specific nature of learning. Jerome Bruner (1990: 106), for instance, has described this emphasis as a 'contextual revolution' in psychology. Attention has shifted from internal structures and representations in the mind to meaning-making, intention and relationships in the experienced world. This development is of great interest to early childhood practitioners. The traditional separation of the individual from the environment, has been replaced by attaching social and cultural purpose to skills and knowledge, thereby blurring the division between the individual and the learning environment. One way to look at a range of learning outcomes is to describe them as an accumulation. Table 6.2 sets out four outcomes along an accumulated continuum of complexity.

Skills and knowledge

The focus here is on skills and knowledge 'in the head', acquired by the learner. In early childhood there are a number of basic routines and low-level skills that might be, and often are, taught and tested: cutting with scissors, colouring between the lines, saying a series of numbers in the correct sequence, knowing the sounds of letters. Often complex

Table 6.2 Learning outcomes along an accumulated continuum of complexity

LEARNING OUTCOMES
(i)   Skills and knowledge
(ii) Skills and knowledge + intent = learning strategies
(iii) Learning strategies + social partners and practices + tools = situated learning strategies
(iv) Situated learning strategies + motivation = learning dispositions

tasks are seen as learning hierarchies with the assumption that smaller units of behaviour need to be mastered as prerequisites for more complex units later on.

Learning is seen as linear and sequential. Complex understandings can occur only by adding together simpler, prerequisite units of knowledge. Measurement-driven basic-skills instruction is based on a model of learning which holds that 'basic skills should be taught and mastered before going on to higher-order problems' (Shepard 1991: 2–3). Shepard asks (p. 7) 'What if learning is not linear and is not acquired by assembling bits of simpler learning?' We (Carr and Claxton 1989: 133) pointed out that this model of learning encourages didactic adult-controlled teaching strategies which ignore the particular, the situational and the social dimensions of learning.

This basic skills model of learning is often used to predict children's prospects at school. The literature on 'school readiness' does not, however, persuade us that particular items of skills and knowledge, unattached to meaningful activities, predict achievement at school.

Teachers and schools may construct a package of entry skills that, through teacher expectation effects, can become critical. But, while skills and knowledge matter a great deal, they will be fragile indeed if institutional arrangements in classrooms and early childhood settings do not embed them in motivating circumstances and imbue them with social and cultural meaning.

Skills and knowledge + intent = learning strategies

Skills that are attached to meaning and intent have been called 'learning strategies'. Nisbet and Shucksmith suggest that a learning strategy is a series of skills used with a particular purpose in mind: 'Strategies are different from skills in that a strategy has a purpose' (1986: vii). Learning strategies are often associated with the idea that children are 'learning to learn'. Nisbet and Shucksmith described strategies like planning ahead, monitoring one's progress to identify sources of difficulty, asking questions. Cullen (1991) describes the continuity of learning from early childhood to school in terms of learning strategies, as she observed children using the same strategies in play in their kindergarten and then in reading lessons at school. She described these as 'repeated patterns of behaviour and language which indicate an active, strategic approach to learning' (Cullen 1991: 45–6). Cullen noted that in the different context of the primary school classroom, however, such abilities or strategies may not be demonstrated. They will not appear if, for instance, there is little opportunity for the child to use a creative approach to choosing resources appropriate to the task in hand, or for the child to see herself as a resource for others.

Learning strategies + social partners and practices + tools = situated learning strategies

At the third level of accumulation, the purpose or intent is linked to social partners and practices, and tools. The learning strategies are *situated*. The focus is on the individual-in-action in which the action is mediated by social partners, social practices and tools (the technology and languages available). This is sometimes called a 'situative' approach, and the outcomes at this level can be called situated learning strategies. The emphasis is on learning as participation in sociocultural activities. Mediated *action* is, as Elizabeth Graue and Daniel Walsh (1995) commented, 'located within specific cultural and historic practices and time'. They compare this to a behavioural approach in which 'behaviour is stripped of these local characteristics; it is mechanical description without narration'. Writing about cognition, Gavriel Salomon comments that distributed cognition elaborates on the notion that 'People appear to think in conjunction or partnership with others and with the help of culturally provided tools and implements' (Salomon 1993: xiii).

This notion of thinking or learning being distributed across social practice and partners and tools introduces the idea of learning as a product of reciprocal relations between the environment and the mind, of the learning process as a *transaction*. Individual learners engage in activities and their participation changes the activities while at the same time they are changed by those activities. Jason changes the marble-painting activity and becomes a tutor in the process; Moses calls on adults and toys and videos not only to help him develop his fund of knowledge about animals, but to use animals as a metaphor or mechanism for making sense of and manipulating his two-year-old world.

Situated learning strategies + motivation = learning dispositions

The fourth level of accumulation adds *motivation* to situated learning strategies to form learning dispositions (Katz 1993). A vivid way to describe this accumulation of motivation, situation and skill is to say that a learner is 'ready, willing and able' to learn. Lauren Resnick (1987: 40–2) commented that shaping the disposition is central to developing the ability, and that much of the learning to be a good thinker is learning to recognise and even search for opportunities to apply one's capacities. She added (p. 42) that 'dispositions are cultivated by participation in social communities that value thinking and independent judgement'. If we take the example of communication, or expressing one's ideas, then *being ready* is being motivated or inclined to communicate, *being willing* is recognising that the situation is an appropriate one in which to express one's ideas, and *being able* is the communication skills and understandings that will be needed for this occasion. Kathy Sylva writes about the 'will and skill to do' as a legacy of effective preschool education (1994: 163) and inclination, sensitivity to occasion, and ability have been described as the three components of thinking dispositions by David Perkins, Eileen Jay and Shari Tishman (1993). Guy Claxton (1990: 164) has commented that in societies where knowledge, values and styles of relationship are undergoing rapid change: 'it can be strongly argued that schools' (and early childhood settings') major responsibility must be to help young people become ready, willing and able to cope with change successfully: that is, to be powerful and effective learners.' Coping with change means coping with changing situations: social partners, social practices and tools. Learning dispositions that take account of the situation can be defined as participation repertoires from which a learner recognises, selects, edits, responds to, resists, searches for and constructs learning opportunities. These can be referred to in a number of ways, as:

- learning dispositions
- being ready, willing and able

- inclination, sensitivity to occasion, and ability
- participation repertoires.

Summary of outcomes of interest

The four levels make up a conceptual hierarchy, not a developmental one. We can assess children's learning at any of the four levels of accumulation. However, assessment that is appropriate for level one outcomes (skills and knowledge) is not appropriate for level four outcomes (learning dispositions). As Elliot Eisner (2000: 346) has pointed out, 'tests are poor proxies for things that really matter'. We will have to devise something very different. On occasion, it will be appropriate to assess (perhaps to measure) narrow outcomes, but I would argue that if we only assess at the first three levels, then we will be taking a narrow and impoverished view of children's learning. The fourth level deserves our primary attention.

Focus for intervention

In my folk model, assessment was designed to highlight deficits. This notion of the developing child as incomplete, a jigsaw with parts missing, means that the areas in which the child is 'unable' become the sites of greatest educational interest. The deficit model says either 'we'll find the missing pieces' or 'don't worry, the missing pieces will turn up in their own time'.

The alternative approach is a credit model, disposition enhancing. The relevant community decides what domains of learning disposition are important, and in a credit model the examples of successful participation that will contribute to the inclination or *being ready* are foregrounded. They are the sites of educational interest because we want their occurrence to be frequent enough to become an inclination.

Deficit-based assessment is 'how you've been brought up'; a credit-based approach 'turns you around'. Foregrounding achievement is not primarily a matter of encouraging self-esteem; it is a matter of strengthening learning dispositions and of encouraging a view of the self as a learner. Early childhood practitioners frequently foreground the occasion or the situation in order to evaluate their programmes, and assessment often places skills and knowledge in the foreground. Procedures for foregrounding the inclination are less familiar.

Notions of validity

The notion that an external 'objective' measure or standard exists for all outcomes (if only we can find it) was another feature of my folk model of assessment. I looked for performances that could be scored independently by people who had no additional knowledge about the student. In the alternative approach, however, assessment of the complex outcomes outlined above (learning dispositions, the learner-in-action and -in-relationships) is a central puzzle. To be valid, these assessments must go beyond anecdote, belief and hope. They will require interpreted observations, discussions and agreements. This process of assessment is like action research, with the practitioner/researcher as part of the action. Assessment procedures in early child-hood will call on interpretive and qualitative approaches for the same reasons a researcher will choose interpretive and qualitative methods for researching complex learning in a real-life early childhood setting. These reasons include an interest in the learner-in-action or -in-relationships, and an interest in motivation – in understanding the learning environment from the children's point of view. A number of people's opinions will be surveyed, including the children's, and often the assessments will be tentative.

Both research and assessments, in trying to 'make sense' of data and turn in a plausible story, always run the risk of over-simplification: losing the rich and often ambiguous complexity of young children's behaviour. Knupfer warns that to 'tell the story' of a child's learning: 'We can run the risk of not fully addressing the perplexities, the contradictions, and the conflicting perspectives if we attempt to create cohesion at the expense of complexity' (1996: 142). Discussions with and observations by a number of interested parties, including the child, can be a source of what Graue and Walsh (1995) have called 'thick' description, acknowledging contradiction, ambiguity, inconsistency, and situation-specific factors.

Ideas about progress

The folk model of assessment with which I began included the notion that all learning could be described as a progression through a hierarchy of skills. Piagetian stage theory, and the strong influence of the early intervention movement in early childhood, have provided a firm foundation for the viewpoint that skills and understandings have an 'early' stage and that the task of early childhood education is to ensure that specific developmental skills are taught in an orderly sequence.

A particular hierarchy or sequence implies a single *endpoint*, but views about the domains of intelligence have changed substantially. In recent years, that single developmental path has given way to alternatives. The notion of multiple ways of think-ing and knowing has challenged what Shirley Turkle and Seymour Papert (1992: 3) have called the 'hegemony of the abstract, formal, and logical' in particular to give renewed value to the concrete and the 'here and now', originally seen in Piagetian terms as an immature stage of development. Seymour Papert (1993) emphasised action and 'con-creteness' and criticised what he called the 'perverse commitment to moving as quickly as possible from the concrete to the abstract' (p. 143). The value of Piaget's work, he maintained, is that he gave us valuable insights into the workings of a non-abstract way of thinking.

Cross-cultural studies have also challenged beliefs in the universality of one particular endpoint, individual rationalism, indicating that any valued endpoint is a cultural con-struction, not a developmental inevitability. Some West African communities define stages of development to full selfhood using social signposts. Children are assigned different roles at different stages of life, and progress is defined as increased authority and shared responsibility within the social community (Nsamenang and Lamb 1998). Margaret Donaldson, in *Human Minds*, has suggested two major pathways of develop-ment: the intellectual and the emotional. In the 'value-sensing' emotional pathway the imagination is central. She reminds us (1992: 259) that education is about increasing what she calls the 'modal' repertoire: 'It is about suggesting new directions in which lives may go.'

Therefore, new voices have suggested that responsibility, care and intuition are endpoints too. Relationships have been emphasised as central to the trajectory from early childhood experience into later learning, and these relationships may be more than mediating variables, means to cognitive ends. Reciprocal relationships and opportunities for participation, valuable in the here and now of an early childhood setting, are also pivotal to the first messages about the self as a learner that children receive in early childhood settings, messages that have an enduring effect on their capacities to learn in later years. What do they tell us about progress? Writers using ecological and sociocultural frameworks have provided some theoretical guidelines. The theoretical perspectives that I have found useful for this question of progress are as follows. Jean Lave and Étienne Wenger (1991) described development and progress as a shift in participation from the edge (periphery) of the activities of a community to taking on a more central role. Barbara Rogoff (1997) described development as transformation of participation. Her list of features for the evaluation of learning and development from this perspective included: changing involvement and role, approaches to participation flexibly shifting from home to an early childhood setting, an interest in 'learning' versus an interest in protecting the status quo, and the taking of responsibility in cultural activities including 'flexibility and vision' in revising ongoing community practices. Bonnie Litowitz (1997) has also emphasised participation as responsibility and resistance (transaction and reciprocity): the child may bring a very different view from the adult to an activity or a task. Urie Bronfenbrenner (1979: 60, 163, 212) has said that learning and development are facilitated by the participation of the developing person in *progressively more complex activities and patterns of reciprocal interaction*, and by *gradual 'shifts in the balance of power' between the learner and the adult*. His theory also maintains that development and learning are about the learner taking on roles and relationships in an *increasing number of structurally different settings*.

As practitioners and I worked together on assessment projects to implement some of these alternative theoretical approaches, to help the children they were working with, and to share ideas with families, five features of participation emerged. They are:

- taking an interest in aspects of the early childhood setting that might be the same or different from home; coping with transition and changing situations;
- being involved, at an increasingly complex level;
- persistence with difficulty or uncertainty: an interest in 'learning' and a capacity to risk error or failure;
- communicating with others, expressing a point of view, an idea or an emotion;
- taking increasing responsibility in a range of ways.

Procedures

It seems, then, that my checklist was not the only, or the best, way to document learning in early childhood. One of the advantages of a checklist is that it takes little time, whereas qualitative and interpretive methods using narrative methods – learning stories

– are time-consuming. Practitioners using storied approaches of assessment, however, become part of a rich tradition of ethnographic and case study observations in early childhood. Susan Isaacs' observations in the 1930s are, in Mary Jane Drummond's words (1999: 4), 'transformed into a geography of learning, as she charts the children's explorations of both their inner and outer worlds'. However, although I commented earlier that a practitioner is like an action researcher, assessment of ongoing learning in an early childhood centre by practitioners is rather different from observations by a visiting researcher. Staff have had to develop ways in which these more story-like methods can be manageable. Practitioners have had to become increasingly skilled at recognising 'critical' moments and memorising the events while jotting down the conversations, and assessment has become less likely to take them away from the 'real' action of teaching and enjoying working with children. Situated frameworks call for the adult to be included in the observations as well, and for many practitioners this is unusual and difficult.

Value to practitioners

Twenty years ago I saw documented assessment as only valuable to me when my reputation with outside agencies was at stake. It was as if in my mind I had a 'league table' of early childhood centres, and I wanted to be reassured that my children were achieving up there with the others from the early childhood centre down the road. Also, I did not want to be blamed by the school and the families for any child's low level of preparation for school. However, as I have worked together with practitioners on different ways of doing assessment that have linked more closely to curriculum implementation, a number of more valuable reasons for documented assessment have emerged. Value for practitioners has included:

- to understand, get to know, be 'in tune' with individual children
- to understand children by using the documentation as a catalyst for discussion with others
- to share information with others in this setting
- to reflect on practice
- to plan for individuals and groups.

Other values included involving the children in self-assessment, discussing the programme with families, and sharing experiences with families.

Concluding comments

This chapter has outlined a shift in my views of assessment, along seven dimensions, from a 'folk' model of twenty years ago, to my current understanding of what the much more complex parameters of an alternative model might look like. I have come around to Mary Jane Drummond's definition of assessment. She says that assessment is: 'the ways in which, in our everyday practice, we observe children's learning, strive to understand it, and then put our understanding to good use' (1993: 13). Assessment then has four characteristics: it is about everyday practice (in this place), it is observation-based (including talking to children), it requires an interpretation, and it points the way to better learning and teaching.

It is ironic that at the dawn of the twenty-first century, at the same time as we are becoming aware that a key feature of children's learning is that it is situated in activity and social practice, governments are requiring national curricula and universal measures of individual achievement. Early childhood programmes are often besieged by school curricula and school entry assessments as well. At the beginning of this chapter I asked whether assessing learning in early childhood is any of our business. It has become our business as early childhood educators and practitioners to respond to these demands and in doing so, in many cases, to reframe the purpose, the outcomes, the items for intervention, the definitions of validity and progress, the procedures, and the value for practitioners. Reframing the rules and redefining curriculum and achievement may simply be exchanging one form of surveillance for another. But we have a responsibility to ensure that the new communities we are constructing for children, in childcare centres, kindergartens and amongst childminders for instance, are ethical and safe environments in which all children learn. Early childhood practitioners therefore have to make some assumptions about learning, assessment and evaluation (as well as about ethics and safety) that are informed and reflective.

The alternative assumptions about assessment outlined in this chapter have emphasised two major views about learning outcomes. The first view is that learning can be described as transformation of participation, that it is situated in social practice and activities, and includes responsibility and resistance. The second view is that learning of interest will include motivation, and that learning dispositions, that add motivation to situated learning strategies, are very complex outcomes.

References

Bronfenbrenner, U. (1979) *The Ecology of Human Development*. Cambridge, Mass.: Harvard University Press.

Bruner, J. (1990) *Acts of Meaning*. Cambridge, Mass.: Harvard University Press.

Carr, M. (1987) 'A preschool "drill" for problem-solving'. *Investigating* 3 (1), 3–5.

Carr, M. and Claxton, G. (1989) 'The costs of calculation'. *New Zealand Journal of Educational Studies* 24 (2), 129–40.

Claxton, G. (1990) *Teaching to Learn*. London: Cassell.

Cullen, J. (1991) 'Young children's learning strategies: continuities and discontinuities'. *International Journal of Early Childhood* 23 (1), 44–58.

Donaldson, M. (1992) *Human Minds*. London: The Penguin Press.

Drummond, M. J. (1993) *Assessing Children's Learning*. London: David Fulton Publishers.

Drummond, M. J. (1999) *Comparisons in Early Years Education: History, Fact and Fiction*. CREPE Occasional Paper. University of Warwick, Centre for Research in Elementary and Primary Education.

Eisner, E. (2000) 'Those who ignore the past . . .: 12 "easy" lessons for the next millenium'. *Journal of Curriculum Studies* 32 (2), 343–57.

Graue, M. E. and Walsh, D. J. (1995) 'Children in context: interpreting the here and now of children's lives'. In J. A. Hatch (ed.), *Qualitative Research in Early Childhood Settings*. Westport, Connecticut: Praeger, 135–54.

Isaacs, S. (1932) *The Nursery Years: The Mind of the Child from Birth to Six Years*. London: Routledge and Kegan Paul.

Katz, L. G. (1993) *Dispositions: Definitions and Implications for Early Childhood Practices*. Perspectives from ERIC/ECCE: a monograph series. Urbana, Illinois: ERIC Clearinghouse on ECCE.

Knupfer, A. M. (1996) 'Ethnographic studies of children: the difficulties of entry, rappart, and presentations of their worlds'. *Qualitative Studies in Education* 9 (2) 135–49.

Lave, J. and Wenger, E. (1991) *Situated Learning: Legitimate Peripheral Participation*. Cambridge: Cambridge University Press.

Litowitz, B. E. (1997) 'Just say no: responsibility and resistance'. In M. Cole, Y. Engeström and O. Vasquez (eds) *Mind, Culture, and Activity: Seminal Papers from the Laboratory of Comparative Human Cognition*. Cambridge: Cambridge University Press.

Nisbet, J. and Shucksmith, J. (1986) *Learning Strategies*. London: Routledge and Kegan Paul.

Nsamenang, A. Bame and Lamb, M. E. (1998) 'Socialization of NSO children in the Bamenda grassfields of northwestern Cameroon'. In M. Woodhead, D. Faulkner and K. Littleton (eds) *Cultural Worlds of Early Childhood*. London and New York: Routledge in association with The Open University.

Olson, D. R. and Bruner, J. S. (1996) 'Folk psychology and folk pedagogy'. In D. R. Olson and N. Torrance (eds) *The Handbook of Education and Human Development: New Models of Learning, Teaching and Schooling*. London: Blackwell.

Papert, S. (1993) *The Children's Machine: Rethinking School in the Age of the Computer*. Hemel Hempstead: Harvester Wheatsheaf.

Perkins, D. N., Jay, E. and Tishman, S. (1993) 'Beyond abilities: a dispositional theory of thinking'. *Merril-Parker Quarterly* 39, 1 January, 1–21.

Resnick, L. B. (1987) *Education and Learning to Think*. Washington, DC: National Academy Press.

Rogoff, B. (1997) 'Evaluating development in the process of participation: theory, methods, and practice building on each other'. In E. Amsel and K. Ann Renninger (eds) *Change and Development: Issues of Theory, Method and Application*. Mahwah, NJ and London: Erlbaum.

Rogoff, B. (1998) 'Cognition as a collaborative process'. In William Damon (ed.) *Handbook of Child Psychology*. 5th edn. Vol. 2. Cognition, Perception and Language. (Volume Editors: Deanna Kuhn and Robert S. Siegler.) New York: John Wiley, 679–744.

Salomon, G. (1993) 'Editor's introduction'. In G. Salomon (ed.) *Distributed Cognitions: Psychological and Educational Considerations*. Cambridge: Cambridge University Press.

Shepard, L. A. (1991) 'Psychometricians' beliefs about learning'. *Educational Researcher* 20 (6), 2–16.

Sylva, K. (1994) 'School influences on children's development'. *Journal of Child Psychology and Psychiatry* 34 (1), 135–70.

Torrance, H. and Pryor, J. (1998) *Investigating Formative Assessment: Teaching, Learning and Assessment in the Classroom*. Buckingham: Open University Press.

Turkle, S. and Papert, S. (1992) 'Epistemological pluralism and the revaluation of the concrete', *Journal of Mathematical Behavior* 11, 3–33.

Vygotsky, L. S. (1978) *Mind in Society: The Development of Higher Psychological Processes*. Edited by M. Cole, V. John-Steiner, S. Scribner and E. Souberman. Translated by A. R. Luria, M. Lopez-Morillas, M. Cole and J. Wertsch. Cambridge, Mass.: Harvard University Press.

Wertsch, J. V. (1991) *Voices of the Mind: A Sociocultural Approach to Mediated Action*. Cambridge, Mass.: Harvard University Press.

Chapter 7

Listening to children [1]

Alison Clark

This chapter draws on a study which explored ways of listening to the views of young children. The Mosaic approach utilises a range of methods: observation, child-conferencing, cameras, tours and mapping to gain perspectives on children's daily lives in a setting. Alison Clark suggests that this approach can be used as a tool to help children reflect on their own lives and enable them to develop new skills and competencies and increase their ability to communicate with adults. She suggests it can also provide a context for communication between the adults involved in the children's lives.

The Mosaic approach

The Mosaic approach provides a flexible set of methods which provide a platform for consulting children. It is a multi-method approach which aims to open up many different ways for young children to convey their views and experiences. Malaguzzi refers to the 'hundred languages of children' (Edwards *et al*. 1998). This framework seeks to maximise this rich potential for children to communicate and for adults to listen. The value of talking to young children is not overlooked. However, tools are suggested which also enable young children to communicate their ideas and feelings to adults in other ways, for example through photographs, drawing and walking. These methods may in turn serve as a springboard for more talking, listening and reflecting.

The Mosaic approach is about gaining young children's perspectives of their everyday lives. The focus is not on 'learning' but about the routines and patterns of each day. It is just as likely to reveal what children think about the toilets as their experiences of learning to write. The tools described here have been influenced by the participatory methods developed in participatory rural appraisal or PRA. These methods were drawn together in the 1980s and 1990s to enable non-literate adults in the majority world to play an active part in decision-making at a local level. Now non-governmental organisations (NGOs) and researchers are exploring the use of these tools with young people and children. Tools include the use of mapping and modelling, diagrams, drawing and collage, child to child interviewing and drama and puppetry. These participatory methods are about attitudes and behaviour as well as about techniques. PRA is designed to empower those who take part by enabling people to represent their *own* situations, to reflect on their experiences and to influence change.

I will briefly outline five of the tools used in the Mosaic approach; observing, child conferencing, cameras, tours and mapping. These examples are taken from my work with young children, mainly under 5s who attend the Thomas Coram Early Childhood Centre (TCECC), part of the Coram Community Campus.

Observation

Observation has been the starting point for this study, across each age group. However, for the youngest children who are pre-verbal or with limited speech, observation is of particular importance. We are able to build on a strong tradition of using observation in early childhood research and practice. Several models have influenced the framework of observation. Selleck (2001) has devised a detailed method of observation during her three year study of under threes in day care. This is based on the gathering of 'Nursery Stories'. We adapted this qualitative approach to focus on individual children within the TCECC.

We also drew on the 'Children's Questions' devised to evaluate the innovative early years curriculum in New Zealand: *Te Whaariki* (Ministry of Education 1996). These questions are drawn from each of the five strands of the curriculum: belonging, well-being, exploration, communication and contribution. The questions are: Do you know me? Can I trust you? Do you let me fly? Do you hear me? and Is this place fair?

We have used the question, 'Do you listen to me?' as the basis for our observations with children under two. This question has also provided an interesting starting point for dialogue with staff.

Child conferencing

Talking to young children is an important part of the Mosaic approach. What framework could be used for enabling children with differing personalities, verbal skills and backgrounds to tell us what they thought about the setting? In order to achieve this goal, there is the need to include both formal and informal conversations with children. Child conferencing provided one structured way of doing so. This is a short interview schedule devised by Bernadette Duffy, Head of TCECC for use as an evaluation tool with preschool children. The questions, (14 in total) ask children about why they come to nursery, who are their favourite people and who do they like being with, and about their favourite activities. There are also questions about how children see the adults' role in the nursery. The interview ends with an open-ended question to provide the opportunity for children to add any further information they think is important. Some children chose to add a drawing at this point or to sign their name.

Is this a useful tool for consulting young children? Child conferencing has possibilities, especially if used flexibly and in conjunction with other methods. The choice of setting for the interview is critical. The 'interview' may need to be conducted on the move, for example a three- and four-year-old began the interview inside and then proceeded to show the researcher their favourite outdoor spaces. The interview then continued outside. Child conferencing was carried out with one key group in the kindergarten of TCECC in July 1999 and repeated with those children who were still a member in November 1999. This provided opportunities for the children to reflect on their previous responses and to assess what had changed and how they now felt about life in the nursery.

The use of cameras

Visual methods are an essential element of the Mosaic approach. There was the possibility of using photographs taken by the researcher to form the basis of the interviews with young children. This tool has been used with success in research involving children under five (e.g. Candappa 1999).

However, we wanted to go a stage further in this research, particularly as we were also interested in exploring participatory methods. The use of cameras by children had great potential. Cameras provide the opportunity for children to express 'voices' without the need for the spoken or written word. Walker (1993) describes this as 'the silent voice of the camera'. This seems to have particular relevance when working with young children. Photography offers a way of communicating their ideas and feelings which allows young children to be in charge. Children can take control of the camera, choose what to make an image of and produce a final product of which they can be proud. A group of three-and four-year-olds were given a short instruction on how to use a single use camera, including how to operate the flash.

Children were asked to take photographs of things that were important to them about the nursery. Issues of importance to the children emerged during discussions whilst taking the photographs and also looking together at the finished results. These included the use of outside space, changing friendships and relationships with key workers.

Tours and mapping

There was also the opportunity to include other participatory methods in the Mosaic approach. Chambers (1997: 117) explains the use of transect walks as a method of gathering detailed information about an environment from the people who live there. He describes this process as 'systematically walking with local guides and analysts through an area, observing, asking, listening, discussing, learning . . .'. The physical nature of this process appeared to offer possibilities for exploring children's 'local knowledge' of their own environment. Langsted (1994) adopted a similar approach in a Scandinavian study of children's lives. He describes what can be seen as a 'walking interview' with five-year-olds. Children walked the interviewer through their day explaining what happens where.

The Mosaic approach was adapted to include a process of tours and mapping. The children directed a tour of the site, working individually, or in twos or threes. The children also took photographs, produced drawings and notes and made audio-tape recordings as the tour progressed. This initial exercise was followed by a map-making activity using the images produced.

This approach enables young children to be the experts in this stage of the research or evaluation process. The researcher did not know the building as well as the children, nor the staff who the children met on the tour. The use of the children's own photographs was also a significant part of the process. Children seemed to relate more easily to images they had made themselves and were more able to construct them into a map.

Listening about living

We have described the Mosaic approach as a way of gaining young children's perspectives of their daily lives. Johnson and Ivan-Smith describe such participatory tools as enabling adults to 'view the world through the lens of children and young people' (Johnson *et al*. 1998: 8). What potential does this have for work with young children in particular settings? One advantage is moving towards a child agenda for change. The use of tools such as the camera and tours can demonstrate children's priorities which might otherwise have become lost. The issue of the use of outside space was raised by the children in the study. Several of the children recorded the importance of the 'empty' spaces, such as by the shed and beside the fence. This information could then be included in discussion when plans for reordering the outdoor area took place.

The Mosaic approach in use in an educational setting also extends consultation beyond a learning discourse. Exchanges between key workers and parents can have a focus which is not necessarily dominated by academic progress. In the study, the researcher met individually with a number of parents to discuss life in the nursery for their child. In one case, the four-year-old also joined in this discussion. The focus was provided by the documentation gathered using the Mosaic approach. A parent could discuss their child's responses to the child conferencing, see photographs taken by their child and maps made from the photographs. Descriptions of observation accounts were also fed into this discussion. Important issues for both children and parents emerged from this reflection. For example, during a tour of the building, one child had expressed her desire to be old enough to have lunch with the four-year-olds in the special room. This was a new routine, introduced to allow the older children to eat lunch together, in preparation for their moving on to school. Her mother was aware from conversations at home that this child was preoccupied by the idea of going to school and talked everyday about wanting to be old enough to go there. This piece of information provided a new insight for the key worker into this child's wishes and also her feelings about her current status within the nursery.

'Experts in their own lives'

The Mosaic approach can also be used as a reflexive tool for helping young children to reflect on their own lives. This way of working is an attempt to move children's evaluation beyond a 'like/dislike' model to one which allows children and adults to reflect on children's everyday experiences. There is firstly the initial value gained from treating children as 'experts in their own lives' (Langsted 1994: 35). By asking children what they think about being in a place, what they do there, their perceptions of what it is all about, we are beginning to take children seriously. This confidence may enable children to develop new skills and competencies, which in turn can increase their abilities to communicate with adults. Experiences recorded in this way can then be used as a reference point for children and adults to assess change over time. The use of child conferencing twice in a six-month period demonstrated this point. Children were interested in what they had said before, sometimes giggled at what they had said and used their past responses as a springboard for reflecting on what had changed.

Conclusion

We have looked at different tools within the Mosaic approach for listening to young children. This is a portfolio of tools which can be used and adapted for working in particular settings. However, the portfolio is an open one. There is, for example, the possibility of using drama, puppets, drawing, modelling and music. The range is endless. The important ingredients are firstly the methods: the combined use of tools which enable young children to express their ideas and feelings with confidence. Secondly, it is the attitude towards children which this approach represents: children as experts in their own lives. There is a value in each piece of the Mosaic. However, the value is increased by combining with other pieces or perspectives, including those of parents and key workers. The Mosaic approach is not designed to produce facts but will provide a platform for discussion, with children, staff and parents. It is in the interpretation of the information gathered that the possibility for greater understanding of young children's lives will emerge.

Alison Clark and Peter Moss subsequently published the following book: Clark, A. and Moss, P. (2001) *Listening to young children: the Mosaic approach*. London: National Children's Bureau.

Note

1 The study was funded by the Joseph Rowntree Foundation in collaboration with Coram Family. This chapter is based on a paper presented at the Parent Child Conference, 2000.

References

Candappa, M. (1999) *Growing Up in the City: A Consultation Exercise with Children and Young People*. Report to the Corporation of London. London: Coram Family/Thomas Coram Research Unit.

Chambers, R. (1997) *Whose Reality Counts? Putting the First Last*. London: Intermediate Technology.

Edwards, C., Gandini, L. and Foreman, G. (eds) (1998) *The Hundred Languages of Children: The Reggio Emilia Approach to Early Childhood Education*, 2nd edn. New Jersey: Ablex Publishing Corporation.

Johnson, V. et al. (eds) (1998) *Stepping Forward. Children and Young People's Participation in the Development Process*. London: Intermediate Technology.

Langsted, O. (1994) 'Looking at quality from the child's perspective', in Moss, P. and Pence, A. (eds) *Valuing Quality in Early Childhood Services: New Approaches to Defining Quality*. London: Paul Chapman Publishing.

Ministry of Education (1996) *Te Whaariki: Early Childhood Curriculum*. Wellington: New Zealand Ministry of Education.

Selleck, D. (2001) 'Being under three years of age: enhancing quality experiences', in Pugh, G. (ed.) *Contemporary Issues in the Early Years – Working Collaboratively for Children*, 3rd edn. London: Paul Chapman Publishing.

Walker, R. (1993) 'Finding a silent voice for the researcher: using photographs in evaluation and research', in Schratz, Michael (ed.) *Qualitative Voices in Educational Research*. London: Falmer Press.

Chapter 8

Observing children

Jane Devereux

In this chapter Jane Devereux provides a rationale for observing children and offers ways of observing that have direct implications for practice. She discusses how information gathered by watching children at play or involved in other activities, provides insight into their current interests and ways of learning, their next steps and also possible concerns.

Introduction

Watching and listening to children as they play and learn is a stimulating and rewarding activity whether you are professionally or personally involved with the child. Observations help practitioners working with children to develop their knowledge of the child and their developing competences, schemas and personal interests. Key questions that I have asked myself throughout my teaching career, are: Why am I doing this activity or action with these children in this way? Is it the best way to enable the most learning to take place for all of the group? Why do I want them to learn this now? Is it informed by my knowledge of the learners' interests, needs and wishes? How do I know this?

This chapter will explore how watching and listening to children provides the basis for all future actions. It will provide a clear rationale for planned observations of children's learning and for the need to keep objective records of that achievement in order to best serve the needs and interests of the learner. It will highlight how important it is to respect the child as a person and include them in the process. Such knowledge and insight provides an informed basis from which to work to support, challenge and extend children's learning and highlight any concerns.

Why observe?

Observations of young children can be used for a variety of purposes. The *Statutory Framework for the Early Years Foundation Stage* (DfES 2007, p. 16) emphasises that 'ongoing assessment is an integral part of the learning and development process. Providers must ensure that practitioners are observing children and responding appropriately to help them make progress.'

Observations provide information on which to base future action and develop our knowledge of how children think and learn, as well as providing evidence of their developing competences, persistent interests, dispositions (Katz and Chard 1989; Carr 2001) and schemas (Athey 1990; Bartholomew and Bruce 1993). They can also be used for practitioners to review their 'role as provider of care and education' (Nutbrown 2006, p. 98) and for forward planning and summative reporting. It is also important to remember that when observing we bring our own experiences, beliefs and values into the process which can influence the way we interpret what we see.

Observation is seen as a fundamental part of the process of teaching and learning and not an end in itself. Some kind of action should normally be a consequence of those observations, even if it is a decision to do nothing, yet, or to gather further observations before planning changes in provision.

The next part of this chapter explores these aspects further and reflects on the implications for practice.

A. *Observation of children's competence*

Watching and listening to children at play and work I am constantly surprised by their creativeness, inventiveness, persistence and talent. While watching a student practitioner on placement in a nursery I heard the following discourse between two girls at work in the writing corner, set up by the student. Having noted an interest in teddy bears by a group of children, she had provided some teddy note books which these two girls were using and discussing as follows:

> *Victoria* (3 yrs 8 mths): What's that you've put in your writing? [Points] There!
> *Louise* (3 yrs 11 mths): Oh that's a full stop. [She makes it bigger and darker]
> *V*: What's it do?
> *L*: It stops my writing going on.
> *V*: Oh I think I need one of those! Let me put one here. [Puts in large full stop at end of her writing.] That's stopped that writing. Good.

(personal observation)

For me, this was a magical moment – being in the right place at the right time. It is only a short observation but provides a whole wealth of evidence about these young children as learners and of possible lines of development to support with those two girls. It does not imply that one must prepare a formal lesson on the use of full stops, but it does suggest that it would be valuable to gather more evidence of the children's understanding of their use, e.g. to collect samples of their writing over the next few days and weeks to see if there was any consistency or pattern in the use of full stops. I may have done some shared writing with groups, including the two girls, and talked about full stops there. I may also have read some familiar big books at story time, encouraging children to help me with the reading. This would have created opportunities to talk about features of written language, such as full stops.

B. *Raising awareness of our own beliefs and values*

As listening to children's voices has become a more central concern for practitioners it is crucial that we understand how our own beliefs and values can affect our interpretation of what we see. Differences in children's experiences, for example, in relation to gender and culture, will be highlighted by observing what they do and so our expectations of the children may be influenced. It is therefore vitally important in early years settings that all adults are involved in the process of gathering observations so that a range of voices can inform the team's approach to provision and interaction with the children. Included in this notion of 'all adults' must be the parents and carers of the children. They have been the foremost influence in the child's life so far and have provided the crucial basis of their early learning. It is important to note at this time the way that our observations and those of the parent and/or carers can help provide continuity in the learning of the child between home and school. Each can inform the other of concerns and developments that can enable all to enhance the learning experiences of the child.

C. *Gathering observations of competence*

This provides practitioners with evidence to report to parents, receiving teachers, heads, inspectors and advisors, OFSTED and other outside agencies concerned with each child's progress. This summative use of evidence can inform discussions at a significant point in the child's educational life, such as the transfer from nursery to reception or from one school to another,

Vital within this justification for observation is the need for evidence if there are concerns about a child's progress or lack of development. For example, children who have difficulty settling into a new setting, find it hard to relate to others, have difficulty communicating with others or have speech difficulties may benefit. Practitioners may need to seek expert advice and support for the team and/or the child. Gathering information about children and with the children will help to refine our understanding of any problem, or alleviate our anxieties by refuting our initial concerns. Having information and detailed observations enables us to approach the appropriate agency(ies) from an informed basis and so initiate action as quickly as possible. In England, this may involve using the Common Assessment Framework (CAF) which has been developed to help identify earlier children who need more substantial or specialised help across different dimensions of growth and development.

At all times in our work with children we should be building up, as Carr (2001) suggests, a positive model or 'credit' of the child and be able to justify the actions we take, on the basis of our detailed knowledge of their needs and experiences. Observation is, therefore, a vital skill that practitioners need to develop from the very beginning of their careers. However, many experienced practitioners will admit that it is not as easy as it sounds. How, then, do we get started and what do we do with the observations as they are gathered?

Factors to consider when observing

Getting started

Who, how, what, when and where to observe are important questions to address in getting started. This can seem a rather daunting list and inhibit some from even attempting to observe. It will be different for each practitioner as it depends on individual experiences of observation and on the skills already developed. The most important thing is to make a start, and to reflect on that experience and learn from it. Sharing experiences with other team members or colleagues in different situations will help clarify the process of observation and may highlight needs.

Who should do the observations?

The whole team should be encouraged to be involved, but some members may need support and encouragement to begin. First, it is important to just have a go. Watch and listen to an individual who interests you or causes you concern. Record what you see on some form of note pad or proforma. The more people who are involved in the observing the more varied will be the evidence about each child. If that produces a consensus of evidence then the assessment of that child's competence is stronger, and decisions about ways to extend and challenge that child will be better informed. Children and parents, as has already been mentioned, should be part of this process too, but it is important to be sensitive to the different ways that children and parents both want to be and can be involved in the process. The start of a child's time in an early years setting is a crucial one to be in contact with parents, to welcome them but also to share their knowledge of their child's learning up to that point. Parents are the first educators of the child and do not stop being such when children start at a setting, but their role is different and complementary to that of the setting.

Providing opportunities for parents to share their understanding and knowledge of their children as learners, through informal discussion with practitioners, can be linked to initial home visits which may sometimes be carried out prior to children starting at a setting.

Bartholomew and Bruce (1993) develop this idea and show how parents can feed observations into the early years setting to help the child have a smooth transition. This is, of course, a two-way process and settings-based observations may help and inform parents/carers and facilitate learning beyond the classroom and provide continuity for the child.

This discussion may also help assess whether or not the observations are providing the information needed about the child as a learner. If the information from parents does not concur with the team's developing picture of the child it may indicate possible areas for further observation, or changes or additions to the provision already on offer. It may be that the quality of provision does not allow children to operate at an appropriate level, important questions may need to be asked about how the environment is organised, about how children are able or unable to access resources, and about the support and interaction that takes place between children and adults. Tightly prescribed tasks with control in the hands of the practitioner may limit children's opportunities to display their creativity, imagination and expertise, and discussion between children and adults where children's efforts are directed towards guessing what answer is inside the practitioner's head may affect the development of their own thinking strategies and skill in solving problems.

Play is a vitally important part of a child's activity. The provision of opportunities for play can allow children to practise and develop new skills and competences, to explore emotional situations, to experiment with ideas, to take risks and to solve problems. Involving all those who work in the early years team in observing children at play and work is therefore vital to gain a clearer picture of each child's competence.

When is the best time to observe?

In reality, as soon as we enter an early years setting, we begin to watch and look. At first this is to gain an overall view of what is happening within the room, and the provision that is on offer. This will include noting the areas of provision, the adults involved and their location and the forms of interaction that are taking place. However, it is very important that our observations go beyond this since, as Nutbrown (2006, p. 99) suggests, watching and learning is the only way to 'establish the progress that has already taken place and explore the future – the learning that is embryonic'. For the very reason that observation is part of the process of teaching and learning and is happening all the time as we listen to and interact with children, it is important to take care that its vital role is not lost. If observation is not planned for specifically, then it often does not happen. How will we know what children are achieving, if we do not spend time watching and listening to what they do and say? At times we will want to observe as we interact with the children, and many of our questions and actions will be in direct response to the children's actions. The more we know about individuals and about child development in general the better will be our observations and, ultimately, our judgements. Planning for observation is, therefore, important and should be part of the general routine. Questions about how many observations can be made during a session, and by whom, need to be considered. In particular, the goals set for the number and type of planned observations must be both realistic and achievable, if they are to stand any chance of happening.

Many nursery teams meet briefly each day or regularly during the week, to share significant information, including observations about children, provision and resources and to plan the next day's provision in the light of the day's events and the children's experiences. The allocation of people, and time to observe as well as who or what is to be observed, may be some of the decisions taken at such meetings. Observations can be made:

- at regular intervals during a day;
- at incidental or opportune moments;
- at the start and end of sessions/activities;
- during activities while participating with children;
- during activities but not participating.

The timing of the observations and the form they take will be determined, to some extent, by the kind of information it is hoped to collect, and we shall consider *what* to observe later in this chapter.

How can observations be made?

In observing the current interests and schemas that dominate the child's interactions and actions in school or nursery we need to look at the whole child and the interplay of intellectual, social, emotional and physical aspects that are vitally important and feed and support each other. We need to be aware that we can and do bring our own experiences and expectations to bear when we observe any action. The old saying that 'what we look for is what we see' carries an important warning for all those working with children, that we try to see what the children are *actually* doing and not what we *think* they are doing, or even what we *want* to see. As Wood (2008) suggests, it is important to remember that the context within which our values and beliefs operate may be different from that of the child and we must respect this difference and individuality.

Observations should be as objective as possible given all the influences that can come in to play as we watch. The use of language is, therefore, very important. There is a world of difference between recording that a child 'wrote his name from right to left in the top right hand corner of the paper starting with the first letter in the extreme corner and moving along from the right to left' and saying that 'he wrote his name in the top right corner of the paper but it was written wrongly as it was back to front'. The first is both more factual and less judgemental than the second entry. Judgemental language may work to lower practitioner's expectations for individual children, and close down options for them. In this example, use of the word 'wrong' does little actually to describe what the child has done or provide information about how his understanding and competence can be developed. It may also be that this child's first or home language is one in which reading and writing *are* carried out from right to left.

Ignorance or insensitivity to such factors are ways in which our observations can be affected. Statements such as 'has difficulty in concentrating', 'is a slow reader', 'has poor gross motor skills' sometimes appear in children's profiles. What evidence, though, can be given to justify such comments? To reach such conclusions the observers would need to have seen things which led them to believe them to be 'true'. To write such statements, however, sometimes even based upon a single observation, suggests that general conclusions are being drawn too easily. For example if we take the comment 'is a slow reader'. The child in question may have had difficulty with a particular text or been called away while in the middle of another activity in which s/he was deeply involved.

At this stage it is useful to consider two types of observation – participatory and non-participatory. The use of either will be dependent on such issues as staffing levels, resources and the information that is being gathered.

Participatory observation

All practitioners, as part of their everyday work with children, are involved in participatory observation, but this does not always lead to written entries in the child's profile. Participant observation may initially seem more difficult to manage, in that notes must be made either at points during work with the children, or immediately afterwards if the knowledge and evidence is not to be lost. We think that we will remember something and will be able to note it down later. Given the pace at which events can develop in early years settings, however, these observations can easily be lost or inaccurately remembered. Having 'post-it' notes, clipboards with paper or notepads placed strategic-ally around the room will help provide both the incentive and the means with which to record the incident, briefly, as it happens. Another practice is to ensure that you always carry a notepad with you, from place to place. Such pads often become the focus for children's attention, too, with them leaving messages and writing their own 'notes' down – all of which should be valued.

Observations made in this way may often be incidental and unplanned as in the writing corner described earlier. Like the planned observations, these can be incor-porated into the general system of observations which add to the developing picture of a child.

The habit of recording observations almost automatically comes with practice and notes often become shorter, but more telling in their content, with increasing experience. One teacher in the PROCESS Research Project (Stierer *et al.* 1993) said that as she became more experienced at observing she wrote less but it told her more!

Non-participatory observation

Non-participatory observation means that the observer stays outside the activity in order to concentrate on the child or aspect being watched. If a single child is the focus it allows the observer to watch that child both as an individual and in the setting of an activity. Similarly, a focus on an aspect of provision or on a particular activity allows the observer to concentrate on that aspect of the nursery alone, without having to keep an eye on anything else.

If the observation is to be non-participatory, children may need to know which adults are available for help while that person is busy observing. Where to sit while observing in this way is also important, but becomes less of an issue as children become used to seeing adults watch them. Sitting too near or far from an activity may affect the quality of what is seen or heard, and even the observer's ability to do so. What is most important is that where an adult sits does not have a limiting effect on the children's activity.

A range of formats or ways of observing are also possible, which may be appropriate for particular purposes and at specific times.

Time sampling

Time sampling involves making observations at pre-specified intervals, for example every ten minutes during a session, of a targeted child, group or area of provision. Possible questions one might have in mind when observing a particular child, for example, might be:

- Where is s/he?
- Who is s/he with?
- What is s/he doing?
- What is s/he saying?

Similarly, in observing an area of provision, or piece of equipment, the observer might be considering the following:

- Who is using the equipment?
- What are they doing?
- What are they saying?
- Are adults involved?

Time sampling is particularly useful for tracking children's activities and interactions over a period of time, for building up a picture of particular children, and for appraising the value and use of equipment.

Frequency sampling

Frequency sampling is a way of tracking incidences of particular aspects of behaviour in a child or group of children. In this, the observer identifies a feature of behaviour and notes whenever this occurs. For example, a child may appear always to play alone in the nursery. Observations would focus on whether or not this was indeed the case, and would include looking at whether s/he approached another child, children or adults, whether s/he initiated any interaction, how any interaction was initiated, and where in the nursery this occurred. As its name suggests, frequency sampling can be useful in giving an accurate picture of the frequency of aspects of behaviour, and can be used to monitor both progress and concerns.

Duration observation

Duration observation is a way of accurately tracking how long children spend at particular activities or using certain equipment. It may seem sometimes as if a child or group of children spend all of their time in the construction area or riding the bikes: duration observation is a good way of establishing just how much time they *do* spend in these areas, and can help to ensure that the observations we record are accurate. 'Kuldip spends all of his time on the bikes' may, in reality, be 'Kuldip chooses the bikes first, generally spends half an hour on them and then moves on to other activities.'

Focused observation

In this method, the observer selects an activity, child or children and records everything that happens for a pre-specified period of, for example, five minutes. Focused observations can be helpful in giving a complete picture of children's activities and achievements.

Who and what should we observe?

Decisions about who or what to observe will be driven by the individual's or team's responsibility for the children in their care, and their interests. The following list shows something of the wide range of possibilities:

new children
individual children or groups – gathering general information
children giving cause for concern
areas of provision

use of particular areas
resourcing of areas
movement around areas.

How these are to be observed will vary, according to the reasons for the observations, and in relation to the information needed. A look back at the previous section, on how observations can be made, will help in reaching decisions about the most appropriate forms of observation for particular situations. Whether observations are to be of one child, several children, or an area of the nursery or classroom that is being monitored to assess the effectiveness of provision, as was stressed earlier, it is important to write what is actually seen and heard.

Providing a rich and varied environment plays an important part in the observation process. Quality observations are supported by quality provision. What constitutes quality provision will be briefly discussed here. Young children's learning is deeply embedded in the context in which they are operating.

Records should include all areas in which a child has been observed, but if there are gaps then it should raise questions for the practitioners involved. A question such as why a child does not go to some areas is worth asking. It will be useful then to look closely at that provision: is it not interesting to others as well? Is it that the child has 'not had access to that kind of experience' and thus may need the support of an adult to initially explore its potential? What *are* the particular interests of that child? From these records it will be possible to see the balance of observations one has of all of the children and build into planning the times necessary to observe children for whom there is less evidence.

Which children are confident with books? Does Simone ever go into the block area or outside to play? Does Jane settle at a task for more than a few seconds? Does Kuldip use provision other than the bikes? Who does Marcus play with? How good at solving problems is Hassam? Does he persist? Does he ask for help? If so whom? These are all questions that can arise about individuals, for which planned observations may help to find answers.

What happens to the observations?

Management and storage

As the notes and 'post-its' and pieces of paper accumulate it is important to have some way of managing the volume, both in the short and long term. These pieces of paper initially provide support and information for the planning of future work with the children: they have a *formative* purpose. They are building up a 'learning story' for that child (Carr 2001) and can also have a *summative role* such as report-writing. The latter include statements made about the child's progress, often for communication to others, in particular to parents or carers, and other practitioners. In the long term, developing a manageable filing system for the observations (and samples and photographs of children's work and their participation) is important if they are to be useful, and not lost. A pocket file for each child, ring binders and a section in a filing cabinet are all possibilities, but solutions will be individual, dependent upon available space and storage facilities and the time to support them. Keeping these samples of evidence is, however, very important both in order to inform planning, and for the summative stage(s) in a child's time in the early years setting. They give insights into the child that can inform the understanding of parents, practitioners and managers, inspectors, educational psychologists and other agencies, and provide evidence to support statements made of the child's competence, in a wide range of contexts and areas of experience.

The short-term management of observations includes the sharing of these with other staff at the end of the day or at team meetings so that everyone is aware of the successes, efforts and concerns about individuals, areas and resources. Gaps in professionals' knowledge about particular children can be identified, and plans can be made to fill these gaps.

Sharing observations

How these observations and records are shared with parents/carers is an important aspect to consider, and ways of doing so need to be developed. Not all parents are able to collect their children at the end of a day or session. This does not, of course, mean they are not interested in their child or do not care about supporting them. In order for all parents to have the opportunity to share such observations on a regular basis the setting may have to examine ways of making time available for practitioners to do so, time which may involve extra resourcing and have staffing implications. Having another adult come in to take a story session at the end of the morning or afternoon for half-an-hour a week, or putting groups of children together for a period at the end of the day, may give some time, but a range of options need to be considered if as many parents as possible are to have the opportunity to participate. The use of notebooks that go home and back to the setting are just one way to support working parents.

At summative stages, at the end of the year, not all of the observations themselves will go forward to the following setting. They can, however, form the basis for formal records and report-writing, with evidence for the statements being drawn from the observational records. The summative statement or report then goes forward, the observations that fed it are stored or discarded, and the process begins again with the next intake.

Conclusion

Watching children explore and make sense of their world provides valuable insights into their developing competences. In exploring observation as part of the role of the adult working with young children it is hoped that its vital role in relation to many aspects of early years work has been articulated. Collecting evidence of competence, creativity, persistence, imagination and socialisation gives us insights into the child's growing intellect and personality, and enables professionals to provide the best supportive learning environment for each individual. As Wood (2008, p. 119) says about the early years practitioner's role and responsibility: 'a pedagogy of listening [and watching] respects children's understanding of their identity and individuality, and helps practitioners to understand the influences of the wider social systems' as they support young children in their learning and development.

References

Athey, C. (1990) *Extending Thought in Young Children*. London: Paul Chapman.

Bartholomew, L. and Bruce, T. (1993) *Getting to Know You*. London: Hodder & Stoughton.

Carr, M. (2001) *Assessment in Early Childhood Settings*. London: Paul Chapman.

Department for Education and Skills (2007) *Statutory Framework for the Early Years Foundation Stage*. Nottingham: DfES Publications.

Katz, L. G. and Chard, S. C. (1989) *Engaging Children's Minds: The Project Approach*. New Jersey: Ablex Publishing.

Nutbrown, C. (2006) 'Watching and listening: the tools of assessment', in G. Pugh and B. Duffy (2006) (3rd edn) *Contemporary Issues in the Early Years*. London: Sage Publications.

Stierer, B., Devereux, J., Gifford, S., Laycock, L. and Yerbury, J. (1993) *Profiling, Observing and Recording*. London: Routledge.

Wood, E. (2008) 'Listening to young children: multiple voices, meanings and understandings', in A. Paige-Smith and A. Craft, *Developing Reflective Practice in the Early Years*. Maidenhead: Open University Press.

Part 2
Learning and development

Carrie Cable

Introduction

In Part 2 we continue the theme of learning but look more closely at areas or aspects of learning that are often included in curriculum documents or guidance frameworks – personal, social, emotional and physical development, language, communication and literacy, mathematical understanding, knowledge and understanding of the world, science, ICT and creativity. This is not to suggest that learning in the early years can or should be compartmentalised into different 'areas of learning'. Children learn through their play and the experiences and activities that are provided for them. Developing the disposition to learn and the tools to learn are of fundamental importance. However, the types of experiences and activities that are planned, the environment and resources that are provided, children's opportunities to participate, make decisions, problem solve and take responsibility and the support they receive from others, will impact on how and what they are able to learn.

Young children's social and emotional development is often solely understood from a developmental psychology discourse that focuses on discrete stages in human development. In Chapter 9 Naima Browne emphasises the need for practitioners to reflect on the ways young children gain a sense of who they are and how to foster the development of self-confidence and self-esteem. She concludes by offering some practical strategies for supporting children's personal, social and emotional development.

We know that young children grow and learn through moving and doing, both physically and emotionally. In Chapter 10 Julia Manning-Morton and Maggie Thorp focus on the implications this has for the types of physical play experience babies and toddlers encounter and are provided with, both indoors and outside, and the types of resources practitioners make available for them to use. The authors provide examples from practice to illustrate and illuminate their suggestions.

The development of early literacy skills is often a contentious issue embedded in debates around informal versus didactic approaches to teaching and learning. In Chapter 11 Robin Campbell argues very clearly for approaches to literacy which place communication, play and enjoyment of books, songs and rhymes as central. He considers the key elements of a literacy curriculum for the early years, including literacy 'goals'. He explores the role of adults as they support, model, interact and scaffold children's learning and concludes by arguing for a broad-based foundation for children's literacy development.

In Chapter 12 Rosemary Feasey and Margaret Still discuss the use of ICT in supporting learning in science and the development of positive learning dispositions across the early years curriculum. Enabling children to engage with new technologies and ICT is an important aspect of the role of all early years practitioners. While the equipment readily available will vary from setting to setting, the authors suggest that practitioners need to explore the possibilities available to them through collaborations, partnerships, loans and parental and community expertise.

Creative development is one of the key aspects and early learning goals in the *Early Years Foundation Stage* (DCSF 2008). However, the development of children's creativity does not only take place through art and craft activities, music or performance. In Chapter 13 Anna Craft and Bob Jeffrey argue that practitioners can enable children's creativity and creative development through all the experiences and activities they provide for children. They draw on evidence from their research to explore what creativity means for practitioners in terms of their practice and discuss the development of a learner inclusive environment which places children at the centre in decisions about what and how they learn.

Chapter 14 focuses on communication and in this chapter Marian Whitehead explores how babies communicate from birth and develop their communication skills even before they can talk. She examines how children first use words and the multiple meanings a single word or phrase can have. In the second part of the chapter she discusses different views of grammar and cautions against more prescriptive views which have dominated much official guidance. Finally she provides a useful list of suggestions to support practitioners in providing rich linguistic beginnings for babies and toddlers.

We know that most children are competent learners but recent research is allowing us insights into the range and extent of these competences. In Chapter 15 Linda Pound explores how many of these competences relate to mathematical thinking and understanding and provides suggestions as to how practitioners may re-evaluate the experiences and activities that they engage in with children. She suggests ways in which practitioners can support children in problem solving and communicating their ideas. As Chapter 15 notes, children's ability to problem solve is now recognised as a fundamental aspect of their successful mathematical development. This is clearly reflected in the *Early Years Foundation Stage* (DCSF 2008). In Chapter 16 Sue Gifford explores how and why developing this aspect of children's knowledge and understanding is so important. Examples and illustrations provide practitioners with ways of developing their practice and children's learning.

Many settings consider projects an effective means of integrating areas or aspects of learning in the early years, while maintaining a focus on holistic learning and development. In Chapter 17, the last chapter in this part of the book, Jane Devereux and Ann Bridges provide an example of a creative project that was rooted in listening to and involving children and adults in problem solving with a real and tangible outcome for everyone. The garden project described in this chapter clearly illustrates the importance of learning taking place both indoors and outdoors.

Reference

Department for Children, Schools and Families (DCSF) (2008) *The Statutory Framework for the Early Years Foundations Stage*. Nottingham: DCSF.

Chapter 9

Children's social and emotional development

Naima Browne

Young children's social and emotional development is often solely understood from a developmental psychology discourse that focuses on discrete stages in human development. Naima Browne emphasises the need for practitioners to reflect on the ways young children gain a sense of who they are and how to foster the development of self-confidence and self-esteem. She concludes by offering some practical strategies for supporting children's personal, social and emotional development.

This chapter explores children's emotional development from a perspective that emphasizes the importance of practitioners considering identity, equity and children's rights as key issues offering material for practitioners to reflect on together. The chapter will look at the ways in which children's identities and sense of who they are develop within a social context. The relationship between children's growing identities and their emotional wellbeing is explored. The impact of factors such as gender and culture on children's identities and emotional development is also examined. The chapter will look at transitions in relation to young children's emotional development. Recent research into the impact of transition will be discussed. The important role that listening to children plays in supporting their emotional development is briefly discussed, although the issue of listening to children is covered in depth in later chapters.

Introduction

Practitioners must provide experiences and support to enable children to develop a positive sense of themselves and of others. They must support children's emotional wellbeing, helping them to know themselves and what they can do. They must also help children to develop respect for others, social skills and a positive disposition to learn.

(DfES 2006: Section 3.9)

Social and emotional development involves, among other things, a growing understanding of how to behave in different situations, the ability to empathize with others, to be self-controlled and develop positive dispositions towards learning. Young children's emotional and social development includes developing good interpersonal skills, developing positive relationships with others, developing intra-personal understandings, and growing self-confidence and self-esteem. A child's emotional and social development is also inextricably linked with their growing sense of who they are: their personal identity.

Emotional wellbeing and resilience

Thinking about emotional wellbeing may help us as practitioners to think more broadly about emotional development. This concept is increasingly being used: 'Considering children's emotional and social development is clearly an important aspect of professional practice and recent research would suggest that in the foundation stage children's emotional health is becoming a priority in local authorities across England' (Ofsted 2007).

Children's emotional and social development is shaped and influenced by a wide range of factors. A child's early experiences of interactions with others, for example, helps lay the foundations for future relationships and the child's ongoing emotional development. Children's diverse life experiences and how they are related to in different ways by other children and by their parents also set up expectations about their behaviour and their emotional development, and reveal what their parents and others think is 'typical' and acceptable.

Developmental psychology and patterns of emotional development

Practitioners working in the UK, USA and north European settings are used to working within the developmental psychology discourse. This means that practitioners tend to think about children's development in terms of ages, stages and identified markers or milestones of progress and development.

Piaget's work has been hugely influential in the field of early years, not least in terms of presenting the child as learning and developing 'naturally' and progressing through a series of clearly identifiable, universal stages on the journey to adult modes of thinking and behaving. Piaget's findings have been criticized by psychologists such as Donaldson (1978) and Hughes (1986), whose research suggested that young children were able to demonstrate far more sophisticated levels of thinking than Piaget had claimed. Nonetheless, the notion of the naturally developing child remains a very powerful concept for early years practitioners. Comments made by early years practitioners and parents, such as 'What stage is she at?', reveal how this particular view of the child is still firmly established within the early years field.

The ideas of Vygotsky and Bruner led to social constructivism being incorporated into the dominant discourse on early years learning; both emphasized that learning is socially situated. While most practitioners acknowledge the importance of social interaction there has not, however, been a move away from envisaging children's learning in terms of ages and stages. This is evident in guidance provided for settings (e.g. QCA 2000).

The notion that children's learning and development can be quantified, measured and tested is related to the concept of childhood as a 'stage' in human development. In this particular model of human development the desirable end state is seen to be adulthood. In societies where adulthood and childhood are seen as stages and states, adulthood is seen to be the last stage in development, or the 'end state'. Adults come to possess 'adult' characteristics through an unvarying and universal developmental process.

The distinction between childhood and adulthood may seem to be obvious and 'natural' but while the concept of adulthood as a state predominates in western societies, in many other societies adulthood is seen as a process: adults are continually developing and therefore never reach complete maturity (Archard 1993). Archard's analysis of different perceptions of childhood and adulthood shows that conceptions of childhood are socially constructed. Once we begin to accept that 'childhood' is socially constructed and what it consists of will vary from culture to culture we also need to question the validity of the idea of the 'naturally developing child' who passes through universal developmental stages.

The developmental stages and markers evident in official guidance such as the *Curriculum Guidance for the Foundation Stage* (QCA 2000) have arisen from a wide range of research findings over the years. The research has focused on what children seem to understand or can do at various ages and stages with little attention given to the children's real-life experiences as active members of their communities and wider society. The result is that 'the child' in developmental psychology is, in a sense, a synthesis of all the children researched. This synthetic or fabricated child, the child against whom children in settings are measured, is not a real child but only signifies the 'norm' or what is seen by research to be 'typical'. Factors such as culture and gender have been rendered invisible by the distillation process. No child matches this 'typical' child but some children's development will be more 'typical' than others.

The concept of the 'naturally developing' child masks the ways in which culture has an impact on the nature of children's life experiences, the ways in which these life experiences are interpreted by the child and the impact of these experiences on the child's development. Erica Burman, who has looked closely at ideas and assumptions underpinning developmental psychology, has argued that developmental psychologists studying infant behaviour have tended to focus on what is measurable. In Burman's words they have tended to suppress 'the indeterminate, ambiguous, non-instrumental features of infant behaviour' (Burman 1994: 33, cited in Penn 2005: 11). A possible consequence of this is that not only *what* some children learn but also certain life experiences and *how* children learn may have been seen as irrelevant or unimportant by researchers. Failing to take full account of the ways in which diverse experiences and discourses contribute towards children's learning and development leads to differences between children's patterns of development being seen as problematic.

Focusing on sets of measurable outcomes suggests that 'children' are homogenous and those that meet the milestones are fine (i.e. 'normal'), while those that do not are outside the norm and this leads to anxieties about groups of children and individual children who, because of their diverse life experiences, which are influenced by the interaction of race, gender and social class, are not conforming to white, male, middle-class norms of development.

This is important to bear in mind when thinking about young children's social and emotional development as children whose social and emotional development does not seem to match the norm, those who are not 'typical', are seen as different or exceptional, and their development is viewed as a problem that requires attention in order to bring the child's development into the range regarded as 'normal'.

Culture and emotional development

Emphasising the 'naturalness' of children's development has led to practitioners monitoring and measuring individual children's development to ensure that they do not stray too far from the 'norm', but few questions are asked about the validity of these norms.

Cross-cultural research into patterns of adult–child interaction has revealed that culture has an impact on what parents value in terms of their child's emotional development (Commons and Miller 1998). According to Levine *et al.* (1994) parental goals vary in different cultures. In some cultures (e.g. the USA and the UK) Levine *et al.* have argued that parents have a pedagogical model of child rearing and one of the characteristics of this model is that parents aim to ensure that their children learn to feel emotionally independent from a relatively young age. This has led to common child-rearing practices such as ensuring babies sleep on their own, rather than with their mother, and also a higher tolerance of babies' crying. For parents from cultures that adopt a paediatric model of child rearing (e.g. Gussii, Kenya) the main focus is on protecting the health and survival of their very young children. This has led to child-rearing practices that include the child sleeping with the mother, rapid responses to a child's crying, and high levels of holding and touching babies and young children.

Commons and Miller (1998) suggest that these different parenting styles may have long-term effects on the emotional development of babies and young children. Early stressful experiences (such as sleeping apart from the mother or being allowed to cry for periods of time) may result in higher levels of the stress hormone cortisol being secreted, which in turn may result in long-term alterations to secretion patterns of cortisol and other stress hormones in later life, which impacts on an individual's ability to handle emotionally difficult situations (Commons and Miller 1998).

Research by Farver and Shin (1997) has also highlighted the probability that culture has an impact on children's social and emotional development. Farver and Shin found that Korean-American children's pretend play themes focused on familiar everyday activities, while Anglo-American children's pretend play themes were based on more fantastic and dangerous subjects. Farver and Shin have argued that the minimal social conflict and familiar scenarios evident in Korean-American children's play themes may reflect the emphasis on 'harmonious interpersonal relationships' that charac-terizes Korean culture (Farver and Shin 1997: 553). This stands in contrast to the dominant culture of Anglo-American children, which values independence and self-reliance and is then reflected in the play themes through which Anglo-American children pursue their own interests and concerns, even if this involves a degree of conflict. Without acknowledging the impact of culture on children's experiences and learning paths it is probable that many Anglo-American children would be regarded as on track in terms of their developing independence, while their Korean-American peers may be described as needing extra support in this area and may possibly be viewed as a 'disadvantaged' group because their social and emotional development appears to lag behind what is regarded as 'normal' for Anglo-American children of the same age.

The theories arising from cross-cultural research have implications for early years practitioners. Working with families drawn from a diverse range of cultures means that we need to be willing to consider the validity of different ways of caring for young children. We need to acknowledge that it is the dominant educational discourses and culture that determine what counts as 'good practice' rather than universally held ideas about young children's needs. Gussii mothers, for example, watching film of American mothers caring for their babies were very distressed at how long babies, were left to cry before the mothers responded to them (Commons and Miller 1998).

Research findings such as these ought to make practitioners pause and reflect on the extent to which professional practice within their setting and their assessments of children's development indicate an uncritical acceptance of culturally specific ideas about young children's social and emotional development. Is the practice within your setting based on the assumption that the markers and milestones you use are the only way, or even the 'best' way, of supporting and assessing young children's emotional development?

Identity and self-esteem

In everyday conversation we tend to use the term 'identity' to mean 'who someone is'. Children's identity develops as they interact with others during the course of their lives. This is not to suggest that babies are 'things' rather than people, but rather that our life experiences help shape our view of ourselves and our identities shift and are reconstructed over time. Our sense of self, therefore, is not stable and fixed but changes with experience. Furthermore each of us does not have a unified, single identity but instead we have multiple identities. We have this range of identities because we all adopt a range of roles in the various social contexts within which we operate. These multiple identities emerge as children learn to make sense of social interactions and engage in a range of discourses. Not all these discourses will provide the same world-view and some of them will conflict with each other. A young child may know, for example, 'she is dad's little daughter and she makes him laugh; her baby brother's loving older sister when she cuddles him and gives him his bottle; her older brother's noisy little sister when she dances and sings to his records; and Alison the artist at nursery when her teacher admires her paintings' (Dowling 2000: 2).

There are so many facets to identity that it helps to focus on one when thinking about the process by which children develop their sense of self. In British society knowing whether you are a girl or a boy is deemed to be important. As soon as a child is born the parents are asked whether the new baby is a girl or boy, and as a young baby adults will label the child as a girl or boy: 'Who's a tired boy then?' or 'Aren't you a lovely girl?' The young child is expected to learn whether they themselves are a girl or a boy and also to accurately assign others to one of two categories: male or female. Young children growing up in this and many other societies are introduced to the dominant gender discourse that presents female and male, girl and boy, feminine and masculine as mutually exclusive categories: you are either one or the other, you cannot be both. In this society as a whole the dominant or most widely accepted form of masculinity emphasizes, among other things, competitiveness, physical strength and rationality. This masculinity is complemented by an 'emphasized femininity' that is characterized by 'compliance, nurturance and empathy' (Connell 1987: 187–8, cited in Browne 2004: 69). Children are likely to be exposed to other discourses in which ideas of feminity and masculinity may be different from those presented by the dominant discourse. Children need to actively negotiate these different discourses and make decisions about how they would like to position themselves within them and how they would like others to view them. Operating effectively within the dominant gender discourse means that a child can relate unproblematically and unambiguously, in gender terms, with others. It also tends to attract a positive response from those around the child ('He's a real boy isn't he?' or 'You're such a good girl, so kind'). This means that, for some children, 'correctly' positioning themselves within the dominant gender discourse brings about positive emotional feedback. Other children may choose to adopt a different position.

While young children are active agents in constructing their identity they are still influenced by the opinions and views of others and will be particularly sensitive to the views and opinions of people they are close to (e.g. parents, carers, teachers, friends, siblings). Early years practitioners can enable children to explore and develop their sense of self by encouraging children to explore different 'ways of being'.

Self-identity and self-esteem are closely linked. When children are developing their identity they are learning to see themselves as others see them. Self-esteem is the value placed on one's own identity. Just as self-identities are shifting and changing so too does someone's self-esteem. A child may feel very valued in one context but less so in another. These changes in self-esteem will be related to how others respond to the child. If a child feels that important adults in their lives care about them, value them and accept them as they are, she or he is likely to have a high level of self-esteem. If, on the other hand, adults criticize the child for seeming not to possess characteristics valued by the adults the child is likely to have lower self-esteem. A child's chattiness and lively interaction with adults may be valued at home but these same characteristics may not be viewed so positively in another context (e.g. an early years setting). A likely consequence of this is that a child's self-esteem may be high at home but lower in the early years setting. Furthermore, if a child moves into a setting in which the adults have expectations of the child based on a lack of understanding about the child's life and experiences outside the setting the child's self-esteem is likely to drop. This lack of understanding can arise due to a lack of knowledge about the child's cultural experiences and assigning a stereotypical identity to the child.

If a child has a high self-esteem he or she is likely to feel that they are significant, that others value them, that they are competent and capable of success, and they are more likely to feel confident about making decisions and meeting new challenges. There is clearly a link between self-esteem and resilience.

Resilience

Having high self-esteem and a clear sense of their identities is necessary for children to develop resilience. Children who are resilient 'are better equipped to resist stress and adversity, cope with change and uncertainty, and to recover faster and more completely from traumatic events or episodes' (Newman and Blackburn 2002). In everyday terms resilience can be defined as the ability to deal with the highs and lows of life and to adapt to challenging circumstances or situations.

Resilience is an important aspect of emotional development as it encompasses the ability to communicate with others, to be willing to attempt to solve problems, to be able to control and channel negative thoughts and feelings, and to be confident and optimistic that things will work out in the end (Grotberg 1995). Without resilience children may feel powerless, sad, anxious, frightened and unable to rise to new challenges.

Resilience and self-esteem are closely linked in that developing resilience requires, among other things, early attachments, confidence of being valued and loved and a clear sense of self-identity (including a strong cultural identity) (Payne and Butler 2003).

While it is true that some children within our settings will have experienced very traumatic events or episodes (e.g. war, experience of being a refugee, homelessness, death within the family) we also need to recognize that all children face challenges and change within their lives – no child is exempt. Moving home, starting with a new childminder, the birth of a new sibling, making the transition from home to nursery or from nursery to school are the types of challenges and changes all children have to deal with. Fostering resilience in children is an important aspect of their emotional development as it enables them to face change and uncertainty, and to manage negative emotions such as anxiety and insecurity rather than be overwhelmed by them.

Children's rights

Adopting a children's rights perspective enables us to move away from age and stage-related goals and to broaden our understanding of what young children need to support their social and emotional development. In the United Nations Convention on the Rights of the Child (UNCRC) children's rights can be sorted into three categories: provision rights, protection rights and participation rights. The UNCRC has been criticized for presenting and maintaining a western understanding of childhood, not least in that it presents the child as a self-contained individual. In many societies and cultures this concept of the child is unknown or unfamiliar.

There is, however, much that is positive in the UNCRC. There is an emphasis, for example, on children's right to express their opinion and have that opinion taken into account in matters affecting the child (UNCRC: Article 12). The UNCRC provides us with another perspective on children's social and emotional development as it emphasizes the need to listen to children and respond to what the children tell us rather than expecting the children to fit in with the provision we make for them. In listening to children more we may become more aware of what they need to develop their identities, confidence and positive self-esteem.

The UNCRC also stresses that whatever is done must be in the child's best interests. There will always be some debate about what is 'best' for a child. In the New Zealand curriculum guidelines, for example, it is stated of wellbeing in Strand 1 that: 'All children have a right to health, protection from harm and anxiety, and to harmony, consistency, affection, firmness, warmth, and sensitivity . . . They need as much con-sistency and continuity of experience as possible in order to develop confidence and trust' (New Zealand Ministry of Education 1996: 46).

You may agree and feel that children should be protected from harm and anxiety, but a certain amount of anxiety is part of life. So, do you think we should be protecting children from anxiety or enabling children to cope with anxiety and in so doing helping them develop their resilience? Dealing with transition, for example, is a part of everyone's life and transitions may be the cause of much anxiety. It is wiser, therefore, to concentrate on supporting young children through transitions and in so doing help to develop their resilience rather than thinking about ways of avoiding transitions.

Transitions and children's emotional development

Transition can be understood in terms of 'the influence of contexts (for example, family, classroom, community) and the connections among these contexts (e.g. family-school relationships) at any given time and across time' (Pianta *et al.* 1999: 4, cited in Dockett and Perry 2001). If we are concerned about the development of children's confidence, self-identity and self-esteem we need to consider how best to support children during various transitions.

Babies and children experience a wide range of changes and transitions in which they move from the familiar (e.g. their home environment) to the unfamiliar (e.g. their early years setting or school). It is important not to underestimate the range, number and impact of transitions that very young children may experience. A study examining stress levels of toddlers making the transition from home to childcare found that their stress levels were high as much as five months after first attending a childcare setting (Ahnert *et al.* 2004). The study highlights the need to think carefully about how to provide ongoing support for very young children within the childcare setting, and how to manage the transition process sensitively.

If the transition is to be a positive experience it is important to manage it sensitively and with an awareness of the complexity of what transition involves. Transitions are not always smooth for all children. This is acknowledged in various guidance and policy documents, particularly with respect to transitions to school and from one key stage to another (e.g. DfES 2003a, 2003b; ACCAC 2004).

Children's experiences of transition are unlikely to be identical. The transitions will depend upon factors such as the children's ages and their family circumstances. Furthermore, although children will share some of transitions (e.g. the transition from their home setting to your setting/school) each child's experiences of these transitions are unique.

When considering how to support children through transitions it is important to be aware of how each transition may make different demands on the child. In moving from the home environment to a nursery setting a child moves into a new cultural setting. This involves the child in having to learn new rules (many of which are unspoken and therefore implicit). Children also have to learn new routines and also adopt new roles or identities: they move from being the 'baby' at home to the 'child' in the nursery or the 'pupil' at school.

In one study, approximately half of the Foundation Stage teachers involved felt that certain groups of children found the transition to school difficult. The groups included children with SENs, children who were born in the summer, children without a nursery experience and children without a friendship group at the school (Sanders *et al.* 2005).

Earlier research has highlighted how ethnicity may also shape a child's experience of transition to school (Gillborn and Mirza 2000; Sammons *et al.* 2002; DfES 2003a). Early years settings and schools need to look very carefully at how the transition to school may impact on different groups of children, and develop strategies to support children during the transition process. This may entail having to critically reflect on the extent to which the ethos, curriculum and organization within the setting meet children's needs and provide for their interests rather than merely developing strategies to help children 'fit in' to the existing provision.

Strategies aimed at supporting children during transitions need to acknowledge the emotional impact of transitions. Many settings aim to minimize anxieties by encouraging children to visit before they start so that the environment is not completely strange; other produce photo books for children new to the setting to familiarize them with the environment, routines and types of activities (LTS 2007).

Dowling (2000) has emphasized the need for practitioners to be proactive in supporting children during periods of transition rather than waiting until children show obvious signs of distress. Some children communicate their feelings of distress or anxiety by crying or refusing to leave an adult's side, or they may have difficulty concentrating or may appear unable to do things that they were previously able to do. A child's body language provides useful signals of unhappiness or cautiousness.

Research seems to point to the importance of friendships (Dockett and Perry 2001, 2002; Sanders *et al.* 2005) in easing children's transitions. Parents, like their children, feel that friendship groups help children to settle in to new environments. One parent described her small daughter's friends as operating as a 'little support network' (Sanders *et al.* 2005: 59). This aspect of children's social and emotional life is sometimes overlooked by adults, who may feel that making new friends is more important than maintaining existing friendships, but a sizeable proportion of settings seem to have recognized the emotionally supportive role that peers and friends can play during transition and have set up various 'buddy' systems (Ofsted 2007).

Babies and young children may experience numerous transitions within an early years setting, including adapting to staff absences, changeover of staff due to shift systems and holidays, moving to different rooms for naps or meals, experiencing going to sleep with one member of staff present and waking with another. Research suggests that babies and young children need responsive adults to provide a secure base (Murray and Trevarthen 1992; Miller *et al.* 1993, cited in Elfer 2004). Both the *Birth to Three Matters Framework* (Sure Start 2002) and *Birth to Three: Supporting Our Youngest Children* (LTS 2005) emphasize how important a relationship with a key person in the setting is in terms of children's emotional security and development. In an ideal world, the key person provides the secure base babies and young children need and is also able to 'tune in' to the child and help her negotiate some of the transitions and new experiences she encounters. In the real world, often for organizational reasons, the key person may not always be available and settings therefore may need to take a critical look at how young children are provided with the emotional support they need. We should also be asking ourselves whether the emphasis on the need for one key person reflects an uncritical acceptance of the dominant childcare discourse. Are there other ways in which settings can provide a secure emotional base for young children?

Supporting children: some practical strategies for supporting children's personal, social and emotional development

Dowling (2000) has argued that emotional health depends upon children being able to experience and express a range of emotions. Young children need to talk about both positive and negative emotions. Central government has shown an increasing interest in the issue of children's personal, social and emotional health and development. In *Promoting Children's Mental Health within Early Years Settings* (DfES 2001) mentally healthy children are described as those who are able to:

1. Develop psychologically, emotionally, intellectually and spiritually
2. Initiate, develop and sustain mutually satisfying personal relationships
3. Use and enjoy solitude
4. Become aware of others and empathise with them
5. Play and learn
6. Develop a sense of right and wrong
7. Resolve (face) problems and setbacks and learn from them.

(DfES 2001: 6)

Bearing in mind the cultural diversity within this country it is important to reflect on whether these indicators are sufficiently broad to be able to accommodate children's differing patterns of social and emotional development.

In 2005 the DfES published a set of resources known as SEAL (Social and Emotional Aspects of Learning). These curriculum resources were designed explicitly to promote social, emotional and behavioural skills and it is particularly significant that these materials aimed to help children become aware of and able to express and describe their emotions. The materials have been influenced by the work of Howard Gardner and Daniel Goleman and the concept of emotional literacy.

In the early 1990s Howard Gardner's work on multiple intelligences received attention. Two of the multiple intelligences Gardner identified were intra-personal intelligence and inter-personal intelligence (Gardner 1993). Intra-personal intelligence concerns knowing about one's own feelings, while inter-personal intelligence is the ability to identify and understand the feelings of others. Daniel Goleman further developed the concept of emotional intelligence and identified five aspects of emotional intelligence: self-awareness (recognizing your feelings), emotional control, self-motivation, empathy and handling relationships.

Some children will communicate how they are feeling through forms of behaviour that may be described as unacceptable or 'challenging'. One approach to this issue has been to locate 'problem' behaviour or 'emotional problems' within individual children and develop strategies for helping the individual children concerned exhibit more pro-social behaviours. An alternative approach is based on the premise that the identities, skills and behaviours an individual develops are related to the social contexts they experience. Linke (1998) has argued that children's own behaviour and attitudes towards others will be influenced by the cultures in which they grow up. Children growing up in cultures valuing competition and self-reliance are likely to react to and treat others differently to those children who are brought up in cultures valuing community and inter-personal support. Maybin and Woodhead (2003) have drawn on research in Canada and the USA to show how children are encouraged to express their emotions and relate to others. In South Baltimore, white, working-class mothers teach their young daughters to 'stand up for themselves' by encouraging them to react aggressively in response to their mothers' teasing (Miller and Sperry 1987, cited in Maybin and Woodhead 2003). In contrast, through the nature of adults' interactions with them, children in the Inuit Utkuhiksalingmiut community are taught that expressions of anger, hostility, bad temper and greed are disapproved of (Briggs 1970, 1998, cited in Maybin and Woodhead 2003).

If a child communicates their unhappiness through 'challenging' behaviour it is not enough to try to change the individual child. Instead we need to be looking at what experiences the child has and the discourses she or he has access to. This means that practitioners need to reflect on the ethos of their setting and the messages, both overt and covert, that children are getting about how people are genuinely valued. If the early years setting or school does not have an ethos that emphasizes caring, respect, honesty, a sense of community, and so on, then attempts at, for example, helping a child feel more confident or raising children's self-esteem are likely to founder. It would be unrealistic to suggest that there will never be some children who, for a range of frequently complex reasons, will require more individualized support. However, the more effective the provision is in supporting children's personal, social and emotional development the fewer the number of children that will require individual intervention (DfES 2005).

Conclusion

This chapter has looked at how considering young children's social and emotional development involves more than enabling children to meet predetermined goals or markers. We need to think about how to help children gain a sense of who they are and negotiate their way through the range of discourses to which they have access, develop their resilience and foster their self-esteem.

References

ACCAC (Qualifications, Curriculum and Assessment Authority for Wales) (2004) *The Foundation Phase in Wales: A Draft Framework for Children's Learning*. Cardiff: ACCAC.

Ahnert, L., Gunnar, M.R., Lamb, M.E. and Barthel, M. (2004) Transition to child care: association with infant-mother attachmient, infant negative emotion and cortisol elevations, *Child Development*, 75(3).

Archard, R. (1993) *Children's Rights and Childhood*. London: Routledge.

Browne, N. (2004) *Gender Equity in the Early Years*. Maidenhead: Open University Press.

Commons, M.L. and Miller, P.M. (1998) Emotional learning in infants: a cross-cultural examination. Paper presented at the American Association for the Advancement of Science Philadelphia, PA, February.

Department for Education and Skills (DfES) (2001) *Guidance Document: Promoting Children's Mental Health within Early Years Settings*. Nottingham: DfES.

Department for Education and Skills (DfES) (2003a) *Aiming High: Raising the Achievement of Minority Ethnic Pupils*. Nottingham: DfES.

Department for Education and Skills (DfES) (2003b) *Excellence and Enjoyment: A Strategy for Primary Schools*. Nottingham: (DfES).

Department for Education and Skills (DfES) (2005) *Excellence and Enjoyment: Social and Emotional Aspects of Learning (SEAL)*, http://publications.teachernet.gov.uk/ (accessed 30 April 2007).

Department for Education and Skills (DfES) (2006) *The Early Years Foundation Stage – Consultation on a Single Quality Framework for Services to Children from Birth to Five*, DfES, http://www.dfes.gov.uk/consultations/conResults.cfm?consultationId= 1393 (accessed 7 March 2007).

Dockett, S., and Perry, B., (2001) Starting school: effective transitions, *Early Childhood Research and Practice*, 3(2) Fall, http://ecrp.uiuc.edu/v3n2/dockett.html (accessed 7 March 2007).

Dockett, S. and Perry, B. (2002) Who's ready for what? Young children starting school, *Contemporary Issues in Early Childhood*, 3(1): 67–89.

Donaldson, M. (1978) *Children's Minds*. London: Fontana.

Dowling, M. (2000) *Young Children's Personal, Social and Emotional Development*. London: Paul Chapman.

Elfer, P. (2004) Building intimacy in relationships with young children, in L. Miller and J. Devereux (eds) *Supporting Children's Learning in the Early Years*. London: David Fulton.

Farver, J.A. and Shin, Y.L. (1997) Social pretend play in Korean and Anglo-American pre-schoolers, *Child Development*, 68(3): 544–557.

Gardner, H. (1993) *Multiple Intelligences*. New York: Basic Books.

Gillborn, D. and Mirza, H.S. (2000) *Educational Inequality: Mapping Race, Class and Gender. A Synthesis of Research Evidence*. London: Ofsted.

Grotberg, E. (1995) *A Guide to Promoting Resilience in Children: Strengthening the Human Spirit, Practice and Reflections 8*. The Hague: Bernard Van Leer Foundation.

Hughes, M. (1986) *Children and Number: Difficulties in Learning Mathematics*. Oxford: Blackwell.

Learning and Teaching Scotland (LTS) (2005) *Birth to Three: Supporting Our Youngest Children*. Edinburgh: Scottish Executive.

Learning and Teaching Scotland (LTS) Early Years (2007) *Sharing Practice: Emotional, Personal and Social Development*, http://www.ltscotland.org.uk/earlyyears/ sharingpractice/keyaspects/emotionalpersonalsocial/index.asp (accessed 6 March 2007).

LeVine, R.A., Dixon, S., LeVine, S., Richman, A., Leiderman, P.H., Keefer, C.H. and Brazelton, T.B. (1994) *Childcare and Culture: Lessons from Africa*. New York: Cambridge University Press.

Linke, P. (1998) *Let's Stop Bullying*. Watson, ACT: Australian Early Childhood Association.

Maybin, J. and Woodhead, M. (eds) (2003) *Childhood, U212*. Milton Keynes: Open University.

Murray, L. and Trevarthen, C. (1992) 'Emotional regulation of interactions between two month olds and their mothers' in A. Alverez (ed) *Live Company Psychoanalytical Psychotherapy with Autistic, Borderline, Deprived and Abused Children*, London: Routledge.

New Zealand Ministry of Education (1996), *Te Whàriki, Early Childhood Curriculum*. Wellington, New Zealand: Ministry of Education.

Newman, T. and Blackburn, S. (Barnardo's Policy, Research and Influencing Unit) (2002) *Interchange 78: Transitions in the Lives of Children and Young People: Resilience Factors*. Edinburgh: The Scottish Executive Education Department.

Ofsted (2007) *The Foundation Stage: A Survey of 144 Settings*. London: HMI.

Payne, H. and Butler, I. (2003) *Quality Protects Research Briefing – No 9: Promoting the Mental Health of Children in Need*. Nottingham: DfES, Research in Practice.

Penn, H. (2005) *Understanding Childhood: Issues and Controversies*. Maidenhead: Open University Press.

Qualifications and Curriculum Authority (QCA)/Department for Education and Employment (DfEE) (2000) *Curriculum Guidance for the Foundation Stage*. London: QCA/DfEE.

Sammons, P., Sylva, K., Melhuish, E.C., Siraj-Blatchford, I., Taggart, B. and Elliot, K. (2002) Measuring the impact of pre-school on children's cognitive progress over the pre-school period, *EPPE Technical Paper 8a*. London: Institute of Education.

Sanders, D., White, G., Burge, B., Sharp, C., Eames, A., McEune, R. and Grayson, H. (2005) *A Study of the Transition from the Foundation Stage to Key Stage 1* (DfES Research Report SSU/2005/FR/013). London: Sure Start/NFER.

Sure Start (2002) *Birth to Three Matters Framework*. London: Sure Start.

UN (1989) *United Nations Convention on the Rights of the Child, Children's Rights Network*, http://www.crin.org/docs/resources/treaties/uncrc.htm (accessed 12 June 2005).

Chapter 10

Children from birth to three playing, growing and learning through moving and doing

Julia Manning-Morton and Maggie Thorp

In this chapter Julia Manning-Morton and Maggie Thorp focus on how young children grow and learn through moving and doing. This has implications for the types of physical play experience babies and toddlers encounter and are provided with both indoors and outside and the types of resources practitioners make available for them to use. The authors provide examples from practice to illustrate and illuminate their suggestions.

Learning to move, learning to play

Raj is a 20-month-old boy, one of six babies in a community day nursery baby room. Raj was pushing a cart round the garden on a sunny September day. He was wearing a coat, a hat and a scarf.

'His mum worries about him catching a cold if he plays outdoors as he's had so many chest infections,' his key person Jo, said. 'She wanted him kept inside, but now she's agreed he can play outside and I've promised to wrap him up warmly in whatever she brings in.'

Raj appeared confident and engrossed in his task. His circuit of the garden included navigating the narrow space between the sandpit and the fence, adjusting his cartload of SMA tins from time to time and calling 'Bye bye' to Jo, each time he passed her. It also involved pausing when Jasmine (age 2), the leader of this tour of the garden, halted abruptly shouting 'No go' and then 'Ready, ready go'.

Later, at sleep time Raj took off his own shoes and once Jo had got his socks past his heels, he took his socks off too. Placing them carefully in his basket he quickly found his bed by the bookshelf where it always was, and laid down with 'dog-dog'.

Before he fell asleep Jo could hear him chanting, ' 'Eady, 'eady go' and 'No go' like a mantra. He seemed to be reliving his experiences in the garden that morning. Jo made a note to tell his mum about this.

Physical play is important

Anyone caring for or observing babies and toddlers cannot fail to notice their enthusiasm for physical play, as seen in the example above. Stonehouse (1988) describes this as a characteristic of this age group. They are always on the move, busy and curious, exploring everything they can reach with their whole bodies. Physical play is not only what young children love to do, it is what they need to do in order to gain control of their bodies; to grow in mobility, agility, dexterity and as a result, in independence.

Traditionally, learning about the 'milestones' of young children's physical development has been the overriding focus of the early years practitioner's training. In more recent years the focus has shifted towards children's cognitive development and consequently, reflecting on and planning for children's physical play is now sometimes overlooked. Effective practitioners prioritize refining their knowledge of children's physical development because they understand that physical play is fundamental to all aspects of children's development and learning, including the development of the child's brain.

In the observation of Raj's play above, it can be seen how being able to move around freely and to celebrate what his body can do has a direct impact on all areas of his development.

Communication skills

Communication skills and the desire to communicate are increased if there is something interesting to communicate about and someone interested to communicate with, as anyone who has been housebound or in a monotonous job will agree. During Raj's exacting endeavours in the garden he uses well-known phrases and learns new words in the context of his game, which he later plays with as he falls asleep.

Social development

Social development is promoted as a baby's growing agility and dexterity enables them to play with others. This is a rich source of learning. Now mobile, Raj can join in more – he can follow and imitate older 'experts' in the garden, which is another characteristic of his age (Stonehouse 1989) and he is able to move away from and maintain contact with his key person.

Emotional development

Raj's emotional development, high self-esteem, confidence and independence can be observed as he is enabled to gain control and enjoy what his body can do through physical play and as he prepares to sleep. Not being allowed to play out of doors had been the source of a great deal of frustration, anger and low self-esteem. His mother had not appreciated his need to be active, and his limited social skills and strong feelings (which are further characteristics of this age group), resulted in frequent angry outbursts and tears. Raj's mobility now brings him into contact with new, strange experiences and fear and excitement increase.

Creativity

Creativity develops as a direct result of babies' and toddlers' growing agility and dexterity. Once new tools or materials have been thoroughly investigated to see what they are and what they can do, they are played with imaginatively and incorporated into a game. For example:

> The curtain becomes the means for a peep-bo game; a paint-brush swiped from side to side in a horizontal trajectory becomes the action of a fast car, often accompanied by sound effects. In the observation of Raj, we also see Jasmine who is now a competent tricycle rider and uses her physical skill to support her creation of a 'bus stop' game in which she practices her leadership skills.

Learning to move

Those caring for children from birth to three will be familiar with the general sequence of physical development and its relation to play in the first three years. Effective practitioners will also have a good understanding of the impact of wider social, cultural and historical trends as well as the immediate environment on young children's development and therefore the uniqueness of each child's individual physical development.

After nine months curled up in the womb a baby's stretching, vigorous random kicking and arm waving helps the baby uncurl (Karmiloff-Smith 1994). This activity strengthens those early weak muscle fibres and at the same time changes are taking place in the baby's brain. Involuntary actions (subcortex controlled) are being taken over by intentional voluntary actions (controlled by the cerebral cortex). Increasingly specialized structures are being laid down which will lead to even greater muscle control.

Gaining head and neck control

This requires considerable strength, as at birth the baby's head is disproportionately large compared to an adult's. A baby's head flops if not supported, which is great if you need to fit into a very confined space like the womb (Karmiloff-Smith 1994), however it's not so helpful if you want to have a good look round!

> Omar (9 weeks) is laid on his stomach; he strives to hold up his shoulders as well as his head so that he can see and better hear his key person who is sitting on the settee feeding and chatting to another baby. She pauses to chat to Omar as they make eye contact.

Now he is able to see more of the world he is motivated to gain further control so he can explore these sights and sounds and integrate them into his play with movement and sound.

Figure 10.1 Babies and toddlers celebrate what their bodies can do in their enthusiasm for physical play.

Rolling over

As babies vigorously kick and wave their arms and legs and lift their heads they may accidentally discover rolling over. The accidental rolling soon becomes intentional rolling play for the enjoyment of the experience.

> Hannah's key person said that Hannah (7 months) plays at rolling over at every opportunity. She rolls towards the objects she cannot reach, she tries to roll over when being changed, and has rolled off the settee at home two or three times.

(At this age babies do not learn about the danger of drops from experience.)

Sitting up

Sitting up is usually achieved between 5 and 9 months, although different childcare practices will affect when this happens. At first babies may only have sufficient balance to sit briefly; after having been pulled up into this position they may start to topple over as the neuromuscular control which moves from head downwards and from the centre of the baby's body outwards is only halfway there, hence the sag at the waist (Karmiloff-Smith 1994).

As both back muscles and balance improve the baby will sit confidently, spread-legged for balance. Being able to sit up opens up new opportunities for play. Now for the first time the baby is upright and is ideally positioned to reach for and explore objects with their hands. Sarah was able to explore a wealth of materials now that she was able to sit and play with the contents of her Treasure Basket (Goldschmied and Jackson 1994). This position also brought her into face-to-face contact with Gemma and Milo, the sitting babies in her baby room. The objects they explored together often acted as a catalyst for communication between them (Goldschmied and Selleck 1996).

Much as lying babies discover rolling over, sitting babies may fall forward and lift themselves up on their arms. They may notice that they can move themselves around in a circle or that vigorous swimming like movements will propel them forward when they are lying on their front. These movements may become crawling, even though that may be backwards at first due to their disproportionately heavy head (Karmiloff-Smith 1994).

Crawling

Crawling is a complex action to learn; the baby has to plan how and when to move each arm and leg in order to get to where they are aiming. They do not have adult models to imitate, and many end up moving in very different ways. Some babies miss this activity out completely, preferring to pull themselves straight up onto their feet.

Whether a baby crawls conventionally or not is not important; the variations are evidence of the babies' active role in making sense of their actions and learning how to use them effectively.

> Morwenna moves to satisfy her great desire to have control over her body so she can better explore and increase her control over her environment through her play. She has decided she wants to reach the train set her sister is playing with. She recognizes the sound of its motor and knows exactly where to find it – in her sister's bedroom.

The route to this forbidden territory is one of the mental maps she has formed since becoming mobile; this has also enabled her to practice cognitive skills such as memory and intentionality (Gopnik *et al.* 1999).

At around 7 to 9 months old babies' experience of fear greatly increases:

> Kofi (8 months) cries when a visiting aunty tries to pick him up. His mother says that a few weeks ago everyone was greeted with a smile. Now he is only happy to be left with those he knows well.

It is perhaps not surprising that this coincides with the new freedom babies have gained to go off independently as they play. This new surge of fear does have some positive effects. Being able to crawl means babies are able to get into more dangerous situations than before; however, most mature crawlers seem to have a fear of danger not previously evident (Gibson and Walk 1960).

> Wayne (9 months) crawled to the top step of the patio and cried for his key person to come and get him.

However, this is not true for all babies:

Lucy (10 months) crawled off the step from the dining room to the kitchen to reach mum and fell face down on the kitchen floor.

Depth perception is now believed to be present at birth; however, there is much debate whether a sense of danger comes with maturation of visual perception or with experience of locomotion (Karmiloff-Smith 1994).

Rader *et al.* (1980) found babies experienced in using a baby walker were as reluctant to crawl across the 'deep' side of the visual cliff as babies who had only got about by crawling. However, they also found that the babies with baby walker experience did cross if in the baby walkers. Rader concluded that visual clues are disrupted when babies move about in artificial devices. Perhaps the crawlers, who could use tactile clues as well as visual ones, were able to be more sensitive to depth and therefore were more cautious. Other experiments found this was not the case; however the much publicized dangers of baby walkers means that adults should err on the side of caution and avoid the use of walkers whatever the outcome of this particular debate.

Practice at crawling increases muscular strength in the baby's arms and legs.

Wayne uses everything in reach to pull himself up. However, he cannot yet get down. His key person reported that the challenge she currently has it to ensure everything in reach will bear his weight and to be on hand to rescue him when he wants to get down.

A baby soon discovers they can cruise around the furniture until a gap appears that is too large to cross.

Lucy leans towards the next piece of furniture with her hands outstretched but does not move her feet. She falls forward, then if not too shaken, crawls across the gap.

Both Wayne's and Lucys upright position and higher eye level and arm reach affects their play. It means they are experts at clearing low tables and shelves. However, the negative implications for play are that when they are cruising they do not have their hands free for exploration and carrying.

Walking

This commences with a few wobbly steps. The baby is encouraged to persist at refining this new skill by their caregivers' joyous response to this achievement. However walking really slows the baby down at first, so when in a hurry they may still resort to crawling. The baby may also resort to crawling for managing slopes or stairs. They are not just learning to walk but to become mobile, and that means being able to adapt their method of locomotion to particular circumstances.

Jamie (12 months) waddles from side to side as he walks, without bending his knees. Books and the remote control for the TV all get trodden on. He steps on a wax crayon that rolls under his foot and down he goes.

Gradually the splayed feet and stiff legged gait of new walkers improves and they become able to go round objects instead of trampling over them. They can stop, go backwards and soon can run (Karmiloff-Smith 1994); these movements soon become central features of their play.

It is important to remember that walking is just another means of exploring and playing for toddlers. They seem to want to celebrate their newly gained level of mobility in their play. Stonehouse (1988) likens this to a teenager who has just learnt to drive. They may be so attracted to the exciting things they encounter that they cannot resist the temptation to go and explore them.

> Johan's mother reported, 'When going to the shop he seems to have a completely different agenda from me. He often toddles off in the opposite direction or stops, waits, and then sets off again for no apparent reason. When we get to steps he wants to go up and down them three or four times before moving on.'

Many toddlers enjoy the challenge of playing on steps. At first going up stairs involves using one foot to stabilize weight and the other turned out as a lever. Thus they need both feet to arrive on each step before moving on to the next one (Karmiloff-Smith 1994). This is also the case going down. Adults can teach toddlers to go down in a backward crawl for safety.

Gradually between 24 and 30 months further physical changes take place. Legs lengthen, fat is converted into muscle and the baby appears less chubby; they become much more upright, arches develop in the toddler's feet, making them less flat footed, and knees and ankles have greater flexibility (Karmiloff-Smith 1994).

Physical play now includes such composite skills as being able to climb a ladder to reach the top of a slide, steer and scoot themselves along on a tricycle and (as seen in the observation of Raj) steer trucks and prams, loaded with their collections around a complex circuit.

Three-year-olds reach their level of mobility, agility, dexterity and independence through the interplay of three things: the maturation of the nervous system and muscle fibres, the child's insatiable appetite to explore and control their own body and their environment; and the physical play experiences and opportunities they are able to engage in that motivate and support them.

Holding, manipulating and doing

A newborn baby's ability to build on their existing grasp reflex through waving, reaching and gradually refining their grasp is the basis upon which their creative use of tools for both expression and survival is built (Karmiloff-Smith 1994). As babies play with these gestures, muscular strength develops down through the arm eventually to reach the fingertips and they gradually increase their control over their movements. Feedback from the effect of this play encourages practice, bringing the neural pathways for perception and action into synchrony and perfecting skills in measuring distance and force (Gopnik *et al.* 1999).

> Claudia (3 months) lying on her back, accidentally batted some metal measuring spoons strung across her cot. The clatter and swinging of the spoons attracted her attention and motivated Claudia to try again and again to recreate this effect.

Figure 10.2 Feedback from the effect of play perfects skills in measuring distance and force.

When a baby can grasp objects they play with them by exploring them with their mouths to find out more about them. Karmiloff-Smith (1994) states that the mouth, tongue and lips are the first areas to develop in the cerebral cortex. This is the part that controls voluntary action and there are twice as many nerve endings in the mouth as in the fingertips, giving feedback about shape, texture and size. [. . .]

Gradually the ability to grasp is refined and a baby can also let go. Noah has perfected this art.

> Noah is sitting in his cot. He usually has a large collection of stuffed toys in there with him. He calls to his key person, David. David enters the sleep area, and finds that Noah has pushed every toy small enough through the bars on to the floor. He has also taken off and cast his socks out of the cot and his dummy. David goes to take Noah out of the cot but Noah protests. To Noah's delight David understands what is required and retrieves everything so Noah can begin the game again.

This game reinforces pathways in Noah's brain that control planning and prediction and the ability to remember objects after they have disappeared (object permanence) (Gopnik *et al.* 1999).

Developing a pincer grasp (usually between 8 and 12 months) is as important as the first step and first word, yet does not usually attract the same kind of attention. This action, combined with the later development of a rotating wrist and hand and eye coordination can be seen in Una's play:

> Una (2½ years) was sticking. In one hand she held a box of small pieces of coloured paper that she had torn up, holding it against her body for extra support. She was using the other hand to take out the pieces of paper one by one, between her finger and thumb and place them on the surface of a sheet of very sticky paper. She had previously smothered this with layers of glue using a spatula.

She now has the necessary skills to use a whole range of tools to support her growing independence; these enhance her play and enable her to enter into the cultural world of using symbols.

Perceiving, understanding and learning

Babies' learning is founded on their sensory play experiences. Through the experiences that the baby and toddler perceive through their senses, synaptic connections are made in the developing brain. Annette Karmiloff-Smith describes this as a fundamental idea to understanding children's development; that it 'is a constant interaction between the emerging structures of the brain and the baby's experience of the world' (1994: 26).

Rita Carter (1999) describes how this process is interactive in the act of perception; that an initial perceptive experience will alter the structure of the brain, which will in turn influence how an object is perceived and so on, thereby building a more complex synaptic network. The implication of this for practitioners is that the more varied and appropriate the play experience offered to the child, the better the essential connections between the neural cells will be.

> Jeanette, after learning about children's perceptual development, now planned sensory play experiences for the babies. In the non-mobile baby area she displayed faces and black and white geometric pattern pictures around the bottom of the walls. She strung a variety of objects across their rug, such as keys, rice in a small sealed cardboard box and bells. The texture, weight and temperature of the loofah made a good contrast with the metal spoon. The lemon she gave to one baby to hold offered him an interesting smell.

Figure 10.3 Sensory play is a prime source of learning.

Sighted adults tend to over rely on their sense of sight to give them information about the world, but for a new baby vision is the least well-developed part of the sensory system. However, babies' tracking reflexes and attraction to moving objects stimulate the visual areas of the brain and when the retinas merge, they can see more clearly where things are and what they are. Now they can study detailed features of faces, not just outlines and can remember faces too.

Perceptual development does not happen in discrete areas but cross-modally. The baby's interactions with their carer brings together the way their carer looks, smells, sounds and moves.

Sound, taste and smell are often overlooked when practitioners consider sensory play experiences but a baby's hearing is as good as an adult's at birth and sound and smell are key ways in which a baby distinguishes between people they know and those they do not.

> Jeanette also used her new understanding to help settle new babies. She asked parents to teach her how they rocked, comforted and got their babies to sleep. She asked for them to bring cot bedding from home smelling of their detergent, and even laid one of the mum's worn T-shirts over her when feeding a new, unsettled baby.

Babies recognize familiar touch and movement, their sense of proprioception tells them where their limbs are without looking.

These abilities to recognize and recall features of people and objects through sensory information shows the fundamental cognitive process of memory at work early in an infant's life. Being able to draw on a perceptual memory helps young children to recall events Six-month-old babies can form event memories that can be retrieved two years later in the presence of the right reminders. This was shown by children of 2½ years returning to a laboratory where they had played a game at the age of 6 months. Although these children were no more likely than other children to pick out the toy previously used in the game, they were more likely to repeat the required reaching play to find the toy unprompted, especially if they heard the sound of the rattle used in the original game (Perris *et al*. 1990).

Many adults are familiar with the startling clarity of a memory prompted by a smell or sound; such an experience reflects the close connection between these areas of the brain.

> Lydia as a baby of 2 months could often be soothed when crying by singing to her. Her mother was a singer and pianist and music was an integral part of her experience at home.

Our growing knowledge of the important links between mobility, dexterity, perception and brain development seem to support Piaget's view that sensory-motor experiences and abilities are a primary source of information for children like Raj, whose active exploration of the garden has an important role in his acquisition of knowledge.

This means that the core of learning for children like Una, Noah, Raj and Tommy is active, hands-on play experience. This allows them to create images in their minds that have meaning, which form a firm basis for thinking and support for developing abstract ideas and symbolic representation of language, numbers or letters.

[. . .]

References

Carter, R. (1999) *Mapping the Mind*. London: Seven Dials.

Gibson, E.J. and Walk, R.D. (1960) The visual cliff. *Scientific American*, 202: 64–71.

Goldschmied, E. and Jackson, S. (1994) *People Under Three, Young Children in Day Care*. London: Routledge.

Goldschmied, E. and Selleck, D. (1996) *Communication between Babies in Their First Year* (video). London: National Children's Bureau.

Gopnik, A., Meltzoff, A. and Kuhl, P. (1999) *How Babies Think*. London: Weidenfield and Nicolson.

Karmiloff-Smith, A. (1994) *Baby It's You*. London: Ebury Press.

Perris, E.E., Myers, N.A. and Clifton, R.K. (1990) Long-term memory for a single infancy experience. *Child Development*, 61: 1796–807.

Rader, N., Bausano, M. and Richards, J.E. (1980) On the nature of the visual cliff avoidance response in human infants. *Child Development*, 51: 61–6.

Stonehouse, A. (ed.) (1988) *Trusting Toddlers; Programming for 1–3 year olds in Childcare Centres*. Melbourne: Australian Early Childhood Association.

Chapter 11

Young children becoming literate

Robin Campbell

The development of early literacy skills is often a contentious issue embedded in debates around informal versus didactic approaches to teaching and learning. Robin Campbell argues very clearly for approaches to literacy which place communication, play and enjoyment of books, songs and rhymes as central. He considers the key elements of a literacy curriculum for the early years, including literacy 'goals'. He then explores the role of adults as they support, model, interact and scaffold children's learning. He concludes by arguing for a broad-based foundation for children's literacy development.

Introduction

Alice was motivated to look at books on her own before her first birthday, she contributed words and phrases to story readings during her second year and wrote her own name unaided by 3 years 6 months (Campbell 1999). Alice was becoming literate, demonstrating that by her actions. Of course, there are many indicators that tell us a young child is emerging as a literacy user (Hall 1987). Showing an interest in, and enjoyment of, books are often regarded as paramount (Butler 1998) especially in Western Industrialised countries. We know much literacy learning develops from engagements with books (Teale 1984). Singing and nursery rhymes, playing with, and making up their own, rhymes (Chukovsky 1963) supports the child's awareness of phonemes. Responding to environmental print (Miller 1999), and making marks that increasingly looks like writing (Schickedanz 1990) demonstrates important knowledge and understanding. These are evidence of young children becoming literate. Spoken language is central to this learning process, as discussed later in this chapter, as is the role of play as a vehicle for language and literacy learning.

Riley (1996) suggests there are two indicators, which are linked to young children's future success in reading and writing by the end of Key Stage 1 in England. These are children's ability, on entering school at five years of age, to write their own name and knowledge of the alphabet. It is therefore interesting to note that *Practice and Guidance for the Early Years Foundation Stage* (EYFS) in England (DCSF 2008) includes 'writes own name' (p. 60) and 'links sounds to letters, naming and sounding the letters of the alphabet' (p. 53).

However, focusing on the achievement of such indicators, rather than the process by which they are achieved, can lead to unwelcome changes in practice. David *et al.* (2000) noted 'early years practitioners in England have felt pressurised by government initiatives to include more literacy in the nursery school programme' (p. 120). Therefore goal setting can put pressure on how those attainments are achieved.

Tensions may appear between achieving simple literacy goals and the use of developmentally appropriate practices. Therefore, early years practitioners have important questions to consider: What is an appropriate literacy curriculum for the early years? What will working towards goals for literacy learning entail? What is involved in adults promoting literacy learning? Those questions also need to be seen in the context of how communication, language and literacy are encouraged in the EYFS and extended between five and eight years of age, at Key Stage 1 in England.

Learning literacy: from birth to three

Becoming a skilled communicator was a key aspect in the framework for children aged birth to three in England (Sure Start Unit 2002) as it is in the EYFS (DCSF 2008). Important experiences identified include the use of stories and songs in their home language, pretend play and symbolic understanding (making one thing stand for another) and play experiences linked to storybook characters. That initial use of 'the power of story, rhyme, drama and song' (DfES 2007: 6) remains even though there has been mandated in England a particular emphasis upon synthetic phonics by five years of age. Many young children will learn about literacy and emerge as literacy users during their first three years. How do they achieve that when largely they are not taught literacy directly? As Wade and Moore (2000) noted, young children who share books with an adult at home achieve well when they go to school. They do so because they learn from books, they learn about books, and they learn literacy. That learning by three years of age often includes knowing how to use books, being familiar with the structure of stories, contributing to the story readings and knowing some letters and words (Campbell 1999). Much of this happens by being engaged in an enjoyable shared reading of worthwhile books. When Alice was two years and nine months she enjoyed sharing with an adult *Good-Night Owl* (Hutchins 1972):

Grandfather:	*Owl tried to sleep.*
	The owl's sleeping in the tree isn't it?
Alice:	Yes.
	Owl's got his eyes closed.
Grandfather:	*The bees buzzed,*
	buzz, buzz,
	and owl tried to
	sleep.
Alice:	There's the buzzy bees.

(Campbell 1999: 58)

In this short extract the child's involvement, and learning, is evident. Alice indicated her close attention to the pictures, she noted that owl's eyes were closed and she pointed to the bees. She also took part in the reading providing 'sleep' at the end of the sentence. Many books that are read to young children provide support that enables them to take part in shared story readings. Therefore two- and three-year-old children are enabled to act like readers and begin to be readers (Minns 1997).

There are also many examples of a child developing as a reader in Whitehead's (2002) study of Dylan up to three years of age. That study reminds us too that boys can also be attracted to books when the books are of interest to them and they are shared with an adult with time to engage in a pleasurable read. Elsewhere, I noted, the extent of the learning that may be achieved was emphasised when another boy, Louie, shared a book with a grandparent. The book had been read frequently – the attraction for Louie being perhaps the many different 'emergency vehicles' in the text.

Grandfather: Ambulance speeding
Louie: emergency!
                  Whee-oww! Whee-oww! Pull over, make way!
                  Siren screaming, light beam-beaming.
Grandfather: Help is coming –
Louie: it's on the way!

Although Louie was just 2 years 8 months old he had memorised large chunks of this book because it was of such great interest to him; that memorisation enabled him to act like a reader during the story readings. Furthermore, he had parents and grandparents willing to read the book with him frequently whenever requested.

Of course, as noted above, there are other literacy activities that also support that development. For example, opportunities to respond to environmental print and mark making are activities that a child can enjoy with an adult, to support literacy learning. So, children who are provided with such experiences and opportunities develop during the early years knowing about literacy.

What is an appropriate literacy curriculum for the early years?

Those activities that children enjoy at home begin to suggest an early years curriculum. Being able to write one's own name and recognise the letters of the alphabet by shape and sound are important. Supporting children to work towards those goals in developmentally appropriate ways before entering school seems sensible. Therefore, early years practitioners will want to help children acquire that knowledge in early years settings or in the reception year of school. However those two features of literacy development are insufficient if that is all that the child acquires. They need more than the tip of the iceberg in a literacy curriculum. The children need the whole iceberg and that suggests a very wide range of literacy knowledge and experience to underpin the surface knowledge. That raises issues about the content and process of the early years curriculum.

Marian Whitehead (1999) suggested four essential strategies for literacy that could provide a broad framework for the literacy curriculum. Those were talk, play and representation; rhyme, rhythm and language patterns; stories and narrative; and environmental print and messages. All of those strategies remain important as the basis for literacy development (Whitehead 2007).

Talk, play and representation

Corden (2000) argued the case 'for the centrality of spoken language in the learning process' (p. 12). Much of children's initial learning is based on talk with oneself, with other children and adults. During that talk comments are made, questions asked, responses provided, and conversations occur. Often the talk is linked to play as young children explore their world imaginatively and verbalise as they do so. Part of that play includes representation as the child creates a farm with bricks, with a hat becomes a fire-fighter, and creates representations of objects and people with marks that become increasingly recognisable as drawings. In time those representations begin to include letter like marks as the child explores writing.

When role play areas are organised as a vet's surgery, a post office, or supermarket, literacy materials are an integral part of the provision (Hall and Abbott 1991). Commonly adults provide print materials such as message pads by the telephone, writing paper and envelopes with pencils or other writing tools; telephone directories, magazines, brochures and catalogues; possibly too a keyboard, typewriter, or computer.

The presence of adults to model writing and talk about it with the children is important. A writing centre encourages children to write, to think about words and letters (so learning about the alphabet) and to develop as literacy users. Frequently that writing will be linked to drawing and painting as the children represent the world symbolically in different ways.

Rhyme, rhythm and language patterns

Rhyme, rhythm and language patterns are found in nursery rhymes, songs, poems and many stories. Young children get great enjoyment from playing with language and learn much about literacy as they do so. Meek (1990) suggested that when children have frequent opportunities to engage with and enjoy nursery rhymes and songs they also learn and extend their phonological awareness. Children enjoy the rhythm of nursery rhymes such as:

> Mary, Mary, quite contrary,
> How does your garden grow?
> With silver bells and cockle shells
> And pretty maids all in a row.

They are also developing an awareness of the '-ow' rime unit and 'gr' and 'r' onset units, even though that awareness need not be made explicit at this point. Although the enjoyment, and transfer of a cultural heritage, are reason enough to engage in these activities they also teach about letters and sounds (Meek 1990).

Stories and narrative

Stories and narrative are important to young children, as Bruner (1968) indicated narrative is one way of thinking. Children, and adults, make sense of their world by creating a narrative of events that they experience. Children also learn from the stories that they hear told and read by adults. In many of these stories there are rhyme, repetition and rhythm which Wade (1990) refers to as 'the three r's' of language and stories that supports young children's learning. Many books that young children hear include rhyme. In *Slinky Malinki* (Dodd 1990) we read that:

> He was cheeky and cheerful,
> friendly and fun,
> he'd chase after leaves
> and he'd roll in the sun.

The rhyme of 'fun' and 'sun' appeals to young children and informs the children incidentally about onset and rime. Later that will help children to read and write by analogy words such as 'bun' and 'run' (Goswami 1999). Then the repetition of phrases and sentences, rather than of single words, creates a story interest for young children and helps the children to join in as readers and become readers. In *Good-Night Owl* (Hutchins 1972) the repetition of 'Owl tried to sleep' draws children into the reading and supports their literacy development. Often it is the use of rhyme and repetition that creates a rhythm to the story as in the now famous *Green Eggs and Ham* (Seuss 1960) but also the Duck books, e.g. Alborough (2004). Yet story does even more, very young children comment upon words known because they saw them in particular books (Baghban 1984 and Campbell 1999).

A starting point for early years literacy are frequent story readings (Campbell 2001a) and the benefits are well documented (Teale 1984). Children develop a love of books and an interest in reading, they acquire characters as imaginary friends, learn words and sentences, begin to understand story structure, and appreciate the rhyme features of many books. In addition the use of repeated readings enables children to gain 'ownership' of the story. For very young children adults make the story readings interactive and provide opportunities for responses. The repeated interactive story readings support children's literacy learning (McGee and Schickedanz 2007).

Subsequently the children can draw, paint, make models, create puppets (to be used during subsequent re-readings of the book) mark make and write (Campbell 2001a). So they represent the story in a variety of formats. Gregory (1996) discussing children learning English as a second language, refers to the 'Outside-In' approach to literacy that uses story as a means of providing the experiences that lead to literacy. That is balanced by the 'Inside-Out' approach that uses the knowledge, experiences and language that children bring to school from their own communities as a basis for becoming literate in an additional language.

Shared reading with big print that all the children in the class could see is another useful literacy activity for similar reasons (Holdaway 1979). However, when used as part of the literacy hour in England (DfEE 1998) it changed the emphasis to an attention to print features – looking at words, considering letters and sounds, noting punctuation and spelling patterns. The format was used to teach directly aspects of literacy and there was a real danger that instead of exciting children about reading it diminished an interest in books. But shared reading can be used more appropriately for a wider purpose (Whitehead 1999, 2007). Finding 'opportunities to tell and read stories' (DCSF 2008b, p. 55), feeling good about the stories, and wanting to engage with other stories will be key at the EYFS.

Environmental print and messages

In our society a great deal of environmental print is experienced and young children demonstrate that they are inquisitive to find out about it. This inevitably leads to discussions about letters of the alphabet. Currently the yellow *M* is among the first letters to create a response from young children when they spot a McDonald's logo.

Environmental print is brought into the setting and talked about (Miller 1999) and as Kenner (2000) demonstrated linked to the languages of home for bilingual children. Logo displays, creating alphabet environmental print books and having a print party are all suggested. Labelling resources and encouraging children to use labels to guide them provides a real purpose for literacy. Classroom print for a purpose that is talked about adds to the children's literacy learning in a meaningful context.

Learning about letters is developed further when children have the opportunity to mark make and send messages. Sending greeting cards is an activity that children may have witnessed, e.g. Christmas and Chinese New Year. Alice sent a card at 3 years 3 months (Figure 11.1), although at that stage the card included just two words 'To' and 'Gd' (Grandad) (Campbell 1999: 76). Nevertheless, there was evidence of involvement with the letters of the alphabet and an attempt at her own name as she wrote 'Alloo' on the back of the card. Already she recognised the need for five letters: an initial capital 'A' and then an 'l' followed by three other letters – which were not yet accurate. Achievement of the two key learning goals was being attained without any direct attention to those features. They were occurring within the context of children as active literacy learners.

Figure 11.1 A card for grandad.

When children have the opportunity to engage with language and literacy within this broad framework, then the writing of their own name, and knowledge of the alphabet, can be learned easily because it develops as part of wider experiences. Early years practitioners support children by providing learning opportunities that complement activities at home or provide new experiences for some children who have not had these literacy activities.

Working towards goals for literacy learning?

Because the writing of own name and knowledge of the letters and sounds of the alphabet appear to be two easily contained items there is a temptation to think of those being taught directly to the children. The practitioner might even use adult-led and adult-directed activities including worksheets, activity cards and reading schemes. Worksheets are seldom, if ever, the best way of teaching literacy. David *et al.* (2000) suggested 'systematic and explicit 'instruction' is inappropriate during the early years' (p. 46). Indeed, if own name and the alphabet are taught directly it appears that the children have an insufficient background to support their literacy development. Children who have the opportunity to play, sing and use language creatively have a basis for making much more rapid development with literacy (Mills and Mills 1998). It is encouraging children who want to read that is important and as a Northern Ireland curriculum document indicated 'The disposition to read is encouraged by reading rather than by instruction in how to read' (CCEA 1999, p. 9). Such a view is reiterated in the EYFS as teachernet.gov.uk (2008) reminded us that children learn literacy best through play such as opportunities for mark making and writing during role play activities.

The broad range of literacy experiences suggested above as a means of supporting the writing of own name and knowledge of the letters and sounds of the alphabet is needed. Fortunately, young children appear to be naturally interested in writing their own forename. In many of the studies of young children developing as literacy users before attending school we read of the attempts of Giti (Baghban 1984), Cecilia (Payton 1984), Adam (Schickedanz 1990) and Alice (Campbell 1999) to write their own name at about three years of age. Writing materials, support for children's own attempts to write and adults who responded to questions were important. Early years settings provide a wide range of opportunities for young children to recognise and write their fore-name. These include names on coat pegs for recognition, name cards collected at the beginning of the day and at other times, a class birthday chart, an alphabet book of class names, and tapping out the syllables of own name. The children are also encouraged to write their name by signing a register list, writing their own name on paintings, drawings and notes, and creating their own name with different media (Campbell 2001b). Children are encouraged and supported to write their own name rather than being directly taught to do so.

Similarly when considering the alphabet Strickland (1998) suggested that 'the best practice is to help children identify letters in an enjoyable way as they acquire the broader concepts about print and books' (pp. 56–7). She then provided a list of activities that started with a 'focus on letters that have special meaning for children, such as the letters in their own names. This is more effective than simply teaching one arbitrary letter per week' (p. 57). Own name and alphabet are linked as the letters of the children's names provide a focus and context for considering the alphabet.

Of course children learn about the alphabet as they explore the writing of their own name. Singing the alphabet song helps children to learn the names of letters and the alphabet sequence. Making an alphabet book of the environmental print supports a developing knowledge of the alphabet. There are additionally many attractive alphabet books, e.g. *Animalia* (Base 1986); *My first abc book* (Igloo 2008); that can be shared with the children and of course making an alphabet book individually or in a group will bring the alphabet to life. So the children write their own name and gain knowledge of the alphabet as part of a wider based and natural literacy provision (Campbell 2004). They specifically experience those two literacy activities supported by the teacher and other adults not by direct teaching although the adults do have an important role.

Adults promoting literacy learning?

If the practitioner is not directly teaching, because that is not the most developmentally appropriate practice for young children, then what will be their role? We have noted that the adult will read, model, demonstrate, interact, scaffold and support, sing, talk and inform children (Campbell 1996). Those roles have to be performed with skill and thought. When a story is read the adult has to know the book, read at an appropriate pace and read with expression. During shared reading there is a demonstration of reading including how the print is used. When words are written on to a word wall it is writing that is demonstrated. The adult interacts with the children so that there is an opportunity for the children to comment, question and respond.

All of that is made evident when we look at how Adam (Schickedanz 1990) and Alice (Campbell 1999) attained the goal of writing own name. They both did so before attending school because they were surrounded by literacy, with books read to them and familiar books repeated. They had adults who talked with them about what they were trying to achieve. And they had numerous opportunities provided for writing whenever they wanted. When they began to write their own name the adults supported them but accepted a learning process that lasted some months. The adult was there to scaffold, support and inform but did not feel it necessary to dictate what should occur. The outcome was a secure knowledge of writing their own name by three and half years of age. It is a replication of that provision, support and encouragement in early years settings that helps other children to achieve those goals.

Extending literacy learning?

In England the *National Literacy Strategy* (DfEE 1998) indicated the use of a literacy hour at Key Stage 1, from 6 to 8 years of age. The requirement was for the teacher to provide four elements of shared reading/writing; focussed word work; independent reading/writing and review. For many teachers that format was seen as a 'strait jacket' that ultimately bores the children (Anderson et al. 2000). However, teachers often divert from the narrow confines of the literacy hour in order to create more interesting, meaningful and appropriate literacy activities. DfES (2003) give some support to that creativity by suggesting that teachers 'make learning an enjoyable and challenging experience' (p. 29). A similar creativity may occur in relation to more recent suggestions favouring synthetic phonics (Rose 2006).

A Year 1 class teacher read the story *Hairy Maclary from Donaldson's Dairy* (Dodd 1983). Briefly some children acted the story as the teacher reread the book. Then she invited the children to tell about other dogs during shared writing. Eventually the children wrote their own verses into small origami books (Johnson 1995). They captured the nature of the rhyming writing verses such as:

> Billy the Bulldog
> Eats like a hog
> Jumping around
> Just like a frog

Some of the children read their books to the class and the books were placed in the class library for others to read. The activity lasted more than an hour and the structure did not follow sequentially the literacy hour guidelines. Nevertheless the children listened to a story reading, acted the story, took part in a shared writing, engaged with word level work that emphasised onset and rime, produced some independent writing, read their books aloud as part of a review and established some texts for independent reading. The teacher had extended the literacy teaching and there was more of a natural flow to the literacy events based on an enjoyable story. The children were interested and involved as they participated in developmentally appropriate literacy activities. Literacy goals were being achieved.

Conclusion

Adults need to support literacy learning but to do so without concentrating on teaching literacy goals directly. Many early years practitioners in England feel pressure being exerted from various government initiatives towards more direct teaching (David *et al.* 2000). Yet in England the *EYFS* (DCSF 2008) indicates that opportunities need to be provided for play and child-initiated activities to support language and literacy learning. Furthermore, the emphasis towards synthetic phonics by five years of age (Rose 2006, DfES 2007) nevertheless recognises the importance of a strong background of speaking and listening in the early years. It is developmentally appropriate to utilise strategies linked to the children's interests and needs rather than attempting to teach directly particular learning goals. Learning needs to be the product of a wide range of activities and opportunities. Attention given to simple literacy goals is just a part of that much wider provision. So specific learning goals are not neglected but rather they become part of far more broad-based literacy foundations. It is a base for children's whole literacy development.

References

Anderson, H., Digings, M. and Urquhart, I. (2000) Hourwatch: monitoring the inception of the National Literacy Strategy. *Reading*, 34(3), pp. 113–118.

Baghban, M. (1984) *Our Daughter Learns to Read and Write*. Newark, DE: International Reading Association.

Bruner, J. (1968) 'Two modes of thought', in Mercer, J. (ed) *Language and Literacy from an Educational Perspective*, Volume 1: Language Studies. Milton Keynes: Open University Press.

Butler, D. (1998) (Revised edition) *Babies Need Books: Sharing the Joy of Books with Children from Birth to Six*. Portsmouth, NH: Heinemann.

Campbell, R. (1996) *Literacy in Nursery Education*. Stoke-on-Trent: Trentham Books.

Campbell, R. (1999) *Literacy from Home to School: Reading with Alice*. Stoke-on-Trent: Trentham Books.

Campbell, R. (2001a) *Read-Alouds with Young Children*. Newark, DE: International Reading Association.

Campbell, R. (2001b) 'I can write my name I can': The importance of the writing of own name, *Education 3–13*. 29(1), 9–14.

Campbell, R. (2004) *Phonics Naturally Reading and Writing for Real Purposes*. Portsmouth NH: Heinemann.

CCEA (1999) *Key Messages from The Curriculum 21 Conferences and The Curriculum Monitoring Programme 1998*. Belfast: Northern Ireland Council for the Curriculum, Examinations and Assessment.

Chukovsky, K. (1963) *From Two to Five*. Berkeley: University of California Press.

Corden, R. (2000) *Literacy and Learning Through Talk Strategies for the Primary Classroom*. Buckingham: Open University Press.

David, T., Raban, B., Ure, C., Gouch, K., Jago, M., Barriere, I. and Lambirth, A. (2000) *Making Sense of Early Literacy: A Practitioner's Perspective*. Stoke on Trent: Trentham Books.

DCSF (2008) *Practice and Guidance for the Early Years Foundation Stage*. Nottingham: Department for Children, Schools and Families.

DfEE (1998) *The National Literacy Strategy: Framework for Teaching*. London: Department for Education and Employment.

DfES (2003) *Excellence and Enjoyment A Strategy for Primary Schools*. London: Department for Education and Skills.

DfES (2007) *Letters and Sounds: Principles and Practice of High Quality Phonics*. Department for Education and Skills.

Goswami, U. (1999) 'Causal connections in beginning reading: the importance of rhyme', *Journal of Research in Reading*, 22(3), 217–240.

Gregory, E. (1996) *Making Sense of a New World: Learning to Read in a Second Language*. London: Paul Chapman.

Hall, N. (1987) *The Emergence of Literacy*. Sevenoaks, Kent: Hodder and Stoughton.

Hall, N. and Abbott, L. (eds) (1991) *Play in the Primary Curriculum*. London: Hodder and Stoughton.

Holdaway, D. (1979) *The Foundations of Literacy*. London: Ashton Scholastic.

Johnson, P. (1995) *Children Making Books*. Reading: Reading and Language Information Centre, University of Reading.

Kenner, C. (2000) *Home Pages Literacy Links for Bilingual Children*. Stoke-on-Trent: Trentham Books.

McGee, L. and Schickedanz, J. (2007) 'Repeated interactive read-alouds in preschool and kindergarten', *The Reading Teacher*, 60(8), 742–751.

Meek, M. (1990) 'What do we know about reading that helps us to teach?' In Carter, R. (ed) *Knowledge about Language and the Curriculum*. London: Hodder & Stoughton.

Miller, L. (1999) *Moving Towards Literacy with Environmental Print*. Royston, Herts: United Kingdom Reading Association.

Mills, C. and Mills, D. (1998) *Dispatches: The Early Years*. London: Channel 4 Television.

Minns, H. (1997) *Read It To Me Now! Learning at Home and at School*. Buckingham: Open University Press.

Payton, S. (1984) *Developing Awareness of Print: A Young Child's First Steps Towards Literacy*. Birmingham: Educational Review, University of Birmingham.

Riley, J. (1996) 'The ability to label the letters of the alphabet at school entry: a discussion on its value', *Journal of Research in Reading*, 19(2), 87–101.

Rose, J. (2006) *Independent Review of the Teaching of Early Reading, Final Report*. London: Department for Education and Skills.

Schickedanz, J. A. (1990) *Adam's Righting Revolutions*. Portsmouth, NH: Heinemann.

Strickland, D. S. (1998) *Teaching Phonics Today: A Primer for Educators*. Newark, DE: International Reading Association.

Sure Start Unit (2002) *Birth to Three Matters: A Framework to Support Children in their Earliest Years*. London: DfES.

Teale, W. (1984) 'Reading to Young Children: Its significance for literacy development', in Goelman, H., Oberg, A. and Smith, F. (eds) *Awakening to Literacy*. London: Heinemann.

Teachernet.gov.uk (2008) Frequently asked questions about the EYFS.

Wade, B. (1990) (ed.) *Reading for Real*. Buckingham: Open University Press.

Wade, B. and Moore, M. (2000) *Baby Power*. Handforth, Cheshire: Egmont World Ltd.

Whitehead, M. (1999) *Supporting Language and Literacy Development in the Early Years*. Buckingham: Open University Press.

Whitehead, M. (2002) Dylan's routes to literacy: The first three years with picture books. *Journal of Early Childhood Literacy*, 2(3), 269–289.

Whitehead, M. (2007) *Developing Language and Literacy with Young Children* (3rd edition). London: Paul Chapman Educational Publishing.

Children's books

Alborough, J. (2004) *Duck's Key Where Can It Be?* London: HarperCollins.

Base, G. (1986) *Animalia*. New York: Harry Abrams.

Dodd, L. (1983) *Hairy Maclary from Donaldson's Dairy*. Harmondsworth: Puffin Books.

Dodd, L. (1990) *Slinky Malinki*. Harmondsworth: Puffin Books.

Hutchins, P. (1972) *Good-Night Owl*. London: The Bodley Head.

Igloo books (2008) *My First ABC Book*. Sywell: Igloo Books.

Mayo, M. (2002) *'Emergency!'* London: Orchard Books.

Seuss, Dr. (1960) *Green Eggs and Ham*. New York: Beginner Books, Random House.

Chapter 12

Science and ICT

Rosemary Feasey and Margaret Still

In this chapter Rosemary Feasey and Margaret Still discuss the use of ICT in supporting learning in science and the development of positive learning dispositions across the early years curriculum. Enabling children to engage with new technologies and ICT is an important aspect of the role of all early years practitioners. While the equipment readily available will vary from setting to setting, practitioners need to explore the possibilities available to them through collaborations, partnerships, loans and parental and community expertise.

Introduction

In this chapter key issues relating to the relationship between information and communications technology (ICT) and science are discussed. The aims of this chapter are three fold: the first is to suggest how ICT supports learning in science; the second aim is to explore how using ICT in science can assist the development of the whole child, in particular positive learning dispositions; and the third aim is to illustrate these points and issues through a number of ICT applications in early years science. No attempt is made to cover every application of ICT in science. Instead a number of areas have been selected to raise the profile of their potential and challenge some current practices.

This chapter is predicated on the viewpoint that young children have the potential to become ICT literate in science at a very early age and that children should be given access to a wide range of applications in science from the moment they enter formal schooling. It takes an approach similar to that of Carr (2001: 11) who views learning in science as a 'credit model'. As Siraj-Blatchford and Siraj-Blatchford (1995: 2) point out: 'Even the youngest children bring with them into school understandings, skills, knowledge and attitudes, and it is the teacher's role to help them develop and build upon these'. Feasey and Gallear (2001: 5) take this a step further and contextualise the point in relation to ICT in science when they suggest that:

Children at the beginning of the 21st century live in a world where they have access to the Internet, digital clocks, digital bathroom scales, video machines and computers which allow children to scan, take and store photographs and desktop publish.

Today's children expect to have a mobile phone to communicate with friends and family, their watches light up and make strange noises and their leisure time is often spent playing complex computer games. Children's lives are surrounded by the products of the information and communication age; children not only live in a technological age, they are the technological age.

Most young children enter formal schooling with some understanding of ICT and some personal experience and skills. Science must build on this as part of the development of sound foundations to ensure that by the end of the primary years they are competent, confident, motivated and critical users of ICT in this area of the curriculum.

Given that children are the 'technological age', teachers must be prepared to offer children access to a range of ICT regardless of the teacher's own personal capability. The teacher needs to reconsider his or her role and, where necessary, shift from being the 'expert' to the 'learner' alongside the child. Later in this chapter this issue will be raised again in relation to the introduction of the Intel Play Computer Microscope into all primary schools in England.

The key focus regarding using ICT to support teaching and learning in science is not, 'Can I, the teacher, manage to use the equipment?' but rather on the 'fitness for purpose' of ICT in a given situation. As Feasey and Gallear (2001: 5) state, the most important question we must ask ourselves as teachers, is 'How will this enhance the science teaching and learning for these children?'

While the focus of this chapter is the relationship between science and ICT, early years education is about the whole child and not about subjects taken in isolation. It is therefore important to remember that using ICT in science is not just about a child learning, for example, to use a digital camera, a computer or sensors, but also it is a means for contributing to the wider development of each individual child and indeed to the broader aims of science education. De Boo (2000: 6) points out that:

> The ultimate aim of education is to produce well-informed, scientifically literate citizens who can find things out for themselves, look critically at media or other information and make long-term decisions about their world, for themselves and the environment. The future is in their hands – the better we can educate our young children, the better that future will be.

Learning dispositions

To lay the foundations of the scientifically literate individual and to help develop children's understanding of scientific concepts and skills, children need to have a 'positive learning disposition' towards science and the use of ICT.

Early years educators are familiar with the idea of learning dispositions. Carr (2001: 21) explains that a positive learning disposition is:

> Being ready, willing and able to participate in various ways . . . in which the teacher takes the child to the next step in a task, gives some assistance, and then gradually withdraws the assistances so that the child can perform the skill all by her- or himself – assumes, as Goodnow (1990) commented, a picture not only of 'willing' teachers on the one hand but of 'eager' learners on the other.

Carr quotes Lilian Katz (1988: 30) who offers this interpretation of learning dispositions: 'Dispositions are a very different type of learning from skills and knowledge. They can be thought of as habits of mind, tendencies to respond to situations in certain ways'. Carr quotes Claxton (1990: 164) who comments that: 'it can be strongly argued that schools' major responsibility must be to help young people become ready, willing and able to cope with change successfully: that is, to be powerful and effective learners'.

In early years science this is exactly what the teacher is attempting to do, to encourage positive dispositions towards learning in science by engaging children in a range of activities to develop their ability to think and work scientifically. In order for this to be successful the teacher needs to offer children an environment that is sympathetic to developing positive dispositions. In terms of science, this includes providing interesting and stimulating experiences within a planned framework to ensure success for individuals. In science, positive learning dispositions include:

- Taking an interest
- Being involved
- Persisting with difficulty or uncertainty
- Communicating with others
- Taking responsibility.

Successful science relies on developing positive learning dispositions alongside sound teaching and learning approaches. As De Boo (2000: 12) indicates:

> Adult intervention throughout is a vital ingredient. Teachers, classroom assistants, nursery nurses and parents all act as role models for the developing child. Adults who are uninterested or less enthusiastic about the world around them, who show no curiosity or interest in things, will send negative messages about science. Conversely, adults who are enthusiastic, questioning, value new experiences and have an obvious love for learning will provide positive role models for children.

An important role of ICT in science is to support the development of positive dispositions in this area of the early years curriculum. Hence the need for those adults involved in supporting early years science to be creative, enthusiastic and open minded in the teaching and learning approaches they develop in early years settings. The positive use of ICT to support science learning is therefore crucial to the development of not only scientific concepts and skills but also to the whole child:

> It is absolutely essential that we pay particular attention to children's dispositions and feelings if they are to be successful in acquiring knowledge and skills. If we want children to gain a sound knowledge and understanding of science then we must encourage a positive learning disposition towards the subject. Underachievement, apathy, or even resistance in adolescence usually begins with some degree of discouragement in the early years.
>
> (De Boo 2000: 57)

In all of this rhetoric it is the individual child who helps to put things into perspective, reminding us that all children are individuals, with different starting points. Some children have well-developed learning dispositions towards science and ICT, sometimes coming to school confident and competent because of experiences in the home. Others require considerable encouragement to bring them out of their uncertainty and reticence because of their lack of exposure prior to formal schooling to science and ICT. Feasey in De Boo (2000) offers this salutary experience to underpin the need to accept and work with individuals' starting points.

> Two nursery-age children were working at a computer on a simple program for sorting animals. One child was actively involved, the other stood behind watching.

Adult:	You are very busy, you look as though you are an expert at sorting the animals, are you?
Child 1:	Yes, I can put the animals in different squares.
Adult:	(To Child 2) Are you an expert as well?
Child 2:	My name is Philip.

(De Boo 2000: 36)

The role of ICT in science

Acknowledging that science and ICT have an important part to play in different aspects of the individual child's development, let us consider specifically the issue of how ICT can contribute to early years science.

Frost (1995: 9) offers an important point in relation to the use of ICT in science:

> When teachers started using the technology in class, other advantages became apparent. When their pupils became fluent in using sensors, the computer offered a new insight into science: they gained something that helped them to understand and encouraged them to explore. When the children used databases and spreadsheets they didn't just draw graphs, they could go onto interpret them. And when they worked together with a word processor, they started talking with zeal, not the usual gossip, but about science.

Frost continues and suggests that ICT offers very special tools, which he calls 'the tools of the mind'. This is an apt phrase because where ICT applications in science are used appropriately they should support the teacher in challenging children to 'engage brain', by drawing upon personal scientific knowledge and understanding as well as everyday experiences and skills.

When children use any ICT application in science, and 'engage brain', the adult should be encouraging children to participate in making a range of decisions such as what, when and how to use it.

The extent to which children will be able to work independently will depend upon the depth of their experience, personal confidence and disposition to using ICT in science. With very young children there will be a partnership with those adults working with individuals and groups. The role of the adult in the partnership is to scaffold and enable children to use their increasing competence to become more and more independent, in both the ICT and the science. It would be naïve to assume that this transition to becoming expert occurs solely within early years, indeed for most children, the transition will not be completed until they enter secondary schooling and maybe not until later in life.

Frost's 'tools of the mind' encompasses many different aspects of working in science. One of the most important advantages of ICT is the access to data that some applications offer, allowing children to collect data automatically and immediately show the results.

With very young children this is one of the most important advantages of ICT in science. Children can have access to immediate readouts and the computer can create a graph based on the data. The teacher can then challenge children to think about the data and to talk about the patterns, trends, oddities and draw conclusions.

As part of their scientific investigations, children gather information by observing and describing objects, animals and plants. They make collections, ask questions, talk about and describe the objects in front of them. They sort their collections into groups under simple criteria, as they look for and identify similarities and differences. They begin to classify scientifically but at the same time they are developing vital information handling skills, a prerequisite to much work within ICT. Sorting objects is a valuable, concrete experience for young children and, as an extension, these children can use simple computer programs that are designed to group pictures of objects by dragging them around the screen using the mouse. As they sort and group objects, children are beginning to develop skills of classification and the use of keywords. Sorting activities can be extended to producing a binary or classification tree. Children learn to pose questions that require a yes or no answer as they identify and understand similarities and differences. This activity is a process of questioning that encourages children to ask scientific questions using correct scientific vocabulary.

Effective questioning

A crucial part of 'tools of the mind' is developing children as effective questioners. Careful use of ICT in science can support this, and the role of the adult is to model effective questions and gradually share the responsibility with the children. For example:

- What shall we use?
- How will we use it?
- What can we see on the screen?
- What do you think it is?
- What does the graph say?
- What is the story of the graph?
- What do we want to know?
- How could the computer help us to find out what we want to know?

To achieve this children need a supportive environment that encourages questioning and supports approaches to finding an answer. Children need a framework and the teacher needs to model how to ask questions and answer them.

Communication in science

Another important area where ICT provides an excellent partnership with science is in the area of children communicating. ICT offers young children a range of alternatives from using the word processor, either personally or with the help of a scribe, to creating graphs, use paint tools and taking digital pictures. Access to this range can free some children from the shackles of having to write for themselves allowing them to indicate what they know through creating photographic records, tables, graphs, adding labels or matching pictures. The most important issue is not that children write about science but that they are able to communicate their ideas in different ways to a range of audiences.

Collaboration and co-operation

Science is often portrayed as being a solitary occupation carried out by manic-looking individuals with few social skills. The opposite is of course true; science is a social activity, requiring a range of people with differing expertise to work together. Science also relies on the wider community to challenge and validate ideas as well as to share new information. Science in the classroom attempts to emulate this, challenging children to work co-operatively together on an activity or a problem that they need to solve. In the classroom we encourage children to talk, share ideas, think about consequences and consider alternatives, and to do so in a way that does not diminish contributions from different children, but instead values them.

Practical science activities should require children to share resources and also to support each other through peer tutoring, where one child is able to help another.

Instant feedback

ICT in science frequently offers children instant feedback, through sensors or a computer microscope. On one occasion I watched a group of young children using a program that asked them some simple questions related to a science topic. It challenged them to sort objects and generally helped them to revisit and revise some basic subject knowledge. The whole class clamoured to use it, they loved showing what they knew and were delighted when the cartoon character applauded them or the computer made a congratulatory sound. On completion they wanted to start all over again and were always eager to let the teacher know their score. What did they learn? Well they learned that they knew something, that they could succeed, that revising ideas and facts was fun and they were motivated to engage with the subject. Even those less certain who sat back and watched classmates were drawn into offering ideas when they felt confident to do so and were pleased for their friends when their answers were correct. They were, in a small and subtle way, developing positive learning dispositions in science.

In a different but similar way the digital camera, computer microscope and sensors offer children immediate feedback; sometimes, as in the case of the computer microscope, this feedback is unexpected. A group of children looked at parts of their body using a computer microscope and were amazed to see the detail of their eye, hairs in their nose and the pattern of their skin.

Instant feedback of this kind also leads to the development of 'awe and wonder', contributing to the 'wow!' factor of science.

Classroom applications

In this section the focus is placed on three particular applications of ICT in science: the digital camera, computer sensors and the Intel Computer Microscope. These were chosen because of their excellent potential for:

- supporting the development of scientific concepts and skills;
- developing ICT skills;
- encouraging collaboration and communication;
- supporting the development of positive learning dispositions towards science and ICT.

One other important reason for choosing these three applications is that in many early years settings they are underused and their potential underestimated. Some ICT applications in science have, over the years, inadvertently become the province of the upper primary range and used less frequently in early years.

Language

Underpinning use of ICT applications in science is the need for the children to be exposed to three language genres, that of science and ICT as well as everyday language. Both science and ICT use specific language and successful communication in each requires children to become familiar with and use both. Take for example the use of temperature sensors in Table 12.1.

Children will need to be taught the language, as Feasey in De Boo (2000: 28) suggests, 'As adults we take for granted the language we use on a daily basis . . . we are sometimes in danger of forgetting how challenging it can be for children to express themselves, especially in relation to ideas and experiences that are new to them'. Feasey in De Boo (2000) quotes Deforges (1989: 43) who suggests that 'one of the major tasks of early years childhood education is to manage the transition to concepts whose powerfulness depends upon their detachment from direct experience'. The challenge for those involved in early years therefore is to:

- introduce language to children, through direct hands on experiences;
- move children on so that they use the language in a wider range of contexts; and

Table 12.1 The language of science, ICT and everyday: the example of temperature sensors

Science	ICT	Everyday
Temperature	Sensor	Up
Thermometer	Program	Down
Degrees	Probe	Hot
Hot	Display	Cold
Cold		Touch
Change		Feel

- develop depth of language use and understanding that is conceptually based and where children are able to link ideas and experiences to more complex situations and ideas that are removed in terms of time and space.

Some of this development is not evident until later years, when for example, children apply scientific concepts to complex simulations, collect, store and analyse data on spreadsheets. However, the foundations are laid in the early years experiences of linking science and ICT.

Sensors

Sensors are a good example of an ICT application in science that could and should be used in early years science. Many young children do not meet sensors in science until after the age of seven or eight. Yet there are sound reasons why they should be used with young children. Let's consider the teaching of the scientific concept of temperature with young children. This is not an easy concept; young children find it difficult to equate number values to experiences of hot and cold. The standard thermometers (including those developed as 'infant thermometers') used to measure temperature do not readily assist children in developing their understanding. Thermometers have inherent difficulties and present a range of problems for upper primary children, let alone those in early years. For example:

- the spirit in the thermometer is slow to show;
- young children find the numbers difficult to read and understand;
- most scales are too small for children to read easily and with confidence;
- children are unable to equate the temperature reading with the experience of 'feeling' the temperature.

The same applies to using other sensors such as sound and light, similar problems arise using conventional equipment. However, using computer sensors with young children offers a range of advantages, which include:

- children can relate the number value to what is happening;
- readings are displayed immediately;
- children can change the environment, e.g. place the temperature sensor into ice, shout into the sound sensor, place the light sensor under their jumper, and see the change in the reading. Therefore allowing them to manipulate their environment and relate cause and effect immediately;
- a real time graph can be created and children can make changes to the environment and see what happens to the graph. This provides an opportunity for work on predictions;
- sensors are robust pieces of equipment and not easily broken;
- sensors are motivating, they are exciting pieces of equipment and intrinsically interesting, children also have a sense of 'being grown up' when using them.

Young children can learn to use sensors and work independently if provided with appropriate teaching and learning opportunities that include time for them to 'explore' using the sensors.

What should not be underestimated is children's ability to explore and as a result learn how to use sensors (and indeed other items of equipment). Children will need some 'direct teaching' to cover fundamental issues and safety and care, however children very quickly become expert. If allowed to take on the role of teacher and engage in peer tutoring they often 'volunteer' to teach interested adults, illustrating how motivation, confidence and an environment supportive of children taking the lead, can allow a role change in the classroom.

Digital cameras

Perhaps more than any other area of the curriculum, science offers the widest range of contexts for using ICT. Many of the applications, such as sensors, allow children to manipulate measurement in a way that conventional methods do not. Sensors can provide a stimulus for exploration and children delight at creating extremes, for example, making a loud noise so that the graph will show a peak or whispering to create the opposite effect. The Intel Play Computer Microscope (a focus of discussion later in this chapter) offers children views of everyday objects that are unavailable to the naked eye, often making the mundane appear fantastic.

This chapter is based on the premise that one of the key roles of ICT in primary science is to encourage children to become independent and active participants in their own learning. This includes children making decisions on what equipment to use, when to use it and, for purposes of their own choice.

The use of the digital camera is an excellent example of ICT equipment that can offer children a high level of independence. While many teachers are nervous about allowing children to use equipment worth several hundred pounds I have yet to meet a class where a child has dropped or damaged a camera! Quite the opposite: where children are allowed to use a camera they do so with care, eagerness and an eye for what is important to them.

Pedagogically there are many reasons for developing children's ability to use this piece of equipment in the early years. The digital camera offers children an immediate record of what they are observing, and the opportunity to change the view if their attempt to take the photograph is not successful. So children can practise taking photographs without 'wasting film' thus developing proficiency in an inexpensive and immediate way.

As children develop their personal expertise in using the digital camera it then offers the children a range of advantages. Feasey and Gallear (2001) suggest that children are able to:

- record immediately their experiences and phenomena;
- take photographs in their own environment when it is appropriate to them;
- check their own photographs and retake;
- view their photographs on the computer screen;
- print out photographs almost immediately rather than have to wait for film to be processed.

This sits well with the idea of learning dispositions and children being 'ready, willing and able' to engage with their own learning in contexts that are appropriate.

In relation to the development of science skills and understandings the digital camera supports the development of scientific concepts in a variety of ways. Children can take photographs of:

- children carrying out science activities;
- the equipment they use;
- different parts of their activity;
- sequences;
- change, e.g. when cooking, growing plants;
- cause and effect;
- modelling an idea;
- habitats;
- animals;
- concepts in action, e.g. playground and forces;
- seasonal change;
- changes in themselves.

The real challenge though, is not in teaching children to use ICT equipment but to develop an environment where children can access such equipment on their own terms. Of course guidance will be needed, teachers will have to scaffold children's learning and provide explicit opportunities and prompts to encourage children to use such equipment. Support will also be required to store photographs whether as a class book with scribed, written comments from individuals or as a personal book which allows children to locate important experiences which becomes part of their own learning story (an idea based on the New Zealand approach where children participate in documenting their own learning experiences (Carr 2001)). The latter is undoubtedly the ultimate goal for those involved in early years learning.

The Intel Play QXA Computer Microscope

The final ICT application in early years science under consideration is the Intel Play QXA Computer Microscope, which was given to all schools in England, as part of the Year of Science. In 2002 BECTA commissioned a team from Northumbria University to carry out a research project into the use of the Intel Microscope in primary schools in the north-east of England. The researchers worked with teachers and children from nursery through to Year 6, mainly in science lessons, although some teachers used the Intel in language and art lessons. The research findings raise a number of issues for the role of ICT in science.

The research report indicated that in the majority of schools the Intel Microscope had not been taken out of the box, indeed one school tried to return it, believing its delivery to be a clerical error. Where the Intel had been taken out of the box, use was limited and teachers only started to use it when involved in the research project. Most teachers stated that time was the key factor, they did not feel that they had sufficient time to familiarise themselves with the equipment and therefore had limited understanding of its potential.

By the end of the project, the situation was very different, teachers were enthusiastic and considered building it not only into science across the school but also into literacy sessions to support the development of written language, speaking and listening. It was the children who had used the Intel who became the computer microscope's most convincing ambassadors using adjectives to describe using it, such as 'ace', 'brilliant' and 'wicked'.

The Intel research illustrated how quickly new ICT equipment can become the norm in a classroom and how, given the right environment, children can lead learning and development in using new equipment. More importantly, children and teachers can start from almost the same knowledge base and become 'companion' learners, supporting each other. The research findings showed that the preferred learning style for finding out how the Intel Microscope worked was the same for both teachers and the children. Both engaged in 'exploration', trying things out to see how it worked. Many teachers took the Intel Microscope home and admitted to 'playing' with it, and announced that: 'I did exactly the same as the children did, I even looked at my skin, eyes, etc. just like the children' (Feasey *et al.* 2003: 18).

The report stated that:

> The majority of pupils became proficient in using the Intel Microscope very quickly and were keen to explore the different facilities and also to teach other children how to use the micro-scope. It was often the children who became the instigators of using the microscope, frequently suggesting to the teacher that they should use the microscope to view new items or use one of the numerous facilities. The children had the confidence to explore the potential of the Intel Microscope and often carried the teacher along with them. In discussions with children, it became obvious the children soon became experts in the classroom in the use of the Intel Microscope.
>
> (Feasey *et al.* 2003: 30)

The teachers engaged in the research were surprised to find that the children who used the Intel Microscope became highly motivated, not only in using the microscope but also in their willingness to discuss their observations and engage other people in conversation. The following is an extract from a teacher's log:

> Children were animated in their discussion with their peers; children sought an audience, to show them what they could see using the computer microscope; children were so excited about their observations that even the quietest and those with special needs engaged in con-versation at a level that was above the norm for those children; the range of language used by all children, including EAL children and those with special needs was of a higher quality than usual.

Teachers were asked why they thought the Intel Microscope encouraged these kinds of responses from the children; they suggested that:

- children were highly motivated by what they could see;
- the microscope allowed them to observe things that could not be seen with the naked eye;
- observations of everyday objects were 'different' under the microscope;
- showing the views on screen or smart board allowed children to share their reactions, ideas and comments;
- there was a 'wow' factor, which clearly motivated children.

One interesting comment from a teacher was that introducing this piece of equipment that was new to everyone, including the teacher, meant that everyone began from the same starting point; everyone was part of a learning partnership. What is clear is that new and interesting equipment that children can access in science, supports the development of positive learning dispositions and can encourage and develop independence in children.

The research showed that very young children found the microscope difficult to use unaided, but enjoyed viewing objects with the aid of an 'interested' adult. 'Children were quick to recognise some of the inherent difficulties in using the Intel Microscope . . . Getting it to focus was hard for me.' Feasey *et al.* (2003: 31). Older early years children were able to use the microscope independently and teachers found different ways of using images from the microscope in activities with the children.

Summary

The central premise of early years education is developing the whole child. In order to do this, teachers and other adults working with young children need to appreciate the dilemmas that individual learning situations raise. In early years science one of the greatest conflicts is between the adult teaching and the child learning at their own pace and in relation to their own interests. We must not underestimate the ability of young children to be independent learners and make decisions and take control of their environment. ICT in science allows children to do this and, where successful, helps to build positive learning dispositions which become the foundation for successful and confident learners in early years.

References

Carr, M. (2001) *Assessment in Early Childhood Settings: Learning Stories*. London: Paul Chapman Publishing.

Claxton, G. (1990) *Teaching to Learn*. London: Cassell.

De Boo, M. (2000) *Science 3–6 Laying the Foundations in the Early Years*. Hatfield: ASE.

Desforges, C. W. (ed.) (1989) Early childhood education. *The British Journal of Education Psychology*, Monograph series no. 4.

Feasey, R., Gair, J. and Shaw, P. (2003) Evaluation of the Intel Play QX3 Microscope, Report to BECTA.

Feasey, R. and Gallear, B. (2001) *Primary Science and ICT*. Hatfield: ASE.

Frost, R. (1995) *IT in Primary Science*. London: IT in Science Publishers.

Goodnow, J. (1990) The socialisation of cognition: What's involved? In J. W. Stigler, R.A. Shweder and G. Herdt (eds) *Cultural Psychology*, pp. 259–86. Cambridge: Cambridge University Press.

Katz, L. G. (1988) What should young children be doing? *American Educator*, (Summer): 29–45.

Siraj-Blatchford, J. and Siraj-Blatchford, I. (1995) *Educating the Whole Child: Cross-curricular Skills, Themes and Dimensions*. Buckingham: Open University Press.

Chapter 13

Creative practice and practice which fosters creativity

Anna Craft and Bob Jeffrey

Creative development is one of the key aspects and early learning goals in the Early Years Foundation Stage (DCSF 2008). In this chapter Anna Craft and Bob Jeffrey draw on evidence from their research to explore what this means for practitioners in terms of their practice and discuss the development of a learner inclusive environment which places children at the centre in decisions about what and how they learn.

Introduction

In this chapter, we discuss some distinctions between creative practice and practice which fosters creativity. In doing so we draw on case study data from empirical work carried out in English nursery and first schools since the mid-1990s. Throughout the chapter we use the term 'practice' to encompass all early years activity. We suggest that these terms may be relevant across all early years settings, although in this chapter the research we draw on was done with teachers in school and nursery settings.

What do *you* think of when you imagine creativity in early years practice? The following event took place near the start of the school year, in a class of five to six year olds, where one of the authors was working as a researcher, alongside the teacher.

Possibilities and thinking thumbs

A small group of five-year-olds are working with a disparate selection of materials that their teacher has introduced to them. The materials include bread, glue, tissue paper, scissors water and card. During the discussion before they start on their own individual projects, their teacher encourages them to explore the properties of each resource, showing that they are thinking by waggling their 'thinking thumbs'. She talks both gently but purposively with the children, trying to maintain a relationship with each as an individual. As the children come up with ideas of how the materials could be used, she uses language carefully to hint that each person will make up their own mind about how to use these materials. '**You** might be going to do that' she mentions several times in response to ideas.

Is this acting creatively to embrace effective learning or is it a practice which fosters creativity? Or is it both? And what do we mean by these terms?

If we look at education policy documents, we find a distinction made in 1999 by the report of the National Advisory Committee on Creative and Cultural Education (NACCCE 1999). It defined creative teaching as 'teaching creatively' (using imaginative approaches to make learning more interesting and effective) and 'teaching for creativity' (forms of teaching that are intended to develop children's own creative thinking or behaviour). In this chapter, we use the terms 'creative practice' and 'practice which fosters creativity' to encompass the same ground as that intended by the NACCCE report, but in a way which is relevant for all early years practitioners, not simply those who are teachers or teaching assistants in schools. The chapter explores ways in which children can be offered access to decision making, control over some of their activities and acknowledgement for their ideas.

Creative practice

What does creative practice mean for practitioners? Studies of practice have established that practitioners feel creative when they control and take ownership of their practice, are innovative and ensure that learning is relevant to learners.

Woods and Jeffrey (1996) suggest that creative practitioners are flexible about how they apply their philosophies and methodologies to the varied and highly complex situations they meet in the classroom. They find inventive ways into children's learning.

In the example given at the start of this chapter, the teacher invited the children to take control and ownership of what they hoped to do with the materials she had provided them with. She emphasised the need for them to make their own meaning and to develop their own personal plans, by acknowledging that each of them may do it differently. In this way she aimed to make the learning experience relevant to each child. She was, we suggest, inviting them to be innovative in their constructions, by emphasising the individuality of each person's suggestion. She was, of course, the teacher, however there will be equivalent situations for other early years practitioners in which children can be encouraged, through task and language, to take on control and ownership.

Creative practitioners, suggests Jeffrey (1997), are skilled at drawing on a repertoire of approaches to enable children's learning: they 'devise, organize, vary, mix whatever teaching methods and strategies they feel will most effectively advance their aims' (Jeffrey 1997, p. 74). The creative practitioner can envisage possibilities and differences, and see these through. The teacher at the start of this chapter had decided to initiate a series of creative thinking activities. She embedded these activities into the curriculum plans made with the parallel class teacher.

But in order to be creative in her practice, she needed the opportunity to do so.

Teaching assistants and others in support roles in the classroom, as well as practitioners in other early years settings, are not always in the position to initiate activities and experiences in the same way. However, where a practitioner is carrying out the ideas of someone else, there is always room for interpretation, and for using professional discretion where appropriate. The following case study, from field notes written about an observation in a nursery and reception classroom in a Hertfordshire primary school, illustrates this point.

Beverley, a classroom assistant, is leading a cake-making activity with six children, aged three and four. The activity has been suggested by the teacher and Beverley has taken the group to work in an area just outside the classroom, near to the portable oven. Instead of passing around one big bowl with the children taking it in turns to mix its contents, she has decided to give each child their own bowl. Each child experiences the whole process from measuring out the ingredients to mixing them up and putting their mixture into a paper case.

In this example it seemed to us that Beverley took ownership of the planned work and adapted it to suit the situation. She was creative by taking control and transforming the context into an effective learning experience. She encouraged children's creativity by offering them each the opportunity to engage more actively with, and to explore for themselves more fully, each part of the learning activity. What she is doing is more than 'starting with where the child is', which is sometimes described as another feature of 'good teaching'. She was offering children an opportunity to engage individually and in parallel with others, with the process of cake mixing, from start to finish, thus giving each child more space to ask their own questions and make their own discoveries. The example also shows how, even where the framework of a practitioner's work is defined by someone else, it is possible to act creatively within this.

Practice which fosters creativity

The NACCCE report emphasises, as have other Government reports such as the Roberts Review (DCMS 2006), House of Commons Education and Skills Committee (2007) and Government response to this (House of Commons Children, Schools and Families Committee 2008), that creativity is relevant across the curriculum and not purely in the creative and performing arts. This principle is echoed by researchers (Craft 2000, Beetlestone 1998) and embedded in the Early Years Foundation Stage Curriculum (DCSF 2008) which links creativity with critical thinking and sees the two as core to early years provision, encouraging children to make connections, supporting transformation of understanding and engaging children in sustained, shared thinking with adults and with other children. Studying these processes among young children in early years settings, Craft, Cremin, Burnard and Chappell (2008) demonstrate how children can be encouraged to be inventive, to generate possibilities, to ask 'what if?' and to suggest approaches to problems and opportunities in any aspect of their learning. We are all 'naturally' creative in this way, to some degree.

But what exactly does 'practice which fosters creativity' involve? Our recent research in English nursery and key stage one classrooms has highlighted an important approach in practices which foster creativity. We have called this approach 'learner inclusive' (i.e. involving the children and trying to 'hear' their perspectives on their learning, to the extent they have some control over it) (Jeffrey and Craft 2003). This can be seen as a 'child-in-context' practice, in other words an approach to supporting learning in which practitioners observe, reflect and support individual children's learning, as well as giving children many choices and a great deal of control over what they explore and how. Some might argue that it is simply 'good teaching' to adopt a learner inclusive approach. But over time, the dominant views of what has been seen to be 'good teaching' has shifted. The child-centred movement came under much criticism in the 1980s and 1990s for many reasons, one central one being that letting children have too much control led to adults having a lack of overview and direction in terms of children's learning. In schools in particular, a child-centred approach has been continuously threatened at policy level since that time. We would suggest that, given the current curriculum frameworks for young children, and our obligations to provide learning opportunities within these, it is possible and, in the case of creativity in particular, necessary, to re-introduce and reconstruct child-centred education (Sugrue 1997).

The learner inclusive environment

Writing in the late 1990s, Duffy (1998) discusses the creation of conditions which inspire children, and ways of intervening with sensitivity, to enable children's thinking to be valued. Based on recent empirical work, we suggest (Jeffrey and Craft 2003) that practices which foster learner creativity involve the construction of a learning environment appropriate to the children in it. In this approach, the learner is, as the term suggests, often included in the process of what knowledge is investigated, discovered and valued. As discussed earlier, it could be argued that this is what lies at the heart of 'good teaching'. This contrasts with a more outcomes-based definition of good teaching, where the quality of teaching is judged by the outcomes, often achievement-based. The two approaches are not incompatible; it is possible for children to achieve highly within a learning environment where they have a strong input into the process and content of their learning (Jeffrey and Woods 2003). We prefer not to draw a distinction, therefore, between the construction of an inclusive learning environment, and the notion of 'good teaching'. We suggest that in a learner inclusive learning environment, the children's creativity is nurtured and developed through the use of 'possibility thinking' and co-participation in particular.

Possibility thinking can be seen as being a major feature of a learner inclusive environment (Craft 2001, 2002) and involves posing questions such as 'what if?' Possibility thinking includes problem solving as in a puzzle, finding alternative routes round a barrier, the posing of questions and the identification of problems and issues. It thus involves imagination and speculation, as children and adults move from what exists, to what might be. Co-participation (Municipality of Reggio Emilia 1996) is one way in which learners can be included in the sharing of and creation of knowledge (Woods and Jeffrey 1996; Jeffrey and Woods 2003) countering negative feelings of being individually tested and having to compete with peers (Pollard and Triggs 2000; Jeffrey 2003). In another sense, all creative thinking involves engagement with the thinking of others – or some form of dialogue as Wegerif (2003) has argued. In these ways, creativity can be seen as always involving some sort of collaboration or thinking together – even if the other person is not physically there (as, for example, when a child builds on an idea they have come across in a story – or when they are remembering some ideas from the day before in their play).

Being learner inclusive is important because as the child contributes to the uncovering of knowledge they take ownership of it, and if control over the investigation of knowledge is handed back to the learner (Jeffrey and Craft 2003) they have the opportunity and authority to be innovative.

Inclusive learning case study of fostering creativity

Sarah introduces work on the body from two big books to her Year 2 learners. She invites them to tell the group about stories of personal accidents and then she asks the children to imagine what would happen if their bones did or did not grow in relation to the rest of their body. The children use their imagination to create a fuller understanding of their knowledge of the body (Jeffrey and Woods 2003). Some of their comments were as follows:

> I'd be all floppy if my bones didn't grow.
> My skin would be hanging down off the end of my fingers.
> My nose would be dangling down there.
> My earrings will be down touching the floor.
> If my bones grew when my body didn't I would be all skinny.
> I would have extra lumps all-over me.
> My bones would be stretching my body so that's why I would be very thin.
> I'd be like a skinny soldier and bones would be sticking out of my skin.
> My brain would be getting squashed.

Young children like experimenting and problem solving, 'I look forward to doing experiments like the lights and batteries. It is like testing things. I don't care if it goes wrong. If I was a witch and I had to make a new potion in my cauldron I would experiment' (Craig, Year 2).

Being encouraged to pose questions, identify problems and issues together with the opportunity to debate and discuss their 'thinking' brought the learners into the process of possibility thinking as a co-participant (Municipality of Reggio Emilia 1996, p. 206). Sarah wanted to engage her mixed 5–7 year-old children in a discussion about learning. She started with an investigation of how babies learn by asking them how they would fill up an alien's empty brain and the children not only used their imagination but they confronted each other's contributions.

> I would do it in a laboratory.
> I would do it by telling.
> You can't. Because it hasn't got anything in its brain to think with.
> He wouldn't be able to remember anything.
> You could make him go to sleep and then open his head a little to put the right information on his brain.

The process of discussion opened up avenues for learning, which included a philosophical debate:

> The following question came out of the blue and was taken on by the others. 'This question is a hard one because how did the first person in the world know all the things about the world'. 'God taught them' 'But he was a little baby'. 'How did the world get made'? 'How did the first person get made'. 'How did the whole universe get made'. 'How did life grow'? There followed lots of chatter permeated with questions and assertions and answers (Field Note).

These knowledge discussions and investigations opened the possibility of an analysis of the processes of learning:

> The answers not only contribute to knowledge but the contributory climate encourages them to share their knowledge. 'I listen and you teach us'. 'You need to use your ears to listen, your nose to smell and your eyes to see'. 'You need to listen most of the time and to be quiet'. 'It is like you have dots in your brain and they are all joined up'. 'You think about it and stuff like that as well'. 'Your brain is telling you how to use your eyes'. 'The college tells you what to tell us and you tell us and we get the answer' (Field Note).

A learner-inclusive approach includes children in what is being investigated, values their experiences, imagination and their evaluation of the learning experience (Jeffrey 2001).

We have found that practitioners who at first intend only to use creative practice to enhance their effectiveness respond creatively to the potential in situations they meet. Justine, a teacher, commented on how the topic had taken off, having fired the children's imaginations.

> I have been caught up in this. It has encompassed the children's imaginations and sustained the interest of all the children from five to seven, from new children to experienced ones. It has been more successful than I had ever dreamt it was going to be. They ran with it. Children were sneaking off behind me to start instead of waiting for me to say, 'Come on, now let's sit, and let me talk you through it'. I would turn round and there would be children behind me doing it, and doing it correctly. It was a project where children didn't need stimulating. One of the things that I enjoyed about it was sitting with the children and talking about what they were doing, and listening to them enjoying this session. It is very relaxing and I also think they genuinely had a very strong sense of achievement.

Justine provided an environment which led unintentionally to learner creativity, as children came up with their own ideas and put them into practice; for children naturally experiment with imaginative constructions and play with ideas when given the opportunity to do so (Craft 2002).

The topic became learner inclusive, as the children became more interested and involved in the project. For example, this is an extract from an interview with Abigail, who is six years old and who has been involved in a topic in her classroom on the art and craft of William Morris. This project had originally been a light touch look at designs in materials but developed into a major project with children constructing their own designs from materials in the environment. In discussion with the researcher, Abigail said:

> We did our own designs on a piece of paper. They were photocopied at lunchtime to make lots of copies. In the afternoon we stuck them on to a piece of paper how we wanted them. This is the design I chose. I have repeated it. We need to do each section the same colour to make it

look like a design. If I did them all different colours it would not look much like a design. It is all the leaves and flowers on a theme. We brought these things in from outside. There is a fir cone, this is a catkin. I often see this sort of design being done on a computer. You can see designs on walls, cushions, bedclothes, wrapping paper, jars, and clothes.

Abigail shows us how included she felt in this theme of work; her teacher had provided her with an experience of practice which fostered creativity, and a learner inclusive environment. But to return to the ideas of creative practice and practice which fosters creativity, how far do these occur together?

Do creative practice and practice which fosters creativity always occur together?

Creative practice does not necessarily lead to learner creativity, although it may provide suitable contexts for both teacher and learner to be creative as teachers use their own creativity and learners use the spaces provided to maintain and develop their own creative learning. It may also actually encourage children's creativity as teachers model the expression of their own ideas.

A practice which fosters creativity depends on practitioners being creative in providing an ethos which enables children's creativity, in other words, an ethos that is relevant to them and in which they can take ownership of the knowledge, skills and understanding to be learnt. A practice, which fosters creativity, goes further in actively involving the child in the determination of what knowledge is to be investigated and acquired and ensuring children a significant amount of control and opportunities to be innovative.

What does this mean for practitioners?

Creative practice may, but does not necessarily, lead to learner creativity. Practice which fosters creativity is more likely to succeed where learners are included; i.e. where the approach is a learner-inclusive one. Including the learner in the learning process is a risk for practitioners because, once having offered this option, a loss of trust will ensue if they then withdraw it for fear of loss of control. Practitioners interested in teaching for creativity have to accept risk taking as one of their pedagogic tools and to some considerable extent be willing to go wherever the investigation takes the class or group. One strategy for ensuring that control is shared and kept within the boundaries and constraints of the setting is to involve learners in a risk assessment or evaluation of each step in the investigative process and to involve the whole group in that process. In this way a learner inclusive approach can become part of normal practice and of a creative pedagogy.

References

Beetlestone, F. (1998) *Creative Children, Imaginative Teaching*. Buckingham: Open University Press.
Craft, A. (2000) *Creativity Across the Primary Curriculum*. London: Routledge.

Craft, A. (2001) 'Little c Creativity', in Craft, A., Jeffrey, B. and Leibling, M. (eds), *Creativity in Education*. London: Continuum.

Craft, A. (2002) *Creativity and Early Years Education: A Lifewide Foundation*. London: Continuum.

Craft, A., Cremin, T., Burnard, P. and Chappell, K. (2008) Possibility Thinking, in Craft, A., Cremin, T. and Burnard, P. (eds) (2008), *Creative Learning 3–11 and How We Document It*. Stoke-on-Trent: Trentham Books.

DCSF (Department for Children, Schools and Families) (2008) *Statutory Framework for the Early Years Foundation Stage*. Nottingham: DCFS Publications.

Department for Culture Media and Sport (DCMS) and Department for Education and Skills (2006) *Nurturing Creativity and Young People*. London: HMSO.

Duffy, B. (1998) *Supporting Imagination and Creativity in the Early Years*. Buckingham: Open University Press.

House of Commons Children, Schools and Families Committee (2008) Creative Partnerships and the Curriculum: Government Response to the Eleventh Report from the Education and Skills Committee, Session 2006–07. London: The Stationery Office Limited.

House of Commons Education and Skills Committee (2007) Creative Partnerships and the Curriculum. Eleventh Report of Session 2006–07. Report, together with formal minutes, oral and written evidence. London: The Stationery Office Limited.

Jeffrey (1997) The Relevance of Creative Teaching: Pupils' Views, in Pollard, A., Thiessen, D. and Filer, A. (eds.) *Children and their Curriculum: The Perspectives of Primary and Elementary Children*. London: Falmer, pp. 15–33.

Jeffrey (2001) Primary pupils' perspectives and creative learning encylopedeia, Vol. 9 June–July, pp. 133–152 (Italian Journal).

Jeffrey (2003) Countering student 'instrumentalism': A creative response. *British Education Research Journal*, Vol. 29, 4.

Jeffrey, B. and Craft, A. (2003) 'Creative teaching and teaching for creativity: distinctions and relationships'. Paper given at British Educational Research Association National Conference on Creativity in Education (Meeting of Special Interest Group – Creativity in Education), Feb 3rd, 2003, at the Open Creativity Centre, The Open University.

Jeffrey, B. and Woods, P. (2003) *The Creative School*. London: RoutledgeFalmer.

Municipality of Reggio Emilia (1996) *The Hundred Languages of Children*. Reggio Emilia: Reggio Children.

NACCCE (1999), *All Our Futures*. London: DfES.

Pollard, A. and Triggs, P. (2000) *What Pupils Say: Changing Policy and Practice in Primary Education*. London: Continuum.

Sugrue, K. (1997) *Complexities of Teaching: Child Centred Perspectives*. London: Falmer Press.

Wegerif, R. (2003), 'Creativity, Thinking Skills and Collaborative Learning'. Paper presented to the Open University Creativity Research Group, at the Open Creativity Centre, Milton Keynes, March 2003.

Woods, P. and Jeffrey, B. (1996) *Teachable Moments*. Buckingham: Open University Press.

Chapter 14

Great communicators

Marian Whitehead

In this chapter Marian Whitehead explores how babies communicate from birth and develop their communication skills even before they can talk. She examines how children first use words and the multiple meanings a single word or phrase can have. In the second part of the chapter she discusses different views of grammar and cautions against more prescriptive views which have dominated much official guidance. Finally she provides a useful list of suggestions to support practitioners in providing rich linguistic beginnings for babies and toddlers.

> The setting is a fine spring evening in a Cornish seaside town. A young couple with a child of around 12 to 15 months are sitting by the harbour. The child's buggy has been positioned as close as possible to the railings along the harbour wall and the child is leaning forward and gazing intently down at the rising tide, pointing at the lapping water, feet kicking excitedly, shouting 'sea', 'sea', 'sea'. The mother responds by saying 'Yes, it's the sea' several times.

It is all too easy to assume that an interest in children's language development must start with an interest in words and how children learn to use them. In the course of history many parents and scholars have believed just that and waited impatiently for infants to say their first words. Some legends suggest that an emperor with a taste for language study actually conducted an experiment to see if the first words of some unfortunate babies he had kept in isolation would be Latin! Even modern albums of the 'our baby' type, used for recording a child's development, usually include a page for 'first words'. But if we really do wish to understand more about language and support its development in childhood we need to start much earlier: we have to look at what is going on in the first hours and days after birth and not be misled by the excitement of words. Words rest on foundations that are laid down in the earliest communications between babies and their carers.

Communicating

For generations parents and carers have sensed that their newborn infants are attentive, playful and friendly, and modern research now supports such intuitions with clear evidence. It would seem that babies are great communicators from birth and have a range of pre-programmed abilities (instincts) which enable them to form close relation-ships with their carers. For example, babies prefer to look at human faces and eyes and pay attention to human voices. They actually spend remarkably long periods of time just gazing into the eyes of their carers (Schaffer 1977; Stern 1977). The recipients of this adoration are normally entranced and respond by smiling, nodding, talking and stroking the child's face, especially the cheeks, chin and lips. To an observer this behaviour can look remarkably like a real conversation, with turns taken to speak and gaps left for the 'speechless' baby to slot in comments. The adult partner behaves 'as if' this were a conversation and the slightest blink, squeak or squirm from the child is interpreted as a meaningful communication. But the infant partner is also very dis-criminating and will only give this level of attention to people. Although moving objects are tracked and watched, it is familiar adults who are usually treated to smiles, speech-like lip movements and arm waving (Trevarthen 1993). Furthermore, babies can set the pace for communications, making eye contact when they are feeling alert and sociable and dropping their gaze when they no longer wish to play this early language game.

Continuing research into the sociability and communication skills of babies has demonstrated that they can imitate some interesting adult behaviours within minutes of birth (Trevarthen 1993). The list of actions imitated includes mouth opening, tongue-poking, eye blinking, eyebrow raising, sad and happy expressions and hand opening and closing. Perhaps it is not too fanciful to see these actions as crucial ones in the life of a social being who will live in groups, small and large, and communicate face to face by means of voice, expressions and gestures. We cannot dismiss these earliest acts of communication as insignificant flukes; clearly they are pre-programmed (in the genes) and therefore of some survival value to our species. Furthermore, adult carers solemnly imitate their babies and go along with the agendas they set. All this has been observed in recent years by professionals as varied as anthropologists, psychologists, linguists and educators, and the fascinating business of baby watching has attracted popular attention too (Morris 1991). There appears to be general agreement that early communication between babies and carers is a non-verbal form of 'getting in touch' with another person and crucial in the development of language, as well as of understanding and sympathy with others, and of social skills, cooperation and play.

In their earliest communications with a human partner babies also learn about them-selves and how others see them. As they gaze into the eyes of their carers they see a mirror image of themselves and the responses of carers indicate how unique, human and lovable their infants are. This mirroring (Winnicott 1971), if it is a good experience, is the foundation of the child's own self-esteem and ability to love and inspire affection, and is yet another indicator of the significance of this period in a child's development when powerful communications take place without words.

Communicating babies and their carers do not live in vacuum packs and the worlds of particular cultures and communities shape their gestures, expressions, movements, talk and songs, so that from the start a baby enters a culture as well as a language. The basic patterns and timetable of language development are universal, but the fine details of gesture, talk, song and traditional care and beliefs about infants are as varied as the languages children learn. This is an important reminder that the roles of carers, families and cultural communities will always be of great significance in children's linguistic, intellectual and social development. Children do not just learn a language, they learn a way of life.

The kind of communication discussed so far is described by linguists as 'nonverbal communication': it helps to prepare babies for speech and underpins our use of spoken language for the rest of our lives. This wordless communication can also develop into sophisticated signing systems for the deaf, as well as complex signalling systems for occupations as different as dance and mime, racecourse bookmaking and aircraft landing control. The main characteristics of non-verbal communication in infancy are:

- face-to-face intimacy;
- strong feelings (from warm affection to rage and frustration);
- very dramatic use of facial expressions, especially eyes and eyebrows, mouth, lips and tongue;
- whole body movements (including dancing, for example), head nodding and shaking, arm and hand gestures;
- the use of 'mouth sounds' like clicks, whistles, hums, 'raspberries' and loud 'boos'.

The last set of characteristics may seem a little bizarre, but we all make use of 'tuts', grunts, 'mms' and even whistles in our talk, especially on the telephone when we have to keep in touch with our invisible talk partner. In the early days of infant communication, imitating these exaggerated mouth sounds may help the baby to practise a whole range of sounds used in the eventual production of words, but we should also note that such sounds may be funny, outrageous and even rude. Right from the start there is a strong current of playfulness, mucking about and teasing in communication – and babies do as much of the mucking about as do their carers (Reddy 1991; Trevarthen 1993). This teasing is a kind of fibbing, or playful deception, and is thought by some linguists to explain partly how language originated. In group life it was (and still is) important to be able to influence others, guess what was in their minds, and even 'change their minds'. Apparently the great apes, our nearest animal relatives, are 'extremely skilled deceivers' (Aitchison 1997: 26) – especially the chimpanzees – but for purely selfish reasons often connected with food. Human beings, however, can choose to tell a lie which is kind rather than brutally honest, and have turned fibbing into games and 'telling tales' into an art form.

Finding the words

First words, when they come, do not spring perfectly formed after months of silence. As examples of meaningful sounds they emerge from babbling which has been strongly influenced by the sounds of the language, or languages, used constantly with and around the child. As understandable and regularly used labels for people, objects, feelings and events, they can be traced back to the early months of non-verbal communication, when babies develop recognizable 'sounds' for significant people, toys and noisily impressive objects like lorries and aeroplanes. These personal labels evolved by an infant may start out as a 'gaa' or 'brr' but they gradually move closer to the standard words used in the home and speech community (Halliday 1975). In the course of this development they are often 'stretched' in their use by the child so that they can cover a whole range of similar events or ideas. For example, the sound or word for 'car' may be used for lorries, shopping trolleys and lifts; the early word for a significant male carer or parent may be used for any man seen in the street or on the local bus.

This gradual building up of a collection of important words for things is greatly helped by the behaviour of carers who communicate with babies and play the sorts of games which involve highly predictable routines with their own special sounds and words. For example, simply giving and taking things and saying 'please' and 'thank you', or waving and saying 'bye-bye', or pointing at and naming things in homes, streets, magazines, catalogues, picture books and on the television screen. All these important language games really get things going, but words are not just any old random sounds and identifying the first words of immature speakers is not easy (after all, they will have difficulty forming certain sounds for some years in early childhood). Because of this, modern linguists, unlike proud parents and carers, have a set of criteria for what is really a 'first word':

- it is used spontaneously by the child;
- it is used regularly in the same activity or setting;
- it is identified by the carer.

The emphasis on spontaneous use is important because with first words we are looking for evidence of the child's ability to identify and attempt to share meanings by using words – we are not interested in the skills of a well-trained parrot! The best evidence for meaningful word use is the child's reusing of the word in appropriate and similar situations. Treating the carer as the expert who can recognize and identify these first words is essential because only a regular carer has intimate knowledge of the child, as well as detailed knowledge of the contexts in which early words emerge.

The expertise of carers and the contexts in which children use their first words are interesting features of early language learning. Many studies of first words have been conducted and later published by linguists working with their own children – or their grandchildren (Engel and Whitehead 1993) – because carers are best placed to understand their children and their settings. This very powerful insider knowledge has revealed, among other things, that first words start as personal but highly consistent sounds (Halliday 1975); that first words are vivid records of the home life, culture and experiences of children; and that toddlers continue to practise language – especially new sounds, rhymes and words – on their own before falling asleep (Weir 1962; Nelson 1989).

Children's first words indicate how they are sorting out and making sense of their particular worlds and they also provide a guide to what really matters to them. When collections of first words are analysed it soon becomes clear that they can be grouped under such headings as: members of the family, daily routines, food, vehicles, toys and pets (Whitehead 1990). Clearly, people, food, animals and possessions are of great importance to babies and their obvious attractions drive the infants' search for labels.

Having the right words for people and things is an almost foolproof way of getting others to help you get hold of, or stay close to, good things.

Also found among the first words are some simple instructions and requests such as 'up', 'walk', 'out', 'gone' and those really important little words in any language, 'yes' and 'no' (or their linguistic equivalents). All these kinds of words enable a small and fairly immobile person to manage other people, get help and make personal needs and feelings felt. During this 'first words' phase of language development it is obvious to parents, carers and professional linguists that children's single words frequently stand for quite complex sets of meanings, communications and instructions. A word like 'dirty' can in certain situations mean 'my hands are dirty', 'are you putting my paint-splashed T-shirt in the washing machine?' or 'I've dropped my apple on the floor'. Only the carer who is with the child at the time can understand and respond appropriately to such one-word utterances – and may still get them wrong! Human communication is always a sensitive and risky business and single words can only do so much. In order to unlock more of the power of language the young communicator must put words together in meaningful and unique combinations.

The power of language

Once young children begin to combine words together it is even more obvious that they are thinking for themselves and have some powerful understanding about how languages work. The evidence for these big claims can be found in the children's unique language creations which cannot have been imitated from adults and older children. We are likely to hear such requests as 'door uppy' (open the door) and 'no doing daddy' (don't do it daddy), and older infants go on to create new verbs out of nouns, as in 'lawning' (mowing the lawn) and 'I seat-belted myself' (putting on a seat-belt). Professional linguists get very excited about these examples (although other people often dismiss them as 'funny things children say') because they are evidence that all children are born with an innate ability to understand and produce appropriate and meaningful language (Chomsky 1957; Aitchison 1989; Pinker 1994). In fact, this remarkable ability to combine words together so that they make sense is grammar in action and indicates that a child is capable of thought, as well as able to be sociable and influence others.

Professional linguists describe 'grammars' in terms of the things they enable us to do with language (this may come as a surprise to readers reared on a strict diet of adjectives, past participles and the like) and the two highly significant functions of language are: getting things done especially with the help of others – and commenting and reflecting on the world (Halliday 1975). Young children certainly use their emerging skills as speakers in order to get carers and others to do things for them ('chair uppy': lift me onto the chair), and they also make statements which suggest that they can observe the world and comment on what happens ('no more miaow', said as the cat leaves the room). It is worth emphasizing that these early word combinations are evidence of thought, and of an innate ability to share and communicate meanings. Many people are convinced that language is for communication and socializing, which it is, but they overlook its role in our thinking and memory. Yet there is powerful research evidence, as well as common sense, to tell us that language creates and extends our ability to think about abstract and complicated ideas such as 'trust' and 'freedom', or things that are distant in time and space (dinosaurs; Australia; last week's visit to the cinema; my first taste of ice-cream), as well as the entirely invented and non-existent 'little green creatures from Mars', Paddington Bear and Jane Eyre.

These are examples of language as a symbolic system – that is, a way of letting words stand for things, ideas and experiences even in their absence, so that we can hold onto them and think about them. This is so central to human thinking that in cases where disease or genetic damage impair or prevent the development of speech and language other symbolic systems must evolve. The signing and touching 'languages' used by the deaf and the blind provide ways of sorting, ordering, recalling and reflecting on experience as well as gaining the co-operation of others. In early childhood the developmental patterns of affected children may show some personal and some general variations. The emergence of grammatical understanding will be in the normal range because it is pre-programmed and universal, but early word acquisition may show some delay (Harris 1992) because it is triggered and enriched by all the social and cultural naming and labelling games played with babies. It is important that infants who do have some form of sensory impairment have endless opportunities to touch, feel, move rhythmically, sign and name all the people, objects, materials and animals in their environments. We can still learn a great deal from the inspired teacher who placed the hands of the blind and deaf Helen Keller under a gushing water pump and constantly wrote the letter signs w-a-t-e-r on the child's palms as the water poured over them. Such support was left almost too late for Helen Keller who had to retrieve years of loneliness and frustration, but every impaired infant can be helped from the start with a range of stimulating sensory experiences linked to words or signs.

A timetable for speech and language?

In many ways learning languages never stops: we all increase our stock of words and continue to pick up the latest technical terms and fashionable slang of our groups and cultures. Many children start with more than one language, particularly in multilingual societies, or go on to acquire a second and third language at an early age. Some adults learn a new language for professional or social reasons, even to enhance their holidays in foreign countries, and schools in most societies are required to teach one or more other languages. The process of becoming literate and learning the written system of a language is also part of language learning, as is the skilled way in which we all adjust our language (dialect) and our pronunciation (accent) according to particular situations and audiences. But the earliest stages of learning to speak in childhood hold a great fascination for most adults who work with children and/or raise their own families, and some kind of developmental timetable is often asked for. However, such timetables can be rather dangerous if taken too seriously and interpreted with rigidity. Every child and every set of circumstances into which she or he is born is different, which renders timetables both unhelpful and potentially worrying for parents and carers. It is for this reason that no such timetable is included in this book.

A few notes on grammar

Some comments on grammar in this chapter may have seemed strange and require a brief explanation. A great deal of ignorance, prejudice and even fear surrounds the topic of grammar, and the modern study of language – known as linguistics – has not really changed this. The problems arise because there are two very different views of grammar, although few people understand or admit this. The most widespread view is rooted in largely discredited beliefs about what is 'correct' and 'good' in language and emphasises traditional rules of thumb which tell us how we ought to speak and write. This is known as the 'prescriptive' tradition because it 'prescribes' or 'tells us' exactly what the users of a language ought to do. However, the rules prescribed are mainly based on examples from Latin (historically the language of a very few educated and scholarly groups) and from written language, neither of which provide helpful guidance for young contemporary speakers of a living language, or their families. This rather illogical approach is aggravated by a general fear of change and of the ethnic and linguistic diversity in society, plus an excessive and persistent respect for privileged groups whose private education still values classical, 'dead' languages highly. This is sometimes at the expense of living languages, which are caricatured as having no grammar and not best suited for training the mind. Of course the situation is rarely described in such blunt terms, but the damage such unchallenged assumptions can do is considerable.

For example, the prescriptive approach has the effect of dividing a society into those who believe that they speak correctly and those who become convinced that they are bad speakers of their first language. It also promotes a rather nasty view of languages as ranked in league tables with some – mainly English and western European languages – at the top because they are supposedly more logical and sophisticated. This approach not only dismisses some languages (and by implication their speakers) as primitive and limited; it also seriously undervalues their young speakers' remarkable and creative achievements in early language learning.

The study of modern linguistics presents a quite different approach to grammar and actually sees it as a universal feature of human thinking, thus providing us with clues about how the mind works. The essential difference in approach stems from the fact that this linguistics is 'descriptive' not 'prescriptive', and aims to describe how we actually learn to speak and the rules we appear to be following when we speak and write a living language. In order to do this modern linguists attempt to be scientific: they look at what is going on in every aspect of language use. So, they observe, record, analyse and make informed guesses about what is happening in a language and what individual speakers and groups are doing with language in any given situation. They certainly do come up with rules for how a language works, but they get the rules from what speakers and writers are doing with language and they are always ready to change their descriptions over time as a language changes to meet the needs of its speakers.

Educators and carers need to understand a little about what lies behind the endless arguments about language and grammar, if only to realise that the disagreements are like the old quarrels between flat-earthers (a bit like prescriptive linguists) and those who accepted that the earth was round (somewhat like descriptive linguists)! The serious point here is that guidance and statutory regulations for the teaching of language, grammar and literacy are being imposed on early years settings, schools and even parents, and some of these regulations are very prescriptive and closer to a 'flat-earther' position than is admitted. For example, a long list of words to be learnt and recognized out of context was prescribed in the *National Literacy Strategy: Framework for Teaching* (DfEE 1998) for Reception year children, and these words were not memorable ones like 'elephant' or 'banana', but included the likes of 'and', 'my', 'it', 'was', and so on. Further lists of 'high frequency' words were also provided for the rest of the primary years. Although these lists do not appear in the new Framework for the Early Years Foundation Stage (DfES 2007) their legacy is still apparent in some Reception classes. Other sources indicate more sensible, enjoyable and properly language-based approaches to helping young children build up their abilities to recognize such words on sight.

In conclusion, we need to be proud of young children's language, thinking and early literacy behaviours, and able to defend a sensible descriptive view of languages. We can point out that modern grammar is not an undisciplined free-for-all, but describes the rules of a language operating on at least three levels concerned with:

- the organization and patterns of sounds (known as phonology);
- the meaningful combination of words (known as syntax);
- the meanings of words and groups of words (known as semantics).

A fourth level, the *vocabulary* or stock of words in a language (known as lexis), is often included in grammatical descriptions.

This description of several levels of grammatical rules highlights the skill and complexity involved in the everyday use of language by any speakers and the remarkable achievements of young children in learning languages. However, it is not an easy guide to teaching grammar – in most cases these rules are far too complex for direct teaching – but it is a kind of ground plan for basing our approaches in the early years on children's love of language, their desire to communicate and their need to make sense of life and experiences. If simple rules are required, then we could do no better than suggest:

- raising the status of talk and communication;
- ensuring that any language use, spoken or written, is appropriate for its purpose and situation;
- drawing children's attention to print everywhere and making print exciting.

Supporting young communicators

Successful caring, parenting and educating is bound up with paying close and serious attention to young children and helping them to understand their world and manage themselves in it. But taking children seriously as people does not have to be grim and humourless – on the contrary, the best adult carers and educators are the most playful. The child watching the rising tide at the start of this chapter was already at the single-word naming stage of communication, but she (or he!) had been supported just enough to make talk about the sea possible: the buggy was as close as safety allowed to the edge of the harbour wall so that the child could peer down; time was made for uninterrupted watching; the child's recognition and naming of the sea was taken up by the mother and confirmed and expanded into a fuller statement. Above all, the sheer joy of watching the sea was communicated and shared. We can assume that this kind of communication had been repeated in other settings and circumstances many times before and had developed out of months of child and adult play, subtle body language, adult talk and shared communicative sounds and gestures.

We have to value all the non-verbal interactions which occur between infants and adults (or older children) in homes and group settings, create extra opportunities for them, and continue to value a wide range of non-verbal communications after spoken language is established. This will be particularly crucial for children whose first language is not English when they enter care and group settings, because they have to depend on picking up all the non-verbal communicative clues they can. The challenge this presents for the professional adults working with these young potential bilinguals can, however, lead to a wonderful freeing up and transforming of the procedures and curriculum in the setting.

Provision and activities

The following will help ensure rich linguistic beginnings:

- *People.* Play, talk and interaction with other people are the key activities at this stage. At home, parents, other family, siblings, child minders and nannies are the key provision. In group care settings, key workers or stable carers for the youngest babies; a wider number of adults, young adults and older children, as well as same-age peers (babies who are able to sit up enjoy the company of other babies).
- *Places.* In group settings some very small rooms and sheltered areas, inside and out, with cushions, carpeted areas and blankets to lie and sit on; the creation in homes and institutions of safe cupboards, dens (tables with floor-length drapes/cloths over them) or full-length curtains to hide behind; safe garden houses, trees, bushes and improvised tents (blankets, sheets and clothes-airers), and even sturdy fencing to peep through or imagine what lies on the other side.
- *Things to do.* Face-to-face gazing, talking, gesturing, bouncing, singing, dancing, clapping; opportunities for listening and quiet watching (other children and adults, animals, moving trees, mobiles, out of windows, pictures, books); plenty of 'helping and talking' activities like food preparation, clearing up and domestic chores, bath times, getting dressed, gardening, shopping, walks and visits; opportunities to play with collections of natural and manufactured objects presented in 'treasure baskets' (Goldschmied and Jackson 1994) (e.g. wooden and metal spoons, fir-cones, shells, sponges, containers and lids, balls); also, saucepans and lids, rattles, squeakers, simple percussion instruments, wooden and plastic blocks (building bricks), soft toys and dolls; a small collection of picture, story, poetry and alphabet books.
- *Things to talk about.* All the above provide ample opportunities for communication and talk and the development of complex forms of thinking.

References

Aitchison, J. (1989) *The Articulate Mammal: An Introduction to Psycholinguistics*. London: Routledge.

Aitchison, J. (1997) *The Language Web* (1996 BBC Reith Lectures). Cambridge: Cambridge University Press.

Chomsky, N. (1957) *Syntactic Structures*. The Hague: Mouton.

Department for Education and Employment (1998) *The National Literacy Strategy: Framework for Teaching*. London: DfEE.

Department for Education and Skills (DfES) (2007) *Statutory Framework for the Early Years Foundation Stage*. Nottingham: DfES Publications.

Engel, D. M. and Whitehead, M. R. (1993) More first words: A comparative study of bilingual siblings. *Early Years* 14(1), 27–35.

Goldschmied, E. and Jackson, S. (1994) *People Under Three*. London: Routledge.

Halliday, M. A. K. (1975) *Learning How To Mean: Explorations in the Development of Language*. London: Arnold.

Harris, M. (1992) *Language Experience and Early Language Development: From Input to Uptake*. Hove: Lawrence Erlbaum.

Morris, D. (1991) *Babywatching*. London: Jonathan Cape.

Nelson, K. (1989) *Narratives from the Crib*. Cambridge, MA: Harvard University Press.

Pinker, S. (1994) *The Language Instinct: The New Science of Language and Mind*. Harmondsworth: Allen Lane/Penguin.

Reddy, V. (1991) Playing with others' expectations; teasing and mucking about in the first year, in A. Whiten (ed.) *Natural Theories of Mind*. Oxford: Blackwell.

Schaffer, H. R. (ed.) (1977) *Studies in Mother–Infant Interaction*. London: Academic Press.

Stern, D. (1977) *The First Relationship: Infant and Mother*. London: Fontana.

Trevarthen, C. (1993) Playing into reality: conversations with the infant communicator. *Winnicott Studies* 7, 67–84.

Weir, R. H. (1962) *Language in the Crib*. The Hague: Mouton.

Whitehead, M. R. (1990) First words: the language diary of a bilingual child's early speech. *Early Years* 10(2), 53–7.

Winnicott, D. W. (1971) *Playing and Reality*. Harmondsworth: Penguin.

Chapter 15

Born mathematical?

Linda Pound

> We know that most children are competent learners but recent research is allowing us insights into the range and extent of these competences. In this chapter Linda Pound explores how many of these competences relate to mathematical thinking and understanding and provides suggestions as to how practitioners may re-evaluate the experiences and activities that they engage in with children and support them in problem solving and communicating their ideas.

Most adults will readily agree that young children are competent learners but few realise just how competent. Current research techniques (Karmiloff and Karmiloff-Smith 2001) have given us new and exciting insights into very young children's thinking. These techniques have enabled researchers and psychologists to determine babies' interests or preferences, to understand what causes anxiety. Perhaps most startling of all, they have also revealed that babies have a range of surprising, in-born mathematical abilities (Devlin 2000). As Devlin reminds us, mathematics is not only about number but 'about life' (2000: 76) and involves thinking and learning processes such as the identification of pattern, handling information in abstract forms, and a wide range of problem-solving strategies. This chapter also considers the abilities of babies and toddlers to understand something of shape and space, measures and, most strikingly, of number and computation.

Mathematical processes

From birth, humans are programmed to seek out pattern. Our brains are good at recognising pattern, a strategy which we use to identify the thousands of faces with which we come into contact. We enjoy stories because we see in them patterns – 'real or imagined, visual or mental, static or dynamic, qualitative or quantitative, utilitarian or recreational' (Devlin 2000: 11). From their earliest days babies prefer 'complex patterns of high contrast' such as 'checkerboards and bull's-eyes' (Gopnik *et al.* 1999: 64). Pattern is also an integral part of the musical interaction that permeates babies' lives (Pound and

Harrison 2003). In the first year of life babies show a remarkable ability not merely to identify but to anticipate patterns in songs and rhymes (Trevarthen 1998). The young child's giggling sense of anticipation which precedes the final 'tickling under there' in *Walking Round the Garden* develops because he or she is aware that we are deviating from the rhythmic pattern of the rhyme.

The ability to think about things that are not present or do not exist at all is 'one characteristic feature of the human brain that no other species seems to possess' (Devlin 2000: 117). This ability is at the heart of mathematics. The ability to categorise according to shape, colour or sound – one manifestation of abstract thought – is present at birth (Butterworth 1999). Language is itself a symbolic system and as language use is extended, young children's ability to deal with abstract information develops. Use of language also accompanies young children's increasing ability to categorise – which reflects their desire to deal with abstract information. At around fifteen to eighteen months of age they ask the names of objects obsessively. The words heard during this 'naming explosion' (Gopnik *et al.* 1999: 115) in response to the oft-repeated question 'what's that, what's that?' are learnt very rapidly because at this stage the baby is interested in categorising (Karmiloff-Smith 1994). New words can be linked together as a group or category and thus remembered or recalled more readily – a process known as 'fast-mapping' (Gopnik *et al.* 1999). Many young men have been embarrassed by a baby pointing persistently at them and shouting 'dada' – this familiar scene is simply evidence of fast-mapping. The unknown young man is being placed in the same category as the child's familiar father.

Humans also make use of a wide range of problem-solving strategies. Logic is commonly thought of as central to mathematical thinking. However, it is clear that logic is not the only means of reasoning at our disposal (Claxton 1997). Even the youngest baby hypothesises, reasons, predicts, experiments and guesses in just the way that scientists do (Gopnik *et al.* 1999, Devlin 2000), using these skills to make sense of the world. Gopnik *et al.* (1999) describe experiments where young babies learn to move a mobile when a ribbon is tied from it to their ankle. Several days later they will repeat the movement if the same mobile is used – but not if the mobile has been changed. This suggests that the baby's hypothesis is that the movement has something to do with the mobile itself.

Infants learn early that nappy changing and clattering crockery precede mealtimes. Learning to reach out, clutch an object, pull it towards the mouth and let go is a series of motor actions which require careful sequencing – pulling something towards you before you have grasped it is unrewarding. As children develop, their play includes sequences of action of increasing complexity. Despite their physical dependency, young babies are increasingly seen to be highly competent learners. One of the forces which appears to drive their actions is the desire to seek control of both their social world (Dunn 1988, Trevarthen 1998) and the physical world (Gopnik *et al.* 1999). They learn early that particular actions cause or produce specific effects and responses. Indeed babies' survival depends on being able to capture and hold the attention of another person and make known to them their needs. This ability to act with intent is reflected in the development of language. Babies and toddlers demonstrate through their early use of *there!* or *oh dear!* that they have a plan or intention in mind. This occurs for example where they have succeeded or failed in building a tower of blocks.

Shape, space and measures

Just as these processes permeate our lives, so the more explicitly mathematical aspects of shape, space and measures are fundamental to everyday activity. Awareness of shape is linked to both our enjoyment of pattern and to our interest in abstract thought, as we exercise 'the human brain's ability to reason about the environment'.

Spatial awareness is part of our evolutionary heritage. Survival in trees and life on the savannah required understanding both of two- and three-dimensional space (Devlin 2000). This is reflected in infancy as babies reach out towards a stimulating object, explore their own bodies, the bodies of others and the world around them. Exploratory play reflects children's interest in shape and space as they push paper into cardboard tubes, squash tissues into boxes and use their fingers to probe all manner of objects, including the mouths and ears of others! On a larger scale, dropping objects from a height, throwing them high and steering wheeled toys through a tight space are all part of this learning process, which infants seem driven to seek out in their search for control and problems to solve.

Physical action is used to explore and think about shape and space. Spinning round, running up and down a slope, wriggling through a play-tunnel and hiding inside a blanket tent are a vital part of this process. Language is linked to the young child's growing understanding. Early use of *up* or *down* to signify something to do with direction is commonplace. Either might serve to mean 'pick me up', 'put me down' or 'I want the things on that high shelf'. This is illustrated in two-year-old Xav's afternoon of activity. He placed some circular place mats on the floor – walking round them, repositioning them and walking on them like stepping stones, while maintaining the circular pattern. He ran out to the back garden and walked around and around the tree seat; then running while balancing on the circle of bricks which edged the flower bed. He then ran in increasingly large circles around the tree. Later that afternoon, he repeated similar movements in the front garden – taking a circular path around the flower bed, the tree and the whole garden. Throughout this frenetic activity, so characteristic of this age group, he recited to himself 'round and round, round and round'.

Language also reflects children's understanding of measures. *Big*, *little* and *more* are similarly brought into action to denote height, weight or volume. Here too, physical action remains important. In describing or drawing attention to something that is moving very fast, young children typically move their arms horizontally at speed, often accompanying these actions with running movement and appropriate sounds. Very large or very tall objects are depicted with sweeping gestures in the appropriate direction, arms and legs outstretched.

Understanding number

This is where our new found understanding of what appears to be happening inside babies' heads becomes awe-inspiring. There is a wealth of studies (some of which are described in Dehaene 1997, Butterworth 1999, Devlin 2000) which make it clear that from the first day of life babies have some knowledge of number, or numerosity. (The ages shown below are indicative – the findings of studies should not be taken as representing the age at which some things can or cannot be done. Much depends on the context, the skill of the researcher and the personality of the baby involved. Some of the findings will relate simply to the age of the babies available when the researcher wished to carry out his or her experiments.)

There are studies which indicate that babies as young as a day old can differentiate between cards with two or three dots (Antell and Keating cited in Butterworth 1999); that babies of four days of age can differentiate between words with two or three syllables (Bijecjac-Babic *et al.* cited in Dehaene 1997). Studies looking at slightly older babies from five or six months generate responses which indicate that infants of this age can apply their awareness of number in a range of situations – recognising changes to a set of three or four moving objects on a computer screen; discriminating between the number of jumps made by a puppet; and, when shown sets of pictures and objects, preferring to link pictures and groups of objects which display the same number rather than depicting the same object (Butterworth 1999; Dehaene 1997). That is to say that, for example, babies of this age are likely to be more interested in the fact that a picture of buses is similar to a set of teddy bears because there are three each in each case, than that there are three toy buses and a picture of three buses – numerosity is more important to them than other similarities (Starkey *et al.* cited in Butterworth 1999).

Psychologists have been particularly interested in a link made by babies which appears to make their awareness of number even more surprising. The studies described above involve linking pictures and objects and demonstrate babies' visual awareness. It is clear however from other studies that, in addition, babies have an innate oral awareness of number. When, for example, they are played a series of words with the same number of syllables, babies notice when the number of syllables changes. Perhaps even more interesting is the fact that they also make links between visual and oral information. Presented with sets of two or three objects, they will, when played a number of drum beats, choose to look at the set of objects which matches the number of drum beats heard (Starkey *et al.* cited in Dehaene 1997). So not only are babies interested in the numbers of things they can see but they are able to make links between the number of things they can see and the number of sounds they can hear.

Counting or guessing?

Clearly in none of these studies were the babies involved able to articulate the number of objects in any group or set – they were making connections or comparisons between the number within groups. The numbers involved in the studies outlined above were small – usually up to three or four. This ability is not the same process as counting – counting involves (Gelman and Gallistel 1978) being able to:

- use one number name for one object (one-to-one principle);
- remember to use the number names in the same order (stable-order principle);
- understand that the last number name used gives the size of the group (cardinal principle);
- recognise that anything can be counted – you can count a set of similar objects such as dolls, or a set of dissimilar objects which might include knives, forks, plates, cups and oranges (abstraction principle);

- accept that no matter what order you count things in the answer will always be the same – so long as you apply the one-to-one and stable-order principles (order-irrelevance principle).

What the babies in the studies cited by Butterworth and Dehaene were doing was not applying these principles and therefore counting but recognising a group of objects at a glance – a process known as subitizing. Over time it appears that young children come to be able to recognise larger groups of objects – alongside, but different from, the development of the abilities which contribute to counting.

Macnamara (1996) has studied this ability and has shown that children in nurseries are sometimes able to recognise groups of objects of five, six or seven in this way. Her studies also show that many children on entering formal schooling lose this ability and rather than simply being confident that there are enough sweets for the group begin to count everything. Macnamara (1996: 124) gives the example of a boy who had been a very confident 'subitizer' in the nursery. When asked to repeat the same test in the Reception class he became distressed because his teacher had told him he must count everything.

There are some important lessons to be learnt from Macnamara's work. Any failure to support and build on young children's abilities may cause them to lose confidence. A very important aspect of mathematics is the ability to estimate. Indeed much of the mathematics that we use in our day to day lives requires approximate answers – in instances like buying paint, deciding how much money to take on holiday or planning a journey we are not trying to come up with accurate answers, merely good enough estimates. We do this alongside the important job of learning to recite number names and count groups of objects using Gelman and Gallistel's five principles.

Macnamara gives further examples of children in the Reception class who remained good at recognising groups – to the point where some could identify groups of nine or ten objects at a glance. When questioned it appeared that these children achieved success by a combination of subitizing and counting on. One child commented 'I remember some and then I count the rest', by which he meant that while looking at the group of dots or objects he was able to identify (by subitizing) a group of six or seven objects and then to count on mentally the three or four additional objects which had not been part of the first group. Given that much time is often taken up early in formal schooling helping children to learn to count on – being able to hold one number in mind while adding a second set or number to the first – it may be that our failure to recognise children's ability to make use of both sets of skills is contributing to their later difficulties. Both guessing (or subitizing) and counting have a part to play in children's mathematical development and practitioners need to support both.

Adding and subtracting

As if all of this were not surprising enough, it seems that in the first half of the first year of life babies seem able to predict what ought to happen when objects are added to or taken away from an existing set of objects. A mother's naturalistic observation of her 5-month-old daughter (cited by Karmiloff-Smith 1994: 173) perfectly reflects the phenomenon unveiled in complex experiments:

Sometimes we play games after she's finished eating in the high chair. She loves one where I take a few of her toys, hide them under the table top shouting 'all gone' and then making them pop up again just after. She squeals with delight. I once dropped one of the three toys we were playing with by mistake, and I could swear she looked a bit puzzled when I put only two toys back on her table.

These studies of addition and subtraction underline what was found in the studies of recognition of groups. The baby is more interested in number than in the objects themselves. The toys used could be exchanged – cuddly toys being replaced by coloured balls – but so long as the number of objects was correct the baby was not concerned (Butterworth 1999).

Counting on our fingers

Human understanding of number appears to be linked to our use of fingers for counting and computation. This is because the two functions are governed by closely related areas of the brain (Ramachandran and Blakeslee 1999). Understanding of number is from the earliest stages of learning linked to the use of the hands – the control of which takes up a larger proportion of the brain than any other part of the body (Greenfield 1997). The relationship between this part of the body and numbers can be seen in babies and toddlers, as they take up one, then two objects in their hands. They may signal a number of objects by using their fingers, holding up all ten fingers fully spread to signify a large number – sometimes accompanied by language – 'I want this many'.

At this stage the ability to recognise a group of objects is not linked to an ability to count. A group of two objects is recognised as a group of two, without any link to language or any facility to compare one group to another. Learning to recite number names in order – although a vital skill at a later stage – is a separate part of a highly complex learning process. Here too the human mind has, in addition, two important advantages. One is the use of fingers and the other is the role of music in infant development (Pound and Harrison 2003). Cultures around the world use songs and action rhymes, which combine the use of fingers, the role of rhythm and the pleasure of physical and playful contact to make number memorable.

So what should practitioners do?

Many of these exciting findings related to the mathematical abilities of young children demand only what practitioners working with young children have thought of as common sense. Providing a rich range of experiences and materials for problem solving and exploration enables children to develop connections in the brain which will support future thinking, including mathematical thinking. Counting songs – especially those which include the use of fingers and movement – also reinforce learning, enabling children to memorise, represent and recall numbers.

The findings should also encourage practitioners to look for evidence of these apparently innate abilities. Being able to communicate mathematical ideas enables children to think mathematically since communication and thought are mutually supportive (Goldschmeid and Selleck 1996; Siegel 1999). In order to help young children to communicate their ideas we should learn to enjoy their problem-solving abilities; notice when they are identifying or creating patterns – whether musical, based in their movements, talk or in other aspects of their play.

We should also encourage imagination as it contributes to abstract thought – imagining things which are not actually present. This occurs through play, stories and by talking about things that we are going to do and have already done. Where this can be supported by photographs and relevant objects this will support children in visualising abstract ideas.

Above all, adults can support children's considerable abilities by respecting and trying to identify their mathematical intentions. We do this very readily with spoken language – we are delighted when children use a single word and work hard to support them in making their meaning clear. We accept that milk might mean water or orange – what they want is a drink. We also accept their imaginative ideas – taking delight in their ability to pretend that a block is a banana or a mobile phone. Let's work equally hard to ensure that we don't get too caught up in feeling that their mathematical ideas must always be wholly accurate. Let's encourage mathematical play and guessing!

References

Butterworth, B. (1999) *The Mathematical Brain*. London: Macmillan.

Claxton, G. (1997) *Hare Brain and Tortoise Mind*. London: Fourth Estate Limited.

Dehaene, S. (1997) *The Number Sense – How the Mind Creates Mathematics*. London: Penguin Books Limited.

Devlin, K. (2000) *The Maths Gene*. London: Weidenfeld & Nicolson.

Dunn, J. (1988) *The Beginnings of Social Understanding*. Oxford: Blackwell.

Gelman, R. and Gallistel, C. R. (1978) *The Child's Understanding of Number*, Cambridge, Mass.: Harvard University Press.

Goldschmied, E. and Selleck, D. (1996) *Communication between Babies in their First Year*. London: National Children's Bureau.

Gopnik, A. Meltzoff, A. and Kuhl, P. (1999) *How Babies Think*. London: Weidenfeld & Nicolson.

Greenfield, S. (1997) *The Human Brain – A Guided Tour*. London: Weidenfeld & Nicolson.

Karmiloff, K. and Karmiloff-Smith, A. (2001) *Pathways to Language: From Fetus to Adolescent*. London: Harvard University Press.

Karmiloff-Smith, A. (1994) *Baby It's You!* London: Ebury Press.

Macnamara, A. (1996) 'From home to school – do children preserve their counting skills?' in Broadhead, P. (ed.) (1996) *Researching the Early Years Continuum*, 118–127 Cleveland: Multilingual Matters.

Pound, L. and Harrison, C. (2003) *Supporting Musical Development in the Early Years*. Buckingham: Open University Press.

Ramachandran, V. S. and Blakeslee, S. (1999) *Phantoms in the Brain*. London: Fourth Estate.

Siegel, D. (1999) *The Developing Mind*. New York: Guilford Press.

Trevarthen, C. (1998) 'The Child's Need to Learn a Culture', in Woodhead, M. *et al.* (eds.) *Cultural Worlds of Early Childhood*. London: Routledge.

Chapter 16

Problem solving

Sue Gifford

Children's ability to problem solve is now recognised as a fundamental aspect of their successful mathematical development and this is clearly reflected in the *Early Years Foundation Stage* (DCSF 2008). In this chapter Sue Gifford explores how and why developing this aspect of children's knowledge and understanding is so important, and through examples and illustrations provides practitioners with ways of developing their practice and children's learning.

Fadilah (a good counter, aged four) was tackling a sharing problem involving three teddy bears of different sizes and 12 sweets.

Teacher:	How many teddies?
Fadilah:	[counts] 1, 2, 3
T:	Can you count the sweets?
F:	[counts 12 sweets correctly]
T:	Can you share them?
F:	[Lots of taking away and rearranging until the little bear had all the sweets]
T:	Is that fair?
F:	Yes, because the other two have been naughty.
T:	What did they do?
F:	They hit her.
G:	Oh look, there is another bear. Can she have any sweets?
F:	She can only have one because she hit her too!

Fadilah was the youngest of three siblings.

Fadilah clearly saw sharing in terms of social justice rather than mathematical equality. The problem was one we were trying out as part of the Number in Early Childhood project (Gifford 1995). Teachers found that if the bears were different sizes children focused on this: 'If the little bear has the same as the others it will be sick!' or 'The fat bear is on a diet!' Even in 'real life' contexts children did not engage with the intended mathematical problem. For example, when asked to share real biscuits, they sometimes grabbed and made no attempt to share fairly, suggesting that their view of the problem was to get as many as possible. Some teachers decided it was more honest to ask, 'Would you like to solve a maths problem?' and found that children would engage readily in nonsensical tasks like sharing plastic bears between plates. As these examples suggest, trying to engage young children in mathematical problem solving can be problematic.

What does mathematical problem solving look like for three to fives?

Problem solving comes in many sizes and guises: problems can be quite minor and arise incidentally from activities or be part of major projects. They may be posed by children themselves, as in blockplay, where children regularly set themselves the problem of building the biggest arch possible (Gura 1992). Children may decide to make something for collaborative play, such as the car pictured in Fig. 16.1 or be inspired by stories, as with Farrah's houses for the three bears (see Figs 16.2–16.4). These involve mathematics such as choosing shapes according to their properties, deciding how to place them, and in Farrah's case, representing in different ways.

Sometimes design projects may be adult-initiated, such as planning a wild garden or a new role-play area. I planned a party with a reception class who used data handling strategies to decide activities and refreshments, resulting in a novel party which involved 'tennis'. On a smaller scale, children may set up a party in the home-corner and solve the problem of getting the right number of plates either by putting one plate for each person or by counting people then plates. Problem solving is also intrinsic to some apparatus, games or puzzles. For instance, Deloache and Brown (1987) found that two year olds would spontaneously set about putting nesting cups in order. With games, decoding dice numerals is a problem which children solved by using a number frieze either to count pictures or to count the symbols (see Fig. 16.5).

Figure 16.1 A car.

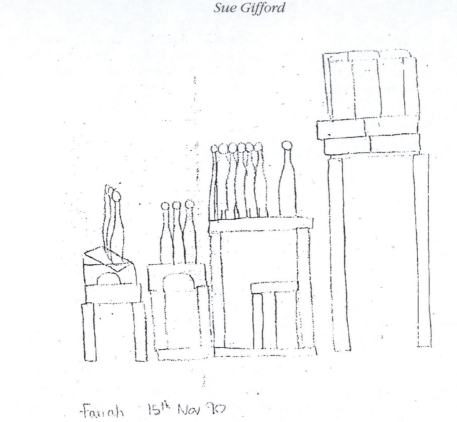

Figure 16.2 Farrah's houses for the three bears (drawn by an adult).

Fadilah's problem was a version of that posed to four and five year olds by Davis and Pepper (1992), whose findings demonstrated some key aspects of problem solving and children's strategies. Twelve biscuits were shared between two dolls: children generally used a 'dealing action schema' of giving one biscuit to each doll in turn, so they had six each. In the 'redistribution' problem, a third doll comes along, who must get an even share before any biscuits are eaten. The children then used a range of strategies to give each doll four biscuits. Some children gathered up the biscuits and dealt them all out again; most did some complicated giving and readjusting. Two children crumbled up all the biscuits and redistributed them as a pile of crumbs each, which the researchers conceded was a successful solution. Some children, including those who were not good counters, seemed to 'just see' a solution, and gave two biscuits from each doll to the third doll.

Davis and Pepper considered this a genuine problem for two reasons: it required 'cogitation' rather than an automatic response like 'dealing'; and there were so many strategies (19 among 74 children, most successful) that children could not be using a learned method. The National Curriculum (DfEE/QCA 1999) characterised mathematical problem solving as presenting difficulties and involving decisions about approaches and materials. Challenge and choice of method are therefore key characteristics of problems. If children know or are told the method to use, then they are not problem solving.

Figure 16.3 Farrah's drawing of a bear in its house.

Why is problem solving important?

Problem solving has been advocated as a major vehicle for learning by Piaget (1973) and Vygotsky (1978), who emphasised collaborative and guided problem solving. In overcoming difficulties children have to connect what they know to new situations. For instance, with the arch problem, children often began by holding an upright and the crosspiece, but found they needed another hand for the third block. Some solved this by finding a friend. Others realised that you could place the two uprights first. Then, wanting to make a large arch, they would place the uprights too far apart, so the crosspiece fell between them. Some children solved the problem by using a 'spacer', which matched the top block, to place under the uprights. The children discovered different ways of making an arch, varying sequence, position, number and length of blocks. Problem solving like this can encourage children to make new connections with existing knowledge and, as Piaget implied, provides motivation for learning. It involves all the major cognitive learning processes, in visualising solutions, checking for errors, and in a collaborative context, imitation and instruction as well as talking and reflecting. It also involves metacognition in evaluating strategies and solutions. Deloache and

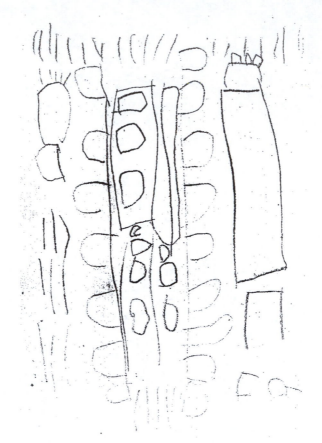

Figure 16.4 Farrah's plan view of the construction.

Brown (1987) described children trying to balance blocks of wood on a metal beam, who persisted in finding a single method to include trick blocks with hidden weights. They called this 'theorising' since the children took feedback into account in order to revise previous theories (such as finding the middle of the blocks). Problem solving can therefore stimulate higher level thinking, including the analysis of problems, synthesis of relevant ideas and creativity when unusual solutions are found, as with the children who redistributed the biscuits as crumbs.

Problem solving also involves important emotional and social learning. Successful problem solving enhances self-esteem and can help children to develop 'mastery orientation'. The children who planned the party became more confident and were keen to tackle new projects. Collaborative problem solving can help forge relationships, giving emotional as well as cognitive support. However, this requires social skills such as gaining entry, giving and taking advice, and resolving disagreements (Broadhead 2004). Moreover, problem solving by definition is difficult and can also threaten self-esteem. Adults therefore have a key role in fostering a supportive climate for problem solving.

Figure 16.5 Decoding numbers using a number frieze.

What do we know about how young children solve problems?

Research reviewing problem solving in mathematics suggests that young children employ similar strategies to older ones. The difference lies in their expertise in the area (Askew and Wiliam 1995). Deloache and Brown (1987) found the following sequence of approaches, for two to three year olds with nesting cups and for four to seven year olds making a train-track circuit:

- brute force: trying to hammer bits so that they fit
- local correction: adjusting one part, often creating a different problem
- dismantling: starting all over again
- holistic review: considering multiple relations or simultaneous adjustments, such as repairing by insertion and reversal.

'Brute force' is a strategy familiar to anyone who has watched young children trying to solve puzzles. Davis and Pepper's redistribution problem provides further examples: those who crumbled the biscuits used 'brute force'; some children got into cycles of 'local corrections' by taking too many from one doll and then having to give back from another; others 'dismantled' and started again. The children who used fewest moves may have considered multiple relations, taking all dolls into account at once. Those who 'just saw' the solution may have considered the problem as a whole.

Askew and William reported that older children planned first, while four year olds tended to start solving practical problems immediately. However, Gura (1992) found that blockplay planning depended on experience rather than age. Deloache and Brown found three year olds used planning to find a hidden toy: when they had to wait before they could start searching, they rehearsed verbally or by looking repeatedly. They reported three year olds looking for a lost camera, who used systematic strategies and searched only in places visited since it was last seen. Some young children, when problem solving, explore possibilities very systematically. One child trying on hats in the nursery hat shop methodically sorted those tried from those untried. Similarly, a five year old ordering fruit by weight carefully separated heavier from lighter after each weighing. Children choosing numbers to add often progress systematically using a pattern of 1 + 1, 2 + 2, 3 + 3. Marion Bird (1991) reported five year olds recording numerical and spatial investigations systematically. The children collecting data for the party showed systems such as making lists when asking who had a tennis racket. Questions like 'How could we make it easier for someone to understand?' can help children to organise their recording.

Successful problem solvers' strategies therefore include:

- getting a feel for the problem, looking at it holistically, checking they have understood, for example talking it through or asking questions
- planning, preparing and predicting outcomes, for example gathering blocks together before building
- monitoring progress towards the goal, for example checking that the bear will fit the bed.
- being systematic, trying possibilities methodically without repetition, rather than at random, for example separating shapes tried from those not tried in a puzzle
- trying alternative approaches and evaluating strategies, for example trying different positions for shapes
- refining and improving solutions, for example solving a puzzle again in fewer moves.

These strategies involve reflection and awareness of thinking. Teachers can help this by modelling strategies and encouraging children to talk about their methods. Children also need a repertoire of alternative methods to choose from, implying a range of expertise. They also need the confidence to be flexible, to be familiar with tackling problems and using what they know. All of this requires support from adults.

Problem contexts and levels of difficulty

Fadilah's response may have been influenced by the difficulty of the problem, prompting her to reinterpret it. Carr (2001) described children reframing challenges to reduce the difficulty, for instance making a hat for an imaginary character instead of a specific toy to avoid measuring. Carr *et al.* (1994) suggested that three things affected the level of difficulty for mathematical enterprises:

- familiar contexts
- meaningful purposes
- mathematical complexity.

For Fadilah, the context clearly resonated. However, children from less advantaged backgrounds can find contextualised problems harder than abstract problems (Jordan *et al.* 2003; Cooper and Dunne 2004). Children perform best in contexts which are culturally familiar to them from home practices, according to Boulton-Lewis (1990). She found that aboriginal children in Australia demonstrated their mathematical potential best in problems about family relationships or playing cards. However, Deloache and Brown (1987) argued for age-appropriate contexts. They found it was only when researchers used hide and seek contexts that young children displayed planning and systematic search strategies, while four to seven year olds displayed theorising and persistence when balancing blocks of wood. Contexts therefore need to be carefully chosen: people of any age 'can display more sophisticated cognition when reasoning about familiar than unfamiliar matters', according to Deloache and Brown (1987: 109).

Purpose may have been a problem for Fadilah: she may simply not have cared about sharing the sweets. Children may be more likely to engage with problems that they have set themselves, like making a car or a satisfying pattern. Deloache and Brown asked about the cups and blocks, 'Why does the child bother?' and concluded that so long as children are 'interested in the outcome and understand the goal even two year olds actively and systematically pursue the solution' (1987: 119). The key factor may be ownership rather than who initiated the problem. Carr *et al.* (1994) argued that the child has to have control of the outcome or else they may just look for the right answer to please the teacher. 'Understanding the goal' also implies that language may be an issue: Fadilah may not have thought that sharing meant equality.

Mathematical difficulty may also have been an issue for Fadilah, although she was a good counter. Children who are not confident in problem solving will generally fall back on less efficient but more secure strategies, according to Boulton-Lewis. This throws doubt on whether it is possible for children to 'use *developing* mathematical ideas and methods' to solve problems, as in the Early Learning Goals (DfES/2007: 74) People seem to need a secure understanding in order to use mathematical methods to solve problems. For instance, children who do not count reliably are unlikely to use counting to find the number of a group.

For children to engage in mathematical problem solving, it therefore seems that they need problems:

- which they understand – in familiar contexts
- where the outcomes matter to them
- where they have control of the process
- which involve mathematics with which they are confident.

How can teachers help?

Gura (1992) noted that some children are more likely to pose problems than others. A problem posing leader can provide opportunities for other children to collaboratively tackle projects like building palaces and roads, which give rise to whole series of problems. Broadhead (2004) argued that long periods of uninterrupted time were necessary for such play to develop and children might need support in developing the necessary social skills.

'Problem solving' in general is difficult to teach, but children can be taught to use strategies involving mathematical ideas, according to Askew and Wiliam (1995). For instance, adults can teach children to check using counting and can provide strategies for puzzles and computer games. Scaffolding can support problem solving: this involves providing support contingent on the child's responses, such as breaking the problem down into smaller steps and drawing children's attention to key features. Coltman *et al.* (2002) gave children clues, such as suggesting they looked more closely at all the faces of the shape when trying to match a solid to a 2D shape. Questioning is a key strategy to focus children's attention, but more subtle strategies such as a comment or look can be effective, as with the adult handing Seema the block to begin her tower at the top. In the Reggio table measuring project (Reggio Children 1997), the teachers used more proactive methods and gathered the children together at intervals during the project, to give them a lesson on non-standard measures or to discuss and vote on alternative methods. Asking children to talk about and show what they have done helps them to analyse and review the situation. Coltman *et al.* (1994) found that encouraging children to check meant they later did this themselves. Burton (1984) suggested that, with older children, self-organising' questions were useful: these are questions which children can use as prompts. Examples for different stages of a problem might be:

Getting to grips:	*What are we trying to do?*
Connecting to previous experience:	*Have we done anything like this before?*
Planning:	*What do we need?*
Considering alternative methods:	*Is there another way?*
Monitoring progress:	*How does it look so far?*
Evaluating solutions:	*Does it work?*
	How can we check?
	Could we make it even better?

Curtis' (1998) conclusion that adults who modelled curious, questioning behaviour encouraged this in children suggests that modelling attitudes may be as important as teaching strategies. Adults who acknowledge difficulties and being 'stuck' but who also demonstrate perseverance can help children to persist and become positive problem solvers. Further suggestions for general problem solving are offered by advocates of thinking skills (see, for instance, www.thinkingskills.com).

Different kinds of problems

Askew (2003: 85) quotes Burkhard's taxonomy of problems:

- action problems, 'the solution to which may directly affect everyday life'
- believable problems, hypothetical or story problems

- curious problems, 'which intrigue'
- dubious problems, 'existing only to provide dressed up exercises'
- educational problems, 'essentially dubious' but which make an important point.

This suggests a framework for providing opportunities for mathematical problem solving. 'Action problems' seems a more appropriate category than 'real life', since it can include children's problems involved in play, which is real to them. Experienced educators may plan 'curious problems', knowing what is likely to 'hook' young children. These may involve matching shapes to holes for younger children or counting large numbers for older ones, as with the children who wanted to know how many stars were on the wall in their spaceship area. 'Dubious problems' or exercises, if they offer no choice or responsibility, are not problems at all. With 'educational problems', teachers can expose muddles for children to resolve. Swan (2003: 117) described using problems to reveal inconsistencies and create cognitive conflict, by discussing children's unaided attempts at problems, calling this 'teaching for meaning'. For instance, when planning the party, I asked the children how they would decide what cakes to cook. They said, 'Ask us and we'll put our hands up.' This resulted in most children putting their hands up for most options, leaving them none the wiser. The children then realised that a more systematic approach was needed, involving recording. I could have organised this for the children, but the muddle posed a problem which helped make an important point about data collection. Different kinds of problem solving can therefore provide a range of learning experiences for children and can provide an effective teaching strategy to assess and clarify misconceptions and to increase understanding.

Opportunities for mathematical problem solving

The following lists provide some suggestions for problem solving contexts, which will involve most of the learning processes.

Adult-initiated

- Preparing: checking there is enough for everyone, for example plates or brushes
- Sharing: checking everyone has the same amount
- Tidying up: organising storage and checking nothing has been lost
- Gardening: arranging plants and bulbs, predicting their growth
- Voting for stories, songs, games or activities
- Planning and setting up: a wild garden or new role-play area
- Communicating: plans, measurements, invitations with times and maps.

Child-initiated

- Construction play and model-making materials: finding like shapes, fitting things together, checking sizes
- Pattern-making materials: creating patterns with rules, using shape properties, movements and positions
- Drawing and picture-making materials; making shapes to represent things

- Open-ended role-play areas: the 'whatever you want it to be place' (Broadhead 2004, for children to construct their own scenarios)
- Mathematical tools for children to use in play, for example calendars for making appointments, calculators for working out prices, scales for weighing a baby.

Games and puzzles

- Turn-taking games with numeral dice
- Nesting, ordering, matching, fitting shapes, for example jigsaws and posting boxes
- Matching numerals and pictures, ordering numerals on a 'washing line'
- Computer games for numbers, directions, shapes
- Hiding games: feely bags with shapes, 'Bears in the Box' game
- Scoring games in children's own ways
- Open-ended game materials, for example pennies, buttons, shells, dinosaurs, dice, spinners, small containers and 'empty tracks'.

Stories for problem posing

- Invented stories
- Adapted versions of books such as *The Doorbell Rang* (Hutchins 1986) or *The Great Pet Sale* (Inkpen 1998)
- Robots as story characters or transport, for example Postman Pat's van delivering letters
- Making settings for stories with small world toys or construction apparatus.

References

Askew, M. (2003). Word problems: Cinderellas or wicked witches? In I. Thompson (ed.) *Enhancing Primary Mathematics Teaching*. Maidenhead: Open University Press: 78–85.

Askew, M. and Wiliam, D. (1995). *Recent Research in Mathematics Education 5–16*. London: HMSO.

Bird, M. (1991). *Mathematics for Young Children: An Active Thinking Approach*. London: Routledge.

Boulton-Lewis, G. (1990). Young children's thinking strategies and levels of capacity. In L. P. Steffe and T. Wood (eds) *Transforming Children's Mathematics Education: International Perspectives*. Hillsdale, NJ: Lawrence Erlbaum Associates: 156–160.

Broadhead, P. (2004). *Early Years Play and Learning: Developing Social Skills and Cooperation*. London: RoutledgeFalmer.

Burton, L. (1984). *Thinking Things Through: Problem Solving in Mathematics*. London: Basil Blackwell.

Carr, M. (2001). *Assessment in Early Childhood Settings: Learning Stories*. London: Paul Chapman.

Carr, M., Peters, S. and Young-Loveridge, J. (1994). Early childhood mathematics: finding the right level of challenge. In J. Neyland (ed.) *Mathematics Education: A Handbook for Teachers, volume 1*. Wellington, New Zealand: Wellington College of Education. 271–282.

Coltman, P., Petyaeva, D. and Anghileri, J. (2002). 'Scaffolding learning through meaningful tasks and adult interaction.' *Early Years* 22(1): 39–49.

Cooper, B. and Dunne, M. (2004). Constructing the 'legitimate' goal of a 'realistic' maths item: a comparison of 10–11 and 13–14 year olds. In B. Allen and S. Johnston-Wilder (eds) *Mathematics Education: Exploring the Culture of Learning*. London: Routledge: 69–90.

Curtis, A. (1998). *A Curriculum for the Pre-school Child: Learning to Learn*. London: Routledge.

Davis, G. and Pepper, K. (1992). 'Mathematical problem solving by pre-school children.' *Educational Studies in Mathematics* 23: 397–415.

Deloache, J. S. and Brown, A. L. (1987). The early emergence of planning skills in children. In J. Bruner and H. Haste (eds) *The Child's Construction of the World*. London: Methuen: 108–130.

Department for Children, Schools and Families (DCSF) (2008) *Statutory Framework for the Early Years Foundation Stage*. Nottingham: DCSF Publications.

DfEE/QCA (1999). *The National Curriculum: Handbook for Primary Teachers in England*. London: Qualifications and Curriculum Authority.

DfES (2007) Practice Guidance for the Early Years Foundation Stage, Nottingham DfES.

Gifford, S. (1995). 'Number in early childhood.' *Early Child Development and Care* 109: 95–115.

Gura, P. (ed.) with the Froebel Blockplay Research Group directed by Tina Bruce (1992). *Exploring Learning: Young Children and Blockplay*. London: Paul Chapman Publishing Ltd.

Jordan, N. C., Hanich, L. B. and Uberti, H. Z. (2003). Mathematical thinking and learning difficulties. In A. J. Baroody and A. Dowker (eds) *The Development of Arithmetic Concepts and Skills*. Mahwah, NJ: Lawrence Earlbaum Associates: 359–383.

Piaget, J. (1973). *Comments on Mathematical Education*. Developments in Mathematical Education, Proceedings of the Second International Congress on Mathematical Education, Exeter: Cambridge University Press.

Reggio Children (1997). *Shoe and Metre: Children and Measurement*. Reggio Emilia: Reggio Children Srl.

Swan, M. (2003). Making sense of mathematics. In I. Thompson (ed.) *Enhancing Primary Mathematics Teaching*. Maidenhead: Open University Press: 112–124.

Vygotsky, L. S. (1978). *Mind in Society*. Cambridge, MA: Harvard University Press.

Chapter 17

Knowledge and understanding of the world developed through a garden project

Jane Devereux and Ann Bridges

Many settings consider projects an effective means of integrating the curriculum in the early years while maintaining a focus on holistic learning and development. In this chapter Jane Devereux and Ann Bridges provide an example of a creative project that was rooted in listening to and involving children and adults in problem solving with a real and tangible outcome for everyone.

Introduction

In the *Statutory Framework for the Early Years Foundation Stage* in England (DfES 2007) it states that to give all children the best opportunities for developing effectively their knowledge and understanding of the world, practitioners should provide first-hand experiences that encourage children to explore, experiment, problem solve and observe amongst other skills in an environment that provides a wide variety of activities, both indoors and outdoors. Appropriate adult support when needed, should be based on sound knowledge of how young children learn and best ways to support and facilitate learning. Knowledge and understanding of the world involves providing experiences that would sow in children the desire in later years to enjoy the study of such subjects as science, design and technology, history, geography and information and communication technology (ICT). The range of key concepts and skills that would support this later subject study include developing children's understanding of time, space, place, forces, energy and materials from many different perspectives.

This chapter describes how one nursery school based in West London used the real experience of developing their nursery school garden to support and extend children's developing knowledge and understanding of the world. Through the short descriptions of some significant episodes it is possible to see how the practitioners and the children planned the project and how the children became engaged and proactive in constructing their own questions and solving some of the problems encountered as they developed their outside area. The examples chosen illustrate areas of the curriculum associated with knowledge and understanding of the world as well as showing how the children's ideas and skills progressed beyond the expectations of the practitioners because the children saw the relevance of what they were doing. Within the garden project children were continually revisiting some of the central concepts listed above, as they handled new materials and changed and modified their outside environment. For instance they found various artefacts and explored what they might be, how old they might be, what they were made of and why they were where they found them; thus engaging in exploring their ideas about place, time and materials to name the more obvious concepts. Each episode described provides an opportunity to examine the kind of knowledge, understanding, attitudes and skills supported by such experiences.

The setting and the context

The nursery school is housed in a small corner of a West London Borough on the edge of an estate built in the early twentieth century. There are 45 full-time equivalent (FTE) children of whom 22 stay all day and the rest of the children attend for half days only. The school has a large indoor room and a small but varied outside area that includes a tarmac area and a grass slope shaded by trees, both of which offer varied experiences to children. There is a large sandpit, an area with a climbing frame and safe landing areas. There is also a large storage shed and a small room situated in the garden that can be used for group work with the children.

In evaluating the kind of provision the nursery was making for the children in its care the staff discussed the development of the garden and it was agreed there was a need to make the garden safer and more usable for longer periods of the year. A steep grass slope was unable to be used safely for lengthy periods of time, because the effects of bad weather made it dangerous. It frequently became totally devoid of grass and very muddy and slippery thus reducing considerably the amount of space available to the children. As the slope afforded children the opportunity to view things from a different perspective the staff were reluctant to lose the height it provided, but it was important to consider its place and value in the garden. Watching what the children did on the slope and which children used it most informed the debate about its potential.

Planning the project

In this particular setting the whole curriculum is frequently planned around a 'real' project, such as developing their garden, and the children are involved in all stages of the planning and solving problems as they arise. Detailed planning stems from different aspects of the project as the work is carried out. Weekly planning is done collaboratively, with an initial evaluation of work and children's progress during that week. From this, key generic learning intentions are formulated for the week or fortnight and activities that would help children towards understanding the learning intentions identified. This project runs alongside a varied array of experiences and areas normally expected in early years settings such as sand and water trays, role play, blocks, painting, craft and music and resource areas that children can access for themselves.

The initial plan was to map out the stages and to consider how to launch the project. It was decided that the initial stage of the project was to look at the garden as it was.

Children and staff discussed what they liked about the garden and what changes they would like to make. In order for everyone to be able to share in this initial planning stage many whole school visits were made to different parks and gardens. These visits included not only practitioners and children but also parents, the secretary and site manager. This provided central shared experiences to which all could refer back and it provided a base from which to progress. It also provided children and adults with different perspectives on what an outside area could include and look like.

Once an initial plan began to emerge from these discussions with all concerned, professional gardeners were consulted and health and safety advice sought. When the final plan was agreed decisions were made as to how to divide the overall project into manageable steps and what the key areas of learning and teaching for each stage would be. It was at this stage that curriculum areas such as science, design and technology, information and communication technology, geography and history were incorporated into the planning cycle under the auspices of knowledge and understanding of the world.

One key factor of re-designing the garden was clearly going to involve digging up large areas of the existing garden. Previous experience had confirmed to adults that there would be a variety of things to be found while digging. The question for them was how to maximise interest and learning from this opportunity. Before beginning any new phase of the work all children were involved in discussions, both to share their ideas and observations and also to be informed of some of the things adults may be focusing on. The sharing of the learning intentions set the scene and gave all children an insight as to what to expect. It in no way precluded their own interests and did not take away the excitement of expectation. The following extract shows how children were encouraged to hypothesis and predict what they might find when they dug up parts of the garden in preparation for moving plants and developing their newly designed garden.

Digging the garden

Practitioner: 'Tomorrow we are going to start digging the big part of the garden. I wonder what might be under the grass?'

At this stage care was taken to ensure that children were not being given information prior to their first-hand experience but was an open invitation to suggest what they might find. This gave the children the chance to share what they already knew and possibly make links with their previous experiences of digging. It also told them that they would be focusing on what they found underneath rather than in just digging. Some of the children suggested they might find treasure and what this might be and these were acknowledged alongside other children's ideas about creepy crawlies and worms.

P: What do you think we'll find?
K: Coins. Coins. My dad found five pence in our garden.
P: We might find coins. Where did you find it in the garden? Was it deep down in the soil?

K: It was in the vegetables where daddy digs lots.

C: We might dig up worms, big wiggly ones.

P: Yes we might. Has anybody else got anything else they think we might find?

M: Rubbish, old bottles.

P: Gosh yes we might. We'll have to be careful in case we find glass or anything sharp. M . . . Why do you think we might find rubbish?

M: Cos I have see a dustbin lorry dropping its stuff in the ground. Near my house is a dump. I go with my grandpa sometimes.

As children predicted what they thought they might find they were encouraged to give a reason why they thought that. Later they would also be given the chance to change their view in the light of their new found evidence. This type of dialogue would give children a chance to reflect on their previous experience of finding creatures, objects etc. and would also give adults a chance to begin to assess how much else they knew about what they might find. Children were encouraged to ask adults at home what they thought so that both home and school were involved in the investigation.

Other questions they were asked were:

'How will we remember what we've found?'

'How will other people know?'

Questions like this give children the chance to reflect on methods of exhibiting, displaying and sharing information and recording what was found. Once the actual digging began adult questioning continued to play a vital role. By constantly striving to ask 'open questions' children were given the chance to think, reflect, modify their views and to reason. For example, when a piece of broken pottery was found children were invited to think about how it got there, who it might have belonged to, if it was old or new.

The children were very excited at the treasure they found and imaginative stories and suggestions about what it was and who it belonged to raised some interesting insights into their understanding of time past, what old meant to them and how artefacts got there.

Reflection

Turner-Bisset (2004: 171) describes history as 'the imaginative reconstruction of the past using what evidence we can find'. The children in the above episode were speculating about the artefact they had found. They were exploring the past and using their imagination in full about what the piece of pottery was, where it came from and how it got there. With sensitive practitioner support, in which the practitioners understood the essence of history and the use of relevant open-ended questions, the children were helped to imagine the story or stories behind the artefact. The ability to hypothesise about what they had found enabled the children to share their understandings of time and cause and effect. As Turner-Bisset (2002) indicates these are important concepts in developing their understanding of the past and the nature of history. As Devereux (2002) suggests, the use of open-ended questions here is important in allowing children to share their own ideas and experiences and collectively build up a shared understanding of what they might find based on their experience. With children using their experiences of the pieces of pottery the practitioners began a display with photographs and drawings that recorded the many finds made and the children's thoughts. Many of the things found were not very old but for the children the understanding that they had been buried for some time and therefore were left or dumped there by someone unknown, at an unknown time, provided a context for them to speculate.

In the next episode the children show how some of the same skills that they were using in exploring the artefact are being reused and developed in a context that is more scientific. This time the children were again speculating, hypothesising and raising questions as they were learning more about what it means when we say something is heavy. The real experience recounted shows how the children were stimulated by the hard work of the initial task to go further and employ their own problem solving and design and technology skills in a game that they devised for themselves.

The story of the bark chips

As part of the garden development project new bark chips were required. Adults planned for the arrival of the sacks of chips and how they perceived the children would be involved. As with any enterprise of this nature there would be numerous cross-curricular possibilities such as communication skills, mathematics, movement and physical development as well as knowledge and understanding of the world, particularly science. In terms of mathematics, estimating how many sacks were needed, tallying and counting them as they arrived were all part of the learning intentions. There would also be the very real experience of what 'heavy' really means as the young children moved the big sacks. How could they do it? Moving heavy objects and developing an understanding of forces would be part of the experience children need to be able to abstract ideas at later stages in their learning and education. Communication, language and literacy would be addressed by discussions before and after the event and in making captions and commentary for displays and books. Physical development would involve the handling of large objects, manoeuvring wheeled toys and developing an awareness of themselves and their cargo within a given space. In making displays and books, that included drawings and paintings about moving the bark chips, various aspects of the creative curriculum would be brought into play.

The knowledge and understanding of the world curriculum would involve problem solving, questioning and investigating, geography, science, the appropriate selection and use of tools and use of information technology. Use of the digital camera and video, by both children and practitioners, enabled all to focus on their own significant learning moments. These possibilities had all been accounted for in the planning and learning intentions relating to skills, attitudes, knowledge and understanding documented.

So far so good, but when over 100 big, heavy sacks were dumped on the pavement outside the school it was a bit daunting for adults and children alike. How do we move these before the end of school into a place where they are safe and will not be damaged or stolen? These children were used to solving problems like this and rapidly devised routes and a one-way system for wheeled vehicles to be pressed into service in the transportation of the sacks into the school garden. They regulated and controlled the flow of traffic and allowed each other time to load and move out of the way before the next group moved in to load and transport the bark chips.

In under an hour the problem was solved by the children using levers to help them lift and load the sacks onto their chosen vehicles. They developed and refined their skills of levering the sacks by trying different length pieces of wood and were soon able to move, lift and slide their sacks efficiently onto their chosen vehicle. The sacks were swiftly stacked in the garden ready for use the following day or that's what the adults who were working in collaboration with the children thought, but the children were only just beginning! The planned curriculum may have finished for the day with the children learning much about moving heavy loads and how to work together and take turns but the spontaneous curriculum was about to be launched.

Some children continued to count and tally the sacks, out of personal interest, but others saw their chance to develop and extend their design and technology skills. Many of them had enjoyed the physical challenge of moving the heavy sacks and it was during this enterprise that they had discovered that the sacks were really very good for jumping and sliding on. For the rest of the afternoon they designed and used their own adventure playground, sharing ideas, helping each other and taking turns to use their creation. They made route ways, paths and devised slides and jumps using the bags as they explored the properties of materials. This child-initiated activity did not mean that the adults became redundant, they still had key roles to undertake. As well as supporting the children's new activities by playing alongside and asking productive questions, they observed what was happening so that future planning could incorporate, develop and extend the children's new discovery and learning.

Reflection

In this episode children were given the chance to explore the reality of forces at work. This real experience of feeling the kind of strength and effort needed to move things is very important in the children's later scientific life as it provides their own internal models of what it felt like. From this foundation it is easier for children in later learning to explore in more abstract ways some of the main theories of science and how forces work because they have a lot of experience to draw on when trying to hypothesise. As Nicholls (1999) says the real exploration experienced by these children provides a way of enhancing their cognitive abilities in science and their investigative skills. It took some groups of children longer to think out how to move their sacks but with support and working alongside the adults they were able to succeed in moving at least one sack per group.

The other significant aspect to this episode was the design technology that occurred as the children applied some of their newly learned skills to move and design their own adventure playground. Design technology as Parkinson and Thomas (1999) suggest can often be seen as the subject that integrates other clearly defined subject areas such as science and geography. Clearly the children who made the route ways were working across the subject boundaries. The making of the pathways is an important element of being able to make and read maps (Mynard 2006). In setting up and modifying their playground as more children joined in the game and as the practitioners too became involved in the play, children engaged in the design technology process. This included designing, making and evaluating the artefacts and systems they had put together. Their earlier learning of how to move the sacks and their refinement of such skills enabled them to be able to quickly modify and extend their adventure playground.

The third episode from the garden project describes some of the issues raised as the children planned to insert a water feature in their garden.

The fountain story

When we made our initial visits with the children to parks and gardens so that they could all have some input into what we would include in our own garden development, it was agreed by adults and children alike that a 'water feature' would be good. A fountain in the far, top corner of the garden was decided upon, where it would provide a focal point for the whole of the outside area. This was the easy part of the plan.

When you think about it, exactly how does a fountain work? In planning much of the children's work around this investigation it became apparent to us as adults that we had a lot of thinking to do as well!

We wanted the children to have the opportunity to experiment with a variety of equipment in the water tray so that they would begin to develop some understanding of water pressure and thus have some real working knowledge of fountains. It soon became clear to us that we were not all that sure ourselves as to the exact workings of fountains and the principles of water pressure. However, the mission statement that referred to 'a learning environment for all' was never intended to be a piece of paper that bore no relation to the day-to-day running of the school. Neither were staff afraid to embark on ventures to which they did not know all the answers. A community of enquiry was well on the way to being established.

Some exciting and challenging activities were set up in the water tray using tubing, funnels and rocks with holes in. At this stage some adults had clarified their own thinking as to how to support the children to try to simulate the workings of a fountain. The children themselves soon discovered that they needed to pour water from a height so that it would have enough momentum to be forced round bends in tubing and back up through holes in rocks. What do you do next? Solve the problem for the children or allow them to work it out for themselves? In this setting problems such as this were always referred back to the children but the adults would have already had some idea in their own minds as to where the investigations might lead and some possible solutions. This was not in order to give the answers but to enable practitioners to ask the appropriate open-ended questions that would allow children to try out their ideas. On this occasion the children tried various ways of raising themselves above the water tray so they could pour the water down. Eventually the climbing apparatus was brought near to the water tray so that children could climb above the water tray easily. This extra height afforded the necessary impetus for the water to rush down the tubes and be forced out of the rock or tubes, but the effect was short-lived.

It is very exciting to pour large containers of water very quickly into a funnel but some children discovered that a little restraint afforded better results. Not all were this disciplined! The following short extract between two children, Ben and Aisha, illustrates some of the ideas that were explored about controlling the water and the height of the fountain.

B: I know if you, if you pour from a high place into the tube it will go higher.
A: Yes, yes let me do it. Hold the tube.

The girl fills the jug and stretches up about 30cms above the tube to pour the water into the tube. She pours slowly but most of the water misses the tube.

B: Its not doing it it's falling out. Stop. Stop. We need something like . . . (he uses his hands to show a funnel shape). (He shouts to the practitioner) Annette, Annette we want a thing like this. (He uses his hands again)

Annette takes Ben into the hut to search for something to help. He comes out with one of the funnels and together the two children fix it to the tube. Aisha pours again and this time more water goes into the tube.

B: It's working. It's working. Yeh. Annette it's working.

This experiment developed over a period of weeks and led to another interesting discussion that involved adults as much as children. Many of us had not really paid much attention to the difference between 'overflow' or 'overspill' and the principles of water pressure that relate to the workings of a fountain. It may be worth considering at this point why we would have ever considered it. The fact is that at this time there was a real reason to think about it and so it interested us in a real, working context. If this was important for us, how much more important is it for children as they constantly try to make sense of their world? It is also worth noting that many young children are very able to take this kind of discussion on board, involving them in real thinking and discovery. During these few weeks all other areas of the curriculum were involved as children discussed, planned, illustrated and many children could describe how a fountain works. None better than one child who said at a group time, 'Well, you have to force the water up somehow and then it goes up the tube and it all comes out and it makes a fountain, but you can buy them in a box you know.' The children were letting us know it was time to move on so a trip to the garden centre was planned to buy the fountain.

Reflection

The important lessons to be learned as practitioners are that of the significance of our own subject knowledge in areas like science, design and technology, history and geography to support children's learning; our willingness and openness to say we do not know the answer and to find out alongside the children, and our ability to know when to stop and move the children on or give them the information needed. For the children during this episode the essential element for them was being allowed the time to explore their ideas about water and pressure. This was developing their scientific understanding of materials and their properties, which when combined together in certain ways and designs could control and regulate the effects of some of the materials. Being allowed to 'wallow' in their new found understanding before moving, on was as Bruce (1991) suggests, a very important part of consolidating their learning and developing confidence as learners, practising and refining what they knew over a period of time, until they were ready to go and buy the fountain. Here the children were able and willing to tell the adults when to move on.

Conclusion

These three episodes from the garden project show how over a period of time a community that was working together learnt together through real shared experiences – a community of practice (Lave and Wenger 1999). Practitioners and children developed their own subject knowledge and confidence in different aspects of knowledge and understanding of the world. At the same time practitioners documented the project with the children using displays, books, the digital camera and the video camera to represent the children's thoughts and ideas. This documenting of children's ideas shows, as Scott (2001) suggests when writing about the Reggio Emilia approach in their nurseries in Northern Italy, 'a strong belief that children are rich and powerful learners, deserving of respect' (22). The documentation also provided an opportunity for practitioners to reflect on their practice and share and develop their understanding of children as learners in a real situation. What was significant and inspiring for the practitioners was the level at which the children were able to operate and think because they were totally involved in the project.

References

Bruce, T. (1991) *Time to Play in Early Childhood Education*. London: Hodder and Stoughton.

Department for Education and Skills (2007) *Statutory Framework for the Early Years Foundation Stage*. Nottingham: DfES Publications.

Devereux, J. (2002) 'Developing thinking skills through scientific and mathematical experiences in the early years', in Miller, L., Drury, R and Campbell, R. (eds) *Exploring Early Years Education and Care*. London: David Fulton.

Lave, J. and Wenger, E. (1999) 'Learning and pedagogy in communities of practice', in Leach, J. and Moon, R. (eds) *Learners and Pedagogy*. London: Paul Chapman Publishing.

Mynard, S. (2006) Geography in the early years update (2006) www.teaching expertise.com/articles/geography-in-the-early-years-1262 (accessed 25 March 2008).

Nicholls, G. (1999) 'Children investigating: adopting a constructivist framework', in David, T. (ed.) *Teaching Young Children*. London: Paul Chapman Publishing.

Parkinson, E. and Thomas, C. (1999) 'Design and Technology: the integrator subject' in David, T. (ed) (1999) *Teaching Young Children*. London: Paul Chapman Publishing.

Scott, W. (2001) 'Listening and learning', in Abbott, L. and Nutbrown, C. (eds) *Experiencing Reggio Emilia*. Buckingham: Open University Press.

Turner-Bisset, R. (2004) 'Meaningful history with young children', in Miller, L. and Devereux, J. (eds) *Supporting Children's Learning in the Early Years*. London: David Fulton Publishing.

Part 3
Learning environments – children and adults

Gill Goodliff

Introduction

Young children are more likely to learn in environments where they experience intimate relationships with adults who are sensitive to their feelings and emotional wellbeing. Knowledgeable and well-trained practitioners, who feel valued and enjoy their jobs, play a vital role in providing the kinds of learning environments which will promote good outcomes for children. Respectful regard for children as learners, and enthusiasm for continuing professional learning – and supporting others in theirs, contribute to vibrant and effective learning environments.

The chapters in the third part of this book encourage you to reflect on aspects of learning environments that foster the emotional wellbeing of both children and adults. Themes that are considered include: the training and professional development of early years practitioners; the significance of involvement in research for developing a reflective approach to professional practice; the emotional responsiveness of practitioners to young children; the potential of the physical environment, including buildings and resources, and the professional learning between and amongst the practitioner participants in an inter-professional collaborative project.

Reflection on practice is generally considered an important aspect of continuing professional development and increased professionalism In Chapter 18 Peter Moss argues for a more professional early years workforce united by an agreed values system and fair pay and conditions for all workers, not just an elite few. He offers a critique of a system which he believes produces 'technicians' rather than reflective and trained professionals. He proposes a way forward through a restructuring of the workforce which draws upon international perspectives. In Chapter 19 Alice Paige-Smith and Anna Craft explore how early years professionals can be considered a community of practitioners through sharing their experiences, discussing issues and negotiating aspects of their roles. They suggest that practitioners' involvement in research can provide a means of developing reflection on practice and contribute to an understanding of leadership in early years settings.

While there is broad consensus that the emotional responsiveness and sensitivity of staff are of high importance in interactions with babies and young children in nursery settings, there is not consensus about how far interactions should be organised to facilitate attachments with particular staff. In Chapter 20 Peter Elfer brings the 'child's voice' into this debate by introducing a method of observation that is particularly suited to the observations of children's emotional responses. He concludes that both individual adult and group relations can be powerful in supporting children's emotional well-being. In Chapter 21 Marion Dowling continues this theme and focuses on the importance of regard for children's feelings. She explores how children's emotional wellbeing is a crucial factor in children who have the potential to be effective learners. Extending the discussion of the previous chapter, she highlights the significant role of adults as key players in children's emotional development and suggests ways in which they can support children through significant experiences, such as transitions and loss.

The importance and potential of the physical environment, both indoors and outdoors, for young children's learning and development is discussed in Chapter 22. Sue Robson considers how the actual environment of the early years setting can give strong messages to children about how they are respected and valued as individuals. She argues for enabling both children and adults to contribute to the way in which their space is, and can be, arranged. Managing risk in early years settings is an important and topical debate. In her short chapter Jennie Lindon picks up the debate on ensuring children's safety and security at the expense of supporting the development of expertise in assessing and managing risk. She highlights the growing concern that children and their environments are becoming too safe for their own good. She argues that children need to be enabled to take risks within a caring environment that offers support if needed. The author identifies practical strategies for early years practitioners to encourage children to learn about risk taking so that they can become competent and confident learners.

An emphasis on multi-disciplinary working is now an expectation in the delivery of services for young children and their families. In Chapter 24, the final chapter of this book, Angela Anning and Anne Edwards report on a project involving collaborations between higher education, local authority officers and early years practitioners in creating an informal community of practice. They consider how this project enabled professional learning for the practitioners concerned, which in turn they argue, supports children's learning.

Chapter 18

The democratic and reflective professional

Rethinking and reforming the early years workforce

Peter Moss

In this chapter Peter Moss argues for a more professional early years workforce united by an agreed values system and fair pay and conditions for all workers, not just an elite few. He offers a critique of a system which he believes produces 'technicians' rather than reflective and trained professionals. He proposes a way forward through a restructuring of the workforce which draws upon international perspectives.

'[The early childhood worker needs to be] more attentive to creating possibilities than pursuing predefined goals . . . [to be] removed from the fallacy of certainties, [assuming instead] responsibility to choose, experiment, discuss, reflect and change, focusing on the organisation of opportunities rather than the anxiety of pursuing outcomes, and maintaining in her work the pleasure of amazement and wonder.'

(Fortunati 2006: 37)

Introduction

English policy on the early years workforce gives a central role to the 'Early Years Professional', who by 2015 is intended to provide graduate-level leadership in all nurseries. Other workers, by implication, will not be professionals, but at best will have a level 3 qualification (equivalent to A level). This chapter argues the need for professionals in early years, but as the core workers in the system, making up over half the workforce, not just leaders; in other words making the quantum jump from a low qualified/poorly paid workforce to a workforce on a par to that in school, taking young children as seriously as we take school children. But I go further, to enquire into the image of this professional: how is this worker understood, with what values is she or he inscribed, and what conditions are needed to achieve the quantum jump? And in doing so, I lift the lid on a can of worms. How can we justify the current devaluation of early years work? What type of services do we want? Is the market model necessary and desirable? How should we fund early childhood education and care (ECEC)?

Integrated responsibility, split system

Early childhood education and care have changed a good deal in Britain over the last decade: sustained policy attention has led to more services, more funding and a more integrated approach, including the bringing together (in England and Scotland) of responsibility for all services within one, education department. Yet much has not changed. Thinking – both in government and public psyches – remains split between 'childcare' and 'early education': hence, government has a 'childcare strategy', a 'childcare tax credit', a 'childcare act'; and whereas 'early education' is treated as a public good for which there is a universal entitlement, 'childcare' is viewed as a private commodity to be purchased by parent-consumers in a private market where suppliers are mainly for-profit providers.

This split thinking is reflected in a continuing split structure: different services for 'childcare' and 'early education', different systems of funding, and different workforces. 'Early education' for 3 and 4 year olds is mainly school-based, where a large part of the workforce are teachers. While 'childcare' is mainly in nurseries, where most of the workforce are nursery or childcare workers, the remainder being family day carers. (I shall focus in this chapter on workers in centre-based services; however, family day carers are a large part of the total early years workforce, and any quantum leap in education and conditions needs to take them into account.)

If we compare teachers and nursery workers, we find a yawning gap separates them. Analysis of the Labour Force Survey shows that, over the period 2001–2005, nursery workers are younger (average age 33), have a relatively low level of qualification (only a fifth have the equivalent of NVQ levels 4 or 5) and are extremely poorly paid (average hourly pay over this period being £5.95). Teachers are older (42 years old on average), predominantly graduates, and earn nearly three times as much (£14.41), not to mention having access to good occupational pension schemes, a key employment condition that childcare workers can mostly only dream of (indeed under current circumstances, childcare and other 'care' workers are at risk of forming a large part of the retired poor in the next generation). The one common theme is gender: both teachers and childcare workers are overwhelmingly female (Simon *et al.* 2007).

Nor is this two tier pattern unique to Britain. *Starting Strong II*, the final report of the major cross-national OECD study of ECEC, concludes that:

> [The situation of staff and levels of training in ECEC across the countries covered] is mixed, with acceptable professional education standards being recorded in the Nordic countries but only in early education in most other countries. . . . Levels of in-service training vary greatly across countries and between the education and child care sectors . . . Figures from various countries reveal a wide pay gap between child care staff and teachers with child care staff in most countries being poorly trained and paid around minimum wage levels.
>
> (OECD 2006: 15)

Why?

At the heart of Britain's continuing split ECEC system is this split workforce: a relatively small group of teacher professionals and a growing army of childcare technicians, whose competences, procedures and goals are all tightly prescribed. Why does this split persist? Why does British society seem to take for granted that work with young children (but also, at the other end of life, elderly people) should largely depend on poorly qualified workers earning, on average, not much above the minimum wage? I would suggest four interlocking reasons.

First, because young children are still widely seen as immature, uncomplicated, incomplete human beings, whose physical and developmental needs can be met through applying simple formulas. Second, because any paid work understood and named as 'care' – 'child care' for example – is widely seen as essentially the commodification of what women do, unpaid and untrained, in the home; understood in this way, 'care work' requires little additional training for women workers and merits only low payment. Third, because successive neoliberal Conservative and Labour governments in Britain have adopted a market model for 'childcare', delivered overwhelmingly by private, for-profit providers and premised on parental fees, mediated for lower income families by tax credits: such private market provision cannot stand the cost of a well educated and paid workforce (any more than schools could do so if parents had to pay most of the costs).

Fourth, and here I am more speculative, there is the hidden hand of paradigm, the overarching system of ideas, values and beliefs by which people see and organize the world in a coherent way. In Britain, and indeed throughout the English-speaking world, ECEC is dominated by a positivistic paradigm, that values certainty and mastery, linearity and predetermined outcomes, objectivity and universality; and believes in the ability of science to reveal the true nature of a real world, giving one right answer for every question (see Dahlberg, Moss and Pence 2007 for a fuller discussion). This paradigm calls for technicians trained in right answers, not professionals trained to reflect and question.

Where do we go from here? One direction, set out for us by government, is basically more of the same, a continuing split workforce but with incremental improvement in the childcare sector giving graduate leadership in nurseries by 2015 and gradual increases in levels of vocational qualification, with level 3 as the main aspiration. But there are other directions that we, as a society, could choose to take. I want to map out here one of those directions, a direction of enhanced and rethought professionalism as part of a wider re-thinking and re-forming of policy that addresses the 'wicked' issues that government has shied away from confronting. My main aim is not, however, to urge this direction on you, the reader, but to stimulate or nurture critical and democratic thinking by 'opening up a new horizon of possibilities mapped out by new radical alternatives' (Santos 1995: 481): we have choices and those choices should be the subject of lively debate and critical thinking.

The case for a different direction

But before explaining my choice, it is worth pausing a moment to consider the case for not following the current route but instead risking a new direction. The case has three legs. First, equality. Why should young children require or get less than school children? Why should the workforce be devalued and treated so inequitably? Second, quality. OECD's *Starting Strong II* report concludes, succinctly, that 'research from many countries supports the view that quality in the early childhood field requires adequate training and fair working conditions for staff' (OECD 2006: 158). Finally, the work demands it: new understandings require different education and structures. Let me unpack this last point more.

Instead of a technology for (re)producing predetermined outcomes in children and a business selling a commodity of childcare, dominant ways of thinking about ECEC services in modern Britain, these services can be understood in very different and far more complex ways. Gunilla Dahlberg, Alan Pence and I have proposed that ECEC institutions may be understood (please note, 'may' – this understanding is a political choice not a necessity) as a children's space or a public forum, where children and adults meet and which are capable of many projects and many possibilities: social, cultural, economic, political, aesthetic, ethical etc., some predetermined, others not predicted at all and, therefore, capable of generating what Fortunati refers to as 'amazement and wonder' (see Dahlberg *et al.* 2007, but see also Moss and Petrie 2002 for elaboration of this concept of 'children's space').

In using the term 'projects', I want to invoke Carlina Rinaldi's use of the word as: 'a dynamic process, a journey that involves the uncertainty and chance that always arises in relationship with others . . . [growing] in many directions, with no predefined progression, no outcomes decided before the journey begins' (Rinaldi 2004: 19). Here are just a few of the possible projects of the ECEC centre, to give a hint of the potential of these social institutions, definitely not a complete inventory:

- Construction of knowledge, values and identities
- Researching children's learning processes
- Community and group support and empowerment
- Cultural (including linguistic) sustainability and renewal
- Gender equality and economic development
- Democratic and ethical practice.

Elsewhere I have explored the possibilities both for democratic and ethical practice (Dahlberg and Moss, 2005; Moss, 2007). For example, bringing democratic politics into the nursery (or other ECEC centre) means citizens having opportunities for participation in one or more of at least four types of activity: *decision-making* about the purposes, the practices and the environment of the nursery; *evaluation* of pedagogical work through participatory methods; *contesting dominant discourses*, by making core assumptions and values visible and contestable; and finally, opening up for *change*, through developing a critical approach to what exists and envisioning utopias and turning them into utopian action.

This possible understanding of the ECEC centre has been further elaborated. Using metaphors that capture the idea of possibility and creativity that are at the heart of this understanding, Carlina Rinaldi, from Reggio Emilia, has spoken of ECEC centres not only as places of encounter but also as construction sites, workshops and permanent laboratories. She uses these metaphors to capture the idea that they offer possibilities for creating new knowledges, new values, new identities, new solidarities. Reflecting on Reggio Emilia's 'municipal schools', Jerome Bruner emphasises their public and communal role; they are "a special kind of place, one in which young human beings are invited to grow in mind, sensibility, and in belonging to a broader community . . . [I]t is a learning community, where mind and sensibility are shared. It is a place to learn together about the real world, and about possible worlds of the imagination" (1998).

It seems to me that if we were to go down this pathway of understanding, then we need to think of an early childhood worker who will be 'at home' in this inclusive, experimenting, creative and democratic early childhood centre. This is the early childhood worker who is a critical thinker and researcher, who works as a co-constructor of meaning, identity and values, and who values participation, diversity and dialogue: in short, a democratic and reflective professional. This understanding of the worker is embodied in the quotation from Aldo Fortunati, with which I began this chapter, and in the concept of what Oberhuemer (2005) has termed 'democratic professionalism': "it is a concept based on participatory relationships and alliances. It foregrounds collaborative, cooperative action between professional colleagues and other stakeholders. It emphasises engaging and networking with the local community" (13).

Values for democratic professionalism

The English government's *Every Child Matters* agenda for children and children's services foregrounds the need for a common core of skills, knowledge and competence for the "widest possible range of workers in children's services", to support the development of more effective and integrated services. I agree that a common framework for a wide range of workers in children's services (including schools) is a good idea. I would, however, go back a step or two: to a common core of understandings and values (I would also want to avoid closure by treating this core as provisional and open, therefore, to critical enquiry and contestation.) The common understanding would be the worker as democratic and reflective practitioner, while I set out below, as a basis for discussion, qualities that I believe this professional might value, as well as some hints, starting points for reflection, of what these values might mean:

- Dialogue: "[Dialogue] is of absolute importance. It is an idea of dialogue not as an exchange but as a process of transformation where you lose absolutely the possibility of controlling the final result. And it goes to infinity, it goes to the universe, you can get lost. And for human beings nowadays, and for women particularly, to get lost is a possibility and a risk" (Rinaldi 2006: 184).
- Critical thinking: "[I]ntroducing a critical attitude towards those things that are given to our present experience as if they were timeless, natural, unquestionable: to stand against the current of received wisdom. It is a matter of introducing a kind of awkwardness into the fabric of one's experience, of interrupting the fluency of the narratives that encode that experience and making them stutter" (Rose 1999: 20).
- Researching: "Research can and should take place as much in the classroom and by teachers as in the university and by 'academics' . . . The word 'research', in this sense, leaves – or rather, demands to come out of – the scientific laboratories, thus ceasing to be a privilege of the few (in universities and other designated places) to become the

stance, the attitude with which teachers approach the sense and meaning of life" (Rinaldi 2006: 148).

- Listening and openness to otherness: "[Listening requires] welcoming and being open to differences, recognising the value of the other's point of view and interpretation . . . It demands that we have clearly in mind the value of the unknown and that we are able to overcome the sense of emptiness and precariousness that we experience whenever our certainties are questioned" (Rinaldi 2006: 65).
- Uncertainty and provisionality: "[Uncertainty is a] quality that you can offer, not only a limitation . . . You have to really change your being, to recognise doubt and uncertainty, to recognise your limits as a resource, as a place of encounter, as a quality. Which means that you accept that you are unfinished, in a state of permanent change, and your identity is in the dialogue" (Rinaldi 2006: 183–184).
- Subjectivity: "There is no objective point of view that can make observation neutral. Point of view is always subjective, and observation is always partial. But this is a strength, not a limitation. We are sometimes frightened by subjectivity because it means assuming responsibility. So our search for objectivity is often driven by the fear of taking on responsibility" (Rinaldi 2006: 128).
- Border crossing, multiple perspectives and curiosity: "We must think of the pre-school teacher as a person who is part of contemporary culture, who is able to question and to analyze this culture with a critical eye . . . An intellectually curious person who rejects a passive approach to knowledge and prefers to construct knowledge together with others rather than simply to 'consume' it" (Rinaldi 2006: 137).

The education and continuous professional development of this reflective and democratic professional involves deepening understanding of these values and learning how to give expression to them in everyday practice. This will involve, as Fortunati puts it so well, being "attentive to creating possibilities", assuming "responsibility to choose, experiment, discuss, reflect and change" and maintaining "the pleasure of amazement and wonder."

Restructuring the workforce

I have deliberately started from understandings and values rather than structures, because it seems to me essential to first ask the critical question: what is my/your image of the professional? Having attempted to answer the question, at least provisionally and sketchily, I can move on to how this image might be realised in practice. In my view, this democratic and reflective professional has a strong, graduate level, initial education, followed by strong continuous professional development supported by collaborative working relations, pedagogical documentation (see Dahlberg *et al*. 2007; Rinaldi 2006), pedagogistas (experienced educators each working closely with a small number of centres), and opportunities for higher degrees. This professional could be designated a 'teacher' specialising in work with younger children (i.e. from birth to 6 or 8 or 10 years) or a 'pedagogue'. Both professions (unlike the 'early years professional', produced out of thin air by the English government) have long traditions, strong theoretical bases and a relationship with the wider children's workforce (the Danish pedagogue, for example, works not only in ECEC services but also in a wide range of child and youth services (Cameron and Moss, 2007); while the teacher is a core profession across a wide range of educational services). In a British context, 'teacher' may make more sense, but that does mean a willingness to rethink 'education' in its broadest sense, and the role of teacher as practitioners of this broad view of education.

This professional would be the 'core' worker of a fully integrated ECEC system, working in all services with children under and over 3 years, and possibly well into primary school; indeed ideally, the reform of the early years workforce would provide the opportunity to rethink and reform the workforce from birth through to (and possibly into) secondary school, based on a shared image of the child, the (pre)school, the educator, and education. What proportion of the workforce should this core worker constitute? Some years ago, the European Commission Childcare Commission (1996) proposed that professional (graduate) workers should account for 'a minimum of 60% of staff working directly with children in collective services' (24), and this still seems to me a good target, as does the proposal that these staff should enjoy pay parity with school teachers.

What is proposed here is not ground breaking, indeed it could be said to be a necessary catching-up exercise. England and Scotland are part of a select group of countries that have taken the brave (and in my view correct) decision to integrate responsibility for the whole ECEC system within education: other countries to have taken the same decision include Brazil, Iceland, New Zealand, Norway, Slovenia, Spain and Sweden. Most of these countries have a core graduate professional, either an early years teacher or a pedagogue. Their proportion of the total workforce varies: for example, in Norway the pedagogue makes up a third, while in Sweden the teacher makes up a half. Most ambitiously, New Zealand has set itself the goal of a 100 percent teacher workforce by 2012 (New Zealand Ministry of Education 2002). Compared then to most countries that have moved ECEC fully into education, England and Scotland have still to make the quantum jump – from a split workforce with a large under-valued childcare sector to a fully integrated workforce organised around a well valued professional.

Putting the right conditions in place

Re-thinking and re-forming the workforce along the lines I have suggested requires re-thinking and re-forming policy. It means developing a truly integrated and inclusive system of ECEC, to replace the current split system. It means new understandings of ECEC centres matched by making 'full service' Children's Centres – capable of many projects and possibilities – the norm for the whole country, not just in disadvantaged areas. It means moving away from the model of markets, parent consumers and competitive private providers to collaborative networks of community services for child and parent citizens provided by a mix of public and private providers, all committed to democracy and inclusion. And it means spending more to develop a valued early years profession.

International comparison confirms the intuitively obvious, that a well qualified workforce requires sustained public funding of services and cannot be achieved if services rely on parental fees and demand subsidies: "demand-side funding [e.g. tax credits] is, in general, under-funding and the burden of costs in market-led systems falls essentially on parents, who, in the market economies pay fees ranging from 35% to 100% of the costs of child care, unless they belong to low-income groups" (OECD 2006: 116). Moreover, parent subsidies may not be passed on fully to providers and they make it difficult for services to plan for the longer term.

Those few countries (I am thinking here particularly of Denmark and Sweden) that have achieved an ECEC system that is available to all children as an entitlement, that offers holistic and community-based services, and that has a workforce at least half of whom are well educated professionals spend between 1.5 and 2% of GDP on supporting this system (OECD 2006: chapter 5). England currently, and despite considerable increases in recent years, still spends only 0.5% (*ibid.*); the difference is made up by parental fees (English parents spend six times as much, on average, for a nursery place as their Swedish counterparts) and the poor education and employment conditions of the workforce. (The gap is also partly accounted for by the Nordic ECEC system covering children up to 6 years, while the English system stops at 5 years or earlier.)

What is, of course, unknowable is the cost of *not* re-thinking and re-forming. As women's educational qualifications continue to rise and their employment opportunities continue to widen, it will prove increasingly hard to recruit the 'childcare' workforce, even with some modest enhancement of training and pay. As the traditional recruitment pool of young, low qualified women dries up, employers will have to find new sources of low paid labour, including migrant workers. There may be increasing differentiation in the private market, with some businesses offering higher qualified staff for higher fees (alongside the French and violin lessons). Large corporations providing nurseries will also spread, using economies of size to keep costs down, including group training programmes and monitoring systems. All this will mean a workforce increasingly governed by detailed procedures and prespecified outcome goals, standardised production methods implemented by a workforce of low level technicians accustomed to measuring themselves and children against external norms. Whether or not this achieves a few points difference on standardised measures remains to be seen; for certain, though, it will leave no space and little will for research, experimentation or democracy.

Summary

This chapter has been about the continuing weakness of the ECEC workforce in Britain today, the poverty of current policy ambition and the reasons for that poverty. I have also offered an alternative direction for the workforce, pursuing the idea of a democratic and reflective professional, inscribed with a number of core values and working in an integrated, inclusive and democratic early childhood centre, a service for which the public take responsibility and which is one of the necessary social institutions for a cohesive society. I have suggested that this professional might make up 60 percent or so, of the total workforce, and would need certain conditions to flourish; I have also indicated that some other countries have already achieved, or else aspire, to this goal.

But the chapter is also an expression of anger and a call for resistance. Anger at the poor education, pay and other employment conditions that we, as a wealthy society, accept for so many of our early childhood workers (but also for other women doing important work, such as the multitude caring for very elderly people). Resistance to the narrow visions, the meagre ambitions, the unchallenged assumptions that constitute current policy. You may not agree with the direction I have proposed for the early years workforce: that is fine, I have little problem with that. But I hope you agree that choices exist and decisions still need to be made; we should not accept current policy as a necessity.

References

Bruner, J. (1998) in Ceppi, G. and Zini, M., *Children, Spaces, Relations: Metaproject for an Environment for Young Children*, Milan: Reggio Children and Domus Academy Research Centre.

Cameron, C. and Moss, P. (2007) *Care Work in Europe: Current Understandings and Future Directions*, London: Routledge.

Dahlberg, G. and Moss, P. (2005) *Ethics and Politics in Early Childhood Education*, London: Routledge.

Dahlberg, G., Moss, P. and Pence, A. (2007) *Beyond Quality in Early Childhood Education and Care; Languages of Evaluation*; 2nd edn, London: Routledge.

European Commission Childcare Commission (1996) *Quality Targets in Services for Young Children*, Brussels: EC Equal Opportunities Unit.

Fortunati, A. (2006) *The Education of Young Children as a Community Project: The Experience of San Miniato*, Azzano San Paolo: Edizioni Junior.

Moss, P. (2007) 'Bringing politics into the nursery: early childhood education as a democratic practice', *European Early Childhood Education Research Journal*, Vol. 15, No. 1, 5–20.

Moss, P. and Petrie, P. (2002) *From Children's Services to Children's Spaces*, London: Routledge.

New Zealand Ministry of Education (2002) *Pathways to the Future: A 10 year Strategic Plan for Early Childhood Education*, http://www.minedu.govt.nz/web/down loadable/dl7648_v1/english.plan.art.pdf (accessed 18 September 2007).

Oberhuemer, P. (2005) 'Conceptualising the early childhood professional', paper given to the *15th Annual EECERA Conference*, Malta, 3rd September 2005.

OECD (2006) *Starting Strong II: Early Childhood Education and Care*, Paris: OECD.

Rinaldi, C. (2004) 'Is a curriculum necessary?', *Children in Europe*, No. 9, 19.

Rinaldi, C. (2006) *In Dialogue with Reggio Emilia: Listening, Researching and Learning*, London: Routledge.

Rose, N. (1999) *Powers of Freedom: Reframing Political Thought*, Cambridge: Cambridge University Press.

Santos, B. de S. (1995) *Towards a New Common Sense: Law, Science and Politics in the Paradigmatic Transition*, London: Routledge.

Simon, A., Owen, C., Moss, P., Cameron, C., Petrie, P., Potts, P. and Wigfall, V. (2007) *Secondary analysis of the Labour Force Survey to map the numbers and characteristics of the occupations working within social care, childcare, nursing and education*, unpublished report for the DCSF.

Chapter 19

Reflection and developing a community of practice

Alice Paige-Smith and Anna Craft

Reflection on practice is generally considered an important aspect of continuing professional development. In this chapter Alice Paige-Smith and Anna Craft explore how early years professionals can be considered a community of practitioners through sharing their experiences, discussing issues and negotiating aspects of their roles. They suggest that practitioners' involvement in research can provide a means of developing reflection on practice and contribute to an understanding of leadership in early years settings.

Reflections on experience

Clough and Corbett (2000) suggest that as practitioners working with young learners, we meld the personal with the professional, drawing on our personal histories. As they put it: 'Tracing origins helps us to understand something of where we find ourselves today' (Clough and Corbett 2000). They refer to the concept of the 'lived relationship', personal and professional 'journeys'. These consist of accounts that include personal and professional views and experiences, and illustrate that, as they put it, 'systematic thought, analysis and theorizing are quite continuous with and expressive of the wider life experience' (2000: 38). They argue that our professional identities and our 'distinctive and influential perspectives' (2000: 38) are determined by what we learn, both professionally and personally, over time.

Such learning is drawn on experience; practitioners therefore engage in 'linking analytical thinking to their own experience of practice' (2000: 38). [. . .] This linking occurs in many ways: through evaluating or researching experience, through a range of means, including documenting the experiences of professionals, parents and children through observations, images, interviews, questionnaire surveys, a reflective diary, listening to children (Clark 2004), and policy analysis or analysis of documents. In becoming who we are as practitioners, then, we build on layer upon layer of experience – our own, and that of others, generated by working within various communities.

In the following extract, Mel Ainscow, Professor of Education, reflects on his role within inclusive education:

> I am engaged in the development of practice. I work with schools. I work with teachers. I work with Local Education Authorities. I think that I am very good at working with people and I, therefore, make things happen or help to make things happen because of that skill. I see myself essentially as a teacher. All the best things I have done have involved me working with groups of people all the time, where we have developed some initiative to make something happen or overcome something. I seem to have a skill in helping people to think together, to overcome problems, to be energetic.
>
> (Ainscow 2000: 41)

Ainscow has conducted large-scale research projects, on a local, national and international level, and has written about 'effective schooling' and inclusive education. At the same time, he reflects on how he sees himself as a teacher, a practitioner in his role, which involves exploring and developing practice.

What he describes reflects a keen awareness of his relationship with others in his practice. For Pollard (2002), [. . .] dialogue with colleagues was a vital element. But rather than being just one of a relatively large number of features, perhaps for those working in the early years in the early twenty-first century, what Wenger calls the 'community of practice' is an encompassing frame/assumption for reflective practice.

Developing a community of practice

The notion of the community of practice, [. . .] has been developed from work by Lave and Wenger (1991), focusing on the socially situated aspects of learning. It signifies the social learning processes that occur when people have a common interest or area of collaboration over an extended time period where they can problem-find, share ideas, seek solutions, build innovative practices. Wenger (1998) has taken the notion of community of practice much further than its initial usage, seeing it in terms of the interplay in negotiation of meaning, and the brokering of shared understanding of change. Effective change or development depends on shared understandings. He discusses a number of tensions. Of these, it is the tension between participation (involvement/shared flux) and reification (congealment of ideas) that has had the greatest influence in the workplace. These tendencies are, according to Wenger, in continual tension between one another; reification, the process of abstracting and congealing ideas (as, for example, represented in symbols and written documents), is necessary in providing structure and a common reference point for understanding. And yet, alone, it is insufficient:

> the power of reification – its succinctness, its protability, its potential physical presence, its focusing effect – is also its danger . . . Procedures can hide broader meanings in blind sequences of operations. And the knowledge of a formula can lead to the illusion that one fully understands the processes it describes.
>
> (Wenger 1998: 61)

At the other end of the spectrum, and in tension with reification, is participation, which demands active social engagement in brokering meaning. Wenger suggests that participation is necessary to temper both the ambiguity and the inflexibility of reification.

And, as he notes, there are practical consequences of this belief, in offering participants in a community of inquiry both the authority and the resource to decision-make:

> If we believe that people in organisations contribute to organisational goals by participating inventively in practices that can never be fully captured by institutionalised processes . . . we will have to value the work of community building and make sure that participants have access to the resources necessary to learn what they need to learn in order to take actions and make decisions that fully engage their own knowledgeability.
>
> (Wenger 1998: 10)

For Wenger it is a dialectical relationship. Neither reification nor participation can be understood meaningfully in isolation from one another in relation to the building of a dynamic community of practice; this is because a community of practice is evolving, learning and not static. When reification and participation interact appropriately, Wenger refers to this as 'alignment' of individuals with the community's learning task, directing energies in a common cause; the challenge, particularly in a multi-disciplinary environment, is to link specific efforts to broader styles and approaches such that others can invest their own energies and interest in them:

> With insufficient participation, our relations to broader enterprises tend to remain literal and procedural: our co-ordination tends to be based on compliance rather than participation in meaning . . . With insufficient reification, co-ordination across time and space may depend too much on the partiality of specific participants, or it may simply be too vague, illusory or contentious to create alignment.
>
> (Wenger 1998: 187)

The notion of the community of practice has fired the imagination of professionals and workers in many different contexts. It is suggested (Hildreth and Kimble 2004) that this may reflect the capacity of the concept of community of practice to provide those working in rapidly and continuously changing environments that may have a strong sense of uncertainty within them, with a means to develop some sense of shared meaning, ownership and even control over what is valued and recognized as 'appropriate practice' in the relevant disciplinary area. Organizations are moving rapidly away from structure, routine, hierarchies and teams, towards much more fluid networks/ communities, which are reliant on shared knowledge. Communities of practice are seen as a fluid self-organizing structure that may facilitate such a shift in practices. In a globalized economy where knowledge is distributed over flexible networks often geographically dispersed, the community of practice has gained huge interest from business in offering a means for knowledge management. But it has also begun to influence and inform the work of many professionals, including those in the early years sector.

 The community of practice, according to Wenger (1998), whose further work on the concept has been and continues to be influential in many contexts, is a collective endeavour and is understood and continuously renegotiated and rebrokered by its members. Membership of a community of practice emerges through shared practices; participants are linked through engagement in activities in common. It is such mutually focused engagement that creates the social entity of the community of practice. The community of practice, which is established on some kind of common ground, endeavour or interest, builds up, collectively, an agreed set of approaches, understandings, values and actual communal repertoire of resources over time. These may include written and other documentation, but also ethos, agreed procedures, policies, rituals and specific approaches. Wenger notes that a community of practice may often be intrinsically motivated – in other words, driven by its members – rather than an external force. Communities of practice share and write an ongoing narrative. They evolve; their function is to reflect collaboratively on shared issues and to develop a story and collaborative approach, together. They often depend heavily on the informal relationships between people and, as ways of working that are often informal, as the relationships develop, so do sources and approaches to legitimation, as well as experiences of trust and identity.

While communities of practice often form within single areas of endeavour or knowledge, they also provide a means for complicated, multi-disciplinary teams to function together to achieve common goals. The concept of community of practice seems to have much to offer the development of practice in the early years, and in particular the notion of brokering across perspectives – or the idea of the 'boundary encounter', which helps each community to define its own particular identity and approach to practice. This depends on the exchange of perspectives from one community of practice to another, and its success depends on skilful 'boundary straddlers' who are able to facilitate reflection on and exchange of perspectives. As Wenger acknowledges, this role is a complicated one, however it facilitates a 'participative connection ... what brokers press into service to connect practices is their experience of multi-membership and the possibilities for negotiation inherent in participation' (Wenger 1998: 109). To an extent this means practitioners recognizing and surfacing their own boundary experiences. For example, many early years practitioners are also parents themselves, their dual roles as parent and professional in a setting may, at times, complement or contradict each other.

Professionals who work with young children in England are required to fulfil a range of policy-based expectations within their provision, relating to curriculum, assessment and access to learning opportunities. Policy frameworks offer a focus that brings colleagues and others (including parents) together as a 'community of practitioners', to develop shared approaches to how they provide for and enhance children's experiences in early years settings. This requires a commitment to shared reflection on practice over time. As Wenger (2005) notes:

> Sustained engagement in practice yields an ability to interpret and make use of the repertoire of that practice. We recognize the history of a practice in the artefacts, actions, and language of the community. We can make use of that history because we have been part of it and it is now part of us; we do this through a personal history of participation. As an identity, this translates into a personal set of events, references, memories, and experiences that create individual relations of negotiability with respect to the repertoire of a practice.
>
> (Wenger 2005: 152)

Wenger notes that when practitioners are in a community of practice they can handle themselves competently and can understand how to engage with others. Apart from being able to negotiate a way of working together through experiences within the workplace, practitioners also draw on shared experiences and, through reflecting together on these, evolve collaborative/shared perspectives: 'We learn certain ways of engaging in action with other people ... It is a certain way of being part of a whole through mutual engagement' (Wenger 2005: 152).

Reflection and inquiry in building communities of practice

Within any setting, whether early years or another context entirely, there will exist varied perspectives, rooted in each practitioner's sense of identity within that setting or context. Born of each person's interpretation of their role in the setting, practitioner identity manifests itself in the tendency to come up with 'certain interpretations, to engage in certain actions, to make certain choices, to value certain experiences – all by virtue of participating in certain enterprises' (Wenger 2005: 153). Developing a community of practice involves the explicit reflection on practice, and sharing of and debate around differences, as well as commonalities.

Reflecting on practice can be carried out through certain types of inquiry/research-based activities and, as Aubrey *et al.* (2002) note, the prevalence of 'action research' within the early years field which includes data collection and change in practice. They also outline the ways in which ethnography presents an appropriate methodology for collecting data with young children. The data can include video- and audio-taped recordings; 'thick description' or contextual data; observations of individual participants, field notes, diaries, and other such documentary evidence from the research setting and the wider context. Both of these methods (action research and ethnography) can be carried out by 'insiders' in the research context, and being a practitioner carrying out action research or ethnographic research can enhance the collection of data. Aubrey suggests that ethnography 'makes explicit to a community, that which they already know implicitly' (Aubrey *et al.* 2002: 138) and the process of finding out about this allows observed communities to understand themselves in more depth. At the same time she suggests there is a lack of a general theory of education or learning in early childhood, and that questions which should be considered, might include 'How do young children learn?' and 'What role do adults play in that learning?'

Collaborative and collective leadership

Essentially reflecting on practice, then, particularly with others, can be seen as an active process of collective meaning-making and assumes that every person is in a position of leadership in the development of a community of practice. For reflection takes every person into a leadership space to an extent.

Reflection may involve taking a 'balcony perspective', where you step back and see the bigger picture, complicated by several factors, including other people's hidden agendas, as Heifetz and Linsky point out:

> Fortunately, you can learn to be both an observer and a participant at the same time. When you are sitting in a meeting, practice by watching what is happening while it is happening – even as you are part of what is happening. Observe the relationships and see how other people's attention to one another can vary; supporting, thwarting, or listening.
>
> (Heifetz and Linsky 2002: 75)

Becoming an observer, they suggest, can also involve sitting back when making a point, pushing the chair a few inches away from the table, resisting the urge to sit forward, ready to defend the point you have made.

Empathy for others and expertise are also considered to be important qualities of leaders – however, as Maccoby (2000) argues, many leaders are narcissists, listening only for the kind of information they seek and behaving over-sensitively to criticism. Leaders may hold the following qualities, according to Goleman (1998: 41):

- a passion for the work itself
- seeking out creative challenges, love to learn and take great pride in a job well done
- an unflagging energy to do things better
- persistent with questions about why things are done one way rather than another
- eager to explore new approaches to their work.

These qualities may be observable among some practitioners in leadership roles – and identifying these, and some of the previous qualities highlighted (such as empathy) may constitute the role of the early years professional in a number of different settings. Empathy for the children is of course essential when working or simply 'being' with young children. Alice Miller (1995), in her book *The Drama of Being a Child*, writes about one situation:

> A family with a boy about two years old was asking for an ice cream. Both parents were licking their ice-cream bars on sticks and offering the boy a lick of their ice cream and telling him that a whole ice cream was too cold for him. The boy refused his father's offer of a lick of his ice-cream, crying out 'No, no' and tried to distract himself, and gazed up enviously at the parents eating their ice cream bars. The more the child cried, the more it amused his parents who were telling him that he was making a big fuss and it wasn't that important. The child then began throwing little stones over his shoulder in his mother's direction, but then he suddenly got up and looked around anxiously, making sure his parents were still there. Once the father had finished his ice-cream he offered the stick to the child and the little boy licked the wood expecting it to taste nice, he threw it away and a 'deep sob of loneliness and disappointment shook his small body'.
>
> (Miller 1995: 81)

Alice Miller observes how the child had no advocate, was unable to express his wishes and was opposed by two adults and their 'consistency in upbringing'. As she notes:

> Why, indeed, did these parents behave with so little empathy? Why didn't one of them think of eating a little quicker, or even of throwing away half of the ice cream and giving the child the stick with a bit of ice-cream left on it? Why did they both stand there laughing, eating so slowly and showing so little concern about the child's obvious distress?
>
> (Miller 95: 82)

Miller suggests that these judgements and types of behaviour by adults are influenced by the adults' own childhood experiences. Being aware of the adult's role and the child's feelings involves empathizing with the child, while at the same time being aware of one's adult values.

Being an early years practitioner, then, in a community of practice, whether a solo nanny or childminder, a nursery worker or a teaching assistant, involves the planning of activities that nurture the child's learning, as well as develop a sense of wellbeing, *and* reflecting on one's own goals for the children, one's own perspectives for specific activities or provision. This may involve complex decision-making based on how children are participating in the setting alongside others, together with an awareness and knowledge of relevant curriculum policy documents. We *also* engage as reflective practitioners at the additional level of connection with other adults, within an evolving community of practice. And, as the early years setting becomes increasingly multi-professional, the development of such communities seems not simply useful but necessary.

References

Ainscow, M. (2000) Journeys in inclusive education; profiles and reflections, in P. Clough and J. Corbett (eds) *Theories of Inclusive Education*. London: Paul Chapman.

Aubrey, C., David, T., Godfrey, R. and Thompson, L. (2002) *Early Childhood Educational Research: Issues in Methodology and Ethics*. London: Routledge Falmer.

Clark, A. (2004) The Mosaic approach and research with young children, in Lewis, V., Kellett, M., Robinson, C., Fraser, S. and Ding, S. (eds) *The Reality of Research with Children and Young People*. London: Sage.

Clough, P. and Corbett, J. (2000) *Theories of Inclusive Education*. London: Paul Chapman.

Goleman, D. (1998) What makes a leader, in *Leadership Insights* (*Harvard Business Review* Article Collection). Cambridge, MA: Harvard Business School Publishing Corporation.

Heifetz, R. and Linsky, M. (2002) A survival guide for leaders, *Leadership Insights* (*Harvard Business Review* Article Collection). Cambridge, MA: Harvard Business School Publishing Corporation.

Hildreth, P. and Kimble, C. (eds) (2004) *Knowledge Networks: Innovation Through Communities of Practice*. Hershey, PA: IGI Publishing.

Lave, J. and Wenger, E. (1991) *Situated Learning: Legitimate Peripheral Participation*. Cambridge: Cambridge University Press.

Maccoby, M. (2000) Narcissistic leaders, *Leadership Insights* (*Harvard Business Review* Article Collection). Cambridge, MA: Harvard Business School Publishing Corporation.

Miller, A. (1995) *The Drama of Being a Child*. London: Virago.

Pollard, A. with Collins, J., Simco, N., Swaffield, S., Warin, J. and Warwick, P. (2002) *Reflective Teaching: Effective and Evidence-Informed Professional Practice*. London: Continuum.

Wenger, E. (1998) *Communities of Practice: Learning, Meaning and Identity*. Cambridge, UK, and New York: Cambridge University Press.

Wenger, E. (2005) *Communities of Practice – Learning, Meaning and Identity*. New York: Cambridge University Press.

Chapter 20

Exploring children's expressions of attachment in nursery

Peter Elfer

While there is broad consensus that the emotional responsiveness and sensitivity of staff are of high importance in interactions with babies and young children in nursery settings, there is not consensus about how far interactions should be organised to facilitate attachments with particular staff. This chapter brings the 'child's voice' into this debate by introducing a method of observation that is particularly suited to the observations of children's emotional responses. Peter Elfer concludes that both individual adult and group relations can be powerful in supporting children's emotional wellbeing.

Introduction

During the last 20 years, consecutive Governments have sought to rapidly expand nursery places for young children. The purposes of this policy are multiple but include facilitating parental employment as well as children's educational attainment, social inclusion and health promotion.

Whilst this policy trend has been broadly welcomed, there has always been anxiety about whether nurseries may have harmful effects, particularly on children under three (McGurk 1993; Leach 1997). There is consensus in the research evidence that nursery is not *per se* harmful. Poor quality nurseries combined with risk factors in home circumstances together constitute an increased risk of insecure attachment, aggression and antisocial behaviour (Rutter 1995; Brooks-Gunn *et al.* 2003; Melhuish 2004). Good quality nurseries, characterised by the sensitivity, responsiveness and consistency of staff (Mooney and Munton 1997; Melhuish 2004) can have positive outcomes for children (McGurk 1993; Rutter 1995; Melhuish 2004).

Intensive case study research (Bain and Barnett 1986; Menzies-Lythe 1989; Dalli 2000) and the literature deriving mainly from practice experience (Goldschmied and Jackson 1994; Elfer, Goldschmied and Selleck 2003; Manning-Morton and Thorp 2001) has supported these findings. This literature has generally called for emotional interactions in nursery to be organised and structured in order to promote attachments relationships

(Bowlby 1993) between children and particular members of staff (widely referred to as the key person or key worker approach), and now adopted in official practice guidance (DfES 2002; DfES/DWP 2006). The main argument, based on attachment theory, is that young children need an additional attachment figure in nursery to promote positive self esteem and reduce anxiety in order to promote exploration.

Two criticisms have been levelled against the application of attachment theory in nursery. First, it has been argued that the assignment of children to individual staff is really an unnecessary attempt to model nursery relationships on family ones and restricts children's opportunities for interactions with a wider group of adults (Dahlberg *et al.* 1999). Second, Helen Penn has argued that an emphasis on attachments to adults ignores the significance of the peer group (1997). Trevarthen too has criticised the 'secure base' concept in attachment theory as inadequate to explain the power of cooperative understanding and exploration (2004).

One of the central questions to ask therefore, about nursery organisation, is how much attachment to particular members of staff does matter to children in nursery and what the links might be between different patterns of nursery organisation and children's overall emotional experience? [. . .]

Researching emotion in nursery

[. . .]

In choosing an observation method that has 'fitness for purpose' in relation to young children's expressions of emotion, it seems important to choose a method that has the sensitivity to register subtle external indicators or expressions of these emotional states and their contexts.

One of the challenges in investigating children's attachment behaviours is that external behaviours can be such deceptive indicators of internal emotional states.
[. . .]
The main points of the Tavistock observation method, usually undertaken in the home, have been fully described (see Rustin 1989; Tavistock Clinic Foundation 2002). I have summarised their application in nursery elsewhere:

> An early years practitioner observes for between 10 and 20 minutes, focussing on one child and her or his interactions with adults, other children and with toys and objects;
>
> The practitioner observes without a notebook, concentrating as far as possible on the chosen child, and being as receptive as possible to the smallest details as well as emotional atmosphere and responses;
>
> After the observation, the practitioner makes a written record of the observation, writing in as free-flowing a way as possible, following the main sequence of events and recording details as they come back to mind;
>
> The written observations are shared with supervisors/colleagues and discussed, differing interpretations and connections being considered and examined;
>
> The practitioner continues to observe, bringing further write ups to the group to be discussed and compared.
>
> (Elfer 2004: 121)

In drawing on this method of home based observation to develop a tool for researching nursery interactions, the central distinguishing feature compared with conventional methods, is the endeavour of the observer to capture as rich as possible information about emotional states. In conventional methods of infant observation, such emotion has been deduced from the external behaviours of the observed. In the current method, the intention is to gain additional access to the emotional communications of the child and the emotional atmosphere of the room, as they evoke emotional responses in the observer. In essence the subjectivity of the observer, the very thing that is normally excluded rather than included as part of the data set, is a central component of this data gathering method.

The observer concentrates her attention on one child, unencumbered by the demanding and immediate task in conventional holistic observations, of having to translate the myriad details into written notes as the basis of a coherent narrative account.

With no immediate requirement to note times, select detail and record this in some written form, the observer can make herself more available to enter the emotional world of the child and be receptive to possible emotional states and the minute details of events and interactions that gave rise to them.
[. . .]

Exploring two children's expressions of emotion in two contrasting nurseries

For the purposes of this chapter, the analysis of observations of two children, one in each of two nurseries, is illustrated. [. . .]

The analysis [. . .] focuses on the patterns of children's emotional and behavioural responses in interacting with adults and other children. Three questions are being asked of the data:

- To what extent do children appear to seek close interactions with particular others, adults or other children?
- If children do make overtures towards particular others, how are these responded to?
- What appears to be the effect of these responses or lack of them?

A brief description of the two children presented in this chapter and the two nurseries that they attend is given in Table 20.1.

Table 20.1 Outline data for the two case study children and their two nurseries

	Nursery 1	Nursery 2
The nurseries		
Status	Private (1 of group of 5)	Charitable Trust (one-off)
Location	Outer London	Inner London
Size (fte)	65	25
Age range	3m to 54m	12m to 54m
Opening hours	8.00 to 6.00	8.00 to 6.00

Table 20.1—*continued*

	Nursery 1	Nursery 2
Tasks and organisation		
Ethos	To be an extended family for each child but with learning and social goals;	Commitment to providing secondary attachment figures. Each staff member is contractually assigned to particular children;
Key Person?	No	Yes
Room organisation	Approx 12m age bands	Mixed groups but some separation based on type of activity rather than age;
Room size	Max of 12 children; 4 staff	Max of 18 children; 6 staff
The children		
Name	Graham	Harry
Age (at start of obs)	16m	12m
Time at nursery.	4.5m	2m
Attend pattern;	8.30 to 5.00 (Mon to Thurs)	9.00 to 4.00 (Mon to Fri not Tues)

Extracts of observation data are presented from each of the four observations in turn. For each child, two of the observations are conventional timed notebook observations and two are based on the Tavistock method.

Graham (16m to 19m)

In the first observation of Graham, one hour before lunch, he reads with a member of staff. As he fetches new books, there is a good deal of half playful, half mildly aggressive vying for and switching between adults' laps. This pattern of alternating attention from a small group of four staff to a small group of perhaps nine children is what the nursery wants to achieve, the children managing with and benefiting from interactions with a small number of different adults, rather than more focussed one to one care.

Graham seems to cope well with this until more firmly excluded from Anne's lap (staff names in bold):

*11.51   Luke has hurt himself and **Anne** draws him closer on to her lap. As they read, the very large picture book seems to form a circle with **Anne's** arm completely enclosing them and with Graham outside this enclosure. But he remains sitting next to **Anne,** looking now at his own book and just occasionally looking up at her . . . Then **Anne** and **Vicky** realise that he has poked out the plastic bubble cover protecting the picture book that he has chosen. "Oh look what Graham has done". . . .*

A number of interpretations can begin to be constructed from the first observation and kept in mind in thinking about subsequent observations of him. Graham seems to express a need for individual adult attention but also his ability, or the necessity, to manage this in different ways that is alternating between different adults and with different degrees of proximity, sitting on a lap or holding onto Anne's leg.

When he cannot actually be on a lap, but only sit adjacent to an adult, physical connection with that adult seems to help reinforce his sense of emotional connection. His confidence to move away from adults when he wants to, for example to get another book, suggests his emotional security with this shared care. However, there are limits to this and when he maybe feels excluded, for example when Anne encircles the hurt Luke, he finds a way of expressing his protest and anger. His feelings of being pushed out are perhaps represented in his own 'pushing out' of the plastic bubbles of the book cover.

What is most striking though is that although so far, the data has pointed to the significance of his close contact with a small number of attentive adults, his experience with the group of children at lunchtime also seems emotionally sustaining:

12.00   Precisely at twelve, the children are given their beakers . . . **Anne** *sits down by the children and begins to sing nursery rhymes . . . Luke seems completely uninterested but . . . Graham is exuberant, making hand movements and gestures, which go with the song.*

In the second observation, Graham arrives with his father:

8.40   . . . warmly greeted by Katy and **Vicky**. *Graham marches in with a big smile and he and Katy embrace. He seems very pleased to see his friends . . . Suddenly Graham seems to get a little anxious and whimpers and runs back to his father as if his enthusiasm to come into the room has rather overtaken him. He has a hug and this seems to enable him once more to turn back into the room.* **Vicky** *picks him up and dad once more says goodbye to him. Graham refuses to look . . . His dad laughs "Oh he's giving me the cold shoulder" and he calls again and again to Graham, trying to encourage him to say goodbye properly.*

*8.45   **Brigid** has been making toast and Graham rushes to sit up . . . looking round with pleasure at the other children, he reaches out an arm to each side to touch the children either side as if in greeting.*

Once again, his protest at being displaced, this time by his father, but the significance of social and physical contact with his friends is shown by the data.

Towards the end of the observation, when the children are singing rhymes together in a group, Graham's attention seems to drift from the group and he turns to grasp my toe. I feel he is experimenting, whether I might be a potential playmate, but wonder too if he feels I might be a source of thoughtful attention to him that he feels is not available to him within the shared care of the group or indeed from the group itself? He seems to develop this contact with me in the third observation.

It is towards the end of the day and a father, not Graham's, arrives.

Graham comes across and pats his leg . . . It is as if Graham almost wants to reassure himself that this is a real father who has really arrived and can really be physically touched.

Once again, does Graham show his need for physical connection in order to reinforce a sense of emotional connection by purposefully moving to touch the father who has arrived to collect his child?

. . . two parents now depart. Graham is blocking the door and the father says in a friendly but commanding way "excuse me Graham". My sense is of his longing to be collected and to leave himself, or to at least stop anyone else leaving . . .

I registered considerable strength of feeling from Graham about his longing to be collected. He is told gently to come away from the door. However, the staff do not come and physically hold him or reassure him that he will be going home soon. It has been a long day for them and they must be tired too. So perhaps Graham feels a little swept aside from the door and he represents this in his play when the parents have left:

suddenly he sweeps a toy off a surface and it crashes to the floor. He laughs at it and in some ways this seems just like a game. But there is no attempt to repeat the action as if it might be an experiment. Nor do I sense curiosity about the process of falling.

The staff are busy and if Graham does have these feelings, he may not feel they have been sufficiently understood by the staff. Might this account for the interaction that occurs next:

Graham continues to play fleetingly. Then comes right up to me, just staring. Close up, I have a rather different impression of him, younger and more vulnerable . . . suddenly he lifts his arm as if to throw something or to strike me, with a little smile of half amusement and half curiosity. I feel he just wants to provoke a reaction, perhaps to feel intimidating.

Has he managed to make me feel something of the vulnerability that he may be feeling? Still his feelings are unacknowledged and he manages to keep them inside. Moving away from me:

he cuddles a little boy bending down and putting his arms round him in an act that seems genuinely affectionate.

There are several instances in previous observations, of Graham embracing other children and it seems important to consider a further possibility arising out of these observations to do with young children's capacity for pro-social behaviour (Eisenberg et al 1999). Sometimes, Graham's hugs of other children seemed more experimental, but the 'feeling' conveyed in this observation is of empathic rather than experimental intention.

Once again, the commitment of the staff to team care but also the link between physical contact and emotion shows itself:

Vicky *changes his nappy and he begins to cry. It is only whimpering/moaning crying to begin with, but when he is put down, he cries more loudly and persistently.*

However, **Vicky** *is now getting Christmas cards ready for each parent to take home. . . . As Graham cries bitterly reaching up to her, she steadfastly continues this job . . . Graham is not to be deflected. . . . So* **Brigid** *actually lifts him away and sits on the floor with him. He cries all the louder . . . Eventually,* **Vicky** *completes the Christmas cards and comes to Graham. He lies in her arms and immediately settles . . .*

The fourth observation, is also at the end of the day, when Graham is tired and waiting to go home. It shows again the possibilities of how Graham may represent his feelings:

Suddenly, he leans forward and snatching (a bucket), sweeps it out of the trolley and behind him, so that the bucket flies across into the space from where he has come. I am startled by the vigorousness of this ejection. . . .

My understanding of this action by Graham, is more about the representation of an emotion, his intention to get rid of something frustrating or painful, perhaps his inability to make his father arrive for him, than the representation of a cognitive idea, for example a trajectory schema.

Parents are beginning to arrive and Graham has to manage seeing other children leave whilst he remains. He seems to want to both facilitate these departures but also to obstruct them in his familiar tactic of blocking the nursery door. This time staff seem more containing of his feelings:

He struggles and cries but **Teresa** *comforts him briefly and when the mother is gone, she puts him down and he seems to settle back into roaming and drifting. But he says several times 'Mummy . . . Mummy . . .?' and staff reassure him, yes Mummy is at work, Daddy is in his Van . . . Daddy will be here soon'. He replies 'Daddy . . .' as if just needing to say the word to remind himself about Daddy.*

Just as before, he then shows the possibility of empathy, in contrast to the harassment of another child:

Graham leans down and kisses a child who is lying on the floor. It seems gentle and affectionate. Another child is sitting in one of the brick trolleys. Every time Joshua pushes the trolley, she breaks into floods of loud crying. She really seems to hate it and Joshua is told to leave her. Graham comes across her in the trolley too and makes some tentative pushes at the trolley and I see her face begin to crumple. But he does not push further.

These observations begin to provide an evidence base concerning Graham's emotional responses in the nursery (anxiety, joy, confidence, omnipotence and vulnerability) and his endeavours to manage them. They also begin to explore the staff responses to Graham, particularly the way in which, as a small team, they emphasise collective shared care. They show too the possible significance of the peer group in sustaining Graham emotionally and the possibilities of his capacity for empathy. Graham shows how he may be able to adapt to the small team collective pattern of care provided in this nursery by a combination of attachments to the staff as a small group of secondary attachment figures, and through his membership of and attachment to the community of the children. The importance of attachment to adults can now be seen, but not necessarily as an exclusive determinant of emotional wellbeing but as one source of it, supplemented by peer interactions.

Harry (12m to 16m)

In the first observation of Harry, he is brought to nursery by his father. The contrast with Graham arriving (Obs 3) is interesting. The fathers both communicate a cheery and perhaps developmentally important confidence to the boys about the manageability of the parting in the face of the boys' anxieties. What is different is their reception by the nursery. Harry is greeted by a specific member of staff (Tina) contracted to be responsible for his daily care whilst Graham is received by one member of a small group of staff allocated to his care as one of a group of children. Harry is also arriving in a mixed age group room (8m–48m) whilst Graham's room was just for 12–24 month olds. Other differences will be at play too, for example their age and home circumstances (Harry had just returned from a holiday with his parents), the impact of which are difficult to gauge but need to be borne in mind.

The boys' responses are different too. Whilst Graham was ambivalent, first enthusiastic but then anxious about leaving his father, Harry is much more directly upset:

*As Dad hangs Harry's coat up . . . moves back across the room towards the door, Harry bursts into tears and protests loudly, leaning out from **Tina's** arms, and stretching his arms towards Dad. Dad laughs, not unkindly . . . he leaves communicating a kind of confidence about the manageability of this separation.*

Tina clearly knows Harry well:

*'I know what Harry likes – "doors" ' and she takes him across to a cupboard and opens the doors but it is clear that Harry is not ready for his distraction. He continues to cry and protest loudly. So she takes him for a walk in the garden returning in about five minutes. She seems quite confident and un-phased by his crying . . . over the next few minutes, he seems to become more contained and **Tina** takes him to a little wooden toy cooker . . . with doors that open like cupboard doors rather than a cooker door. She sets him down in front of the cooker and sits with him.*

Harry's confidence continues to grow and he begins to play with the cooker. He turns the knobs, but he is more interested in swinging open the doors of the cooker. His energy levels and interest seem to visibly rise. His attention switching away from the oven from time to time to intently watch interactions between other children. But the thing that energises him and captures his attention most are the doors. He seems to know exactly how they work, prising his fingers into the little gap between them when they are closed and pulling firmly, his manner one of determined, energetic confidence about how they work. But as the contents of the cooker is revealed, I strongly expect him to look at the objects that are revealed. His interest however is in the door itself, now in a new position. I wondered if the interest might be in the mechanism of the hinge but it is the door, the inner surface now exposed and facing outwards, that seems to intrigue and occupy him.

Graham did not show this intense exploratory engagement and an important question is how much Harry's degree of engagement might be linked to a greater feeling of security deriving from his relationship with Tina.

During the remainder of the observation, Harry continued to play either near or far from Tina but always within visual contact. Only when she disappeared once from view did he stop what he was doing clearly intent on re locating her. The evidence points to Harry's attachment to Tina.

This outcome is not surprising given that the whole organisation of the nursery is directed at the provision of a secondary attachment figures to support primary attachment figures at home. This is in marked contrast to Graham's nursery where the main objective of staff was to minimise individual attachment in favour of collective care by a small team. How were these themes complemented or otherwise in subsequent observations?

The second observation is nearly three months later when Harry is 15m and 1 week. He is already at nursery when the observation starts:

*I realise that he seems quite intimidated by the bigger children and the unpredictability of their movements. He gets knocked and buffeted and although **Tina** is very attentive and protective, she must also give her attention to many other interactions happening in the room. Now Harry is in the all enveloping embrace of Niel, whose hugs seem to be balanced precariously between love and hate. However, **Marina** (Niel's childminder) hovers near to Niel, ready to intervene and shielding and protecting children from his intense overtures.*

Harry climbs up onto a chair at a table where there is no one else, nor any activity, and it seems as if he feels safer here and more comfortable. The children are being summoned for snack time and he gets down:

*and totters with all his might across the room to **Tina** as if running across no man's land from the safety of the table to the safety of **Tina's** arms.*

After snack time, the children have outdoor play in the partially open-air basement of the nursery. It is here that a sequence of episodes shows the power of his relationship with **Tina** in terms of both his emotional wellbeing and supporting his development and learning. The older children rush out to play but Harry is less confident of his walking:

***Tina** stands halfway between him and the outer door, calling to him and encouraging him 'well done Harry'. As he totters towards her, she moves further back towards the door and very quickly, with a look of half delight and half concentration, he covers the distance.*

To begin with, he plays on some car tyres, five in a row, each one propped on the next. Harry:

climbs onto the first and then stays, propped up on the tyre, half contemplating the next one in the row but more looking out to the adults, with a look of pride and excited anticipation.

Throughout this period, lasting some 30 minutes, Harry plays with Tina closely watchful of his safety, but also with an interaction characterised by warmth, engagement and admiration on Tina's part and by pride and loving responsiveness on Harry's. A difference revealed by the richness of this data is the recurring evidence of the intensity of pleasure for both Tina and Harry in their interaction. The significance of this for Harry's emotional wellbeing and development and learning seems inescapable.

Is there a cost to this pattern of nursery organisation? It is striking, in contrast to the evidence from Graham's observations, that there is no evidence in Harry's observation of social interactions with his peers. He shows interest and watchfulness but not actual interaction. Nor is the interest reciprocated by the older children:

he crawls across to the play house, pushing through the swing doors. Mia is outraged 'I don't want babies in here!' and after some huffing and puffing, she leaves the house.

In Graham's nursery, much of his play seemed to resonate with the interests of other children who were close in age. Most children's experience at home will be of older or younger children with some opportunities for joint play but possibly much disdain. In this respect, Graham's nursery provides a different experience to home, rich in the possibilities of same age interactions whilst Harry's seeks to replicate close interactions with family adults but is limited in it's opportunities for those with peers.

In the third and fourth observations, some of the costs of attachment based methods of nursery organisation became more evident. Tina is elsewhere in the nursery and another member of staff, rather peremptorily, removes Harry's plastic apron, as he is no longer playing at the water trough. There is no consultation with Harry or encouragement to return to the water play and the interaction is in marked contrast to Tina's interactions. Harry begins to whimper and then to cry more persistently but this member of staff seems to struggle to be interested. A second member of staff also responds to him but only for a few seconds before she too moves away. Maybe the structuring of relationships in this nursery, whilst facilitating interactions between the individual worker and her allocated children, also has the effect of inhibiting interactions between other adults and these children, a loss of opportunity compared to Graham's nursery.

This observation also shows a second 'cost' to this attachment based pattern of organisation. Tina is singing nursery rhymes to a group of children. The observations so far, outside of meal times, have not shown group activities. Children surround her and she has a new child, Luke, allocated to her and who is on her lap. Harry is on the edge of the group and although he manages to use passing her a toy as an excuse to push through the group to her, claiming back from Luke at least half of her lap, he continues to seem worried and threatened by the group of children clustered around her.

I was to wonder about Harry's struggle to share Tina's attention in the fourth observation too. When the staff have taken their groups of children to the local library,

Tina is very preoccupied with Luke and Harry occupies himself with sharply pulling five or six books at a time from the shelves, dropping them directly onto the floor. As Tina concentrates on Luke, Harry's exuberant play seems to grow, pushing at the buggy to break out of the area where they are sitting, lunging at the revolving DVD rack and continuing his manic clutching at and dropping of books. Eventually Tina feels he needs containing and firmly straps him in the buggy, where he sits quite calmly, perhaps relieved to have managed to force her return of attention.

Conclusion

The aim of this chapter was to bring the voice of the child into the debate about attachment in nursery using a method of observation particularly attuned to children's emotional communications. Close observations of two children (aged 12 months and 18 months), highlights both advantages and disadvantages of different patterns of nursery organisation in terms of degrees of encouragement of attachment.

The analysis of Harry's observations showed how an attachment model of nursery organisation could be understood as facilitating Harry's independent development and learning. He appeared to derive great pleasure and security from this relationship with his allocated worker. However, the observation also began to reveal how the structuring of relationships mainly around interactions with a single member of staff appeared to inhibit interactions with other adults and with children. It also showed Harry's pre-occupation and frustration when his allocated worker had to give her time and attention to other children.

By contrast, Graham's observations in a nursery where there was much less organised commitment to attachment interactions showed how his need for close attention from a consistent member of staff was often not met and reveal how he may have struggled with some difficult feelings arising from this. However, they also show his ability to use his peer group in a way that clearly gave him a sense of participation, recognition as a member of a group and emotional security.

Taken together, the observations of both children show the importance of attachment interactions between these children and adults in nursery, the potential of peer inter-actions to offer emotional security, and the opportunities and costs to children arising from different systems of nursery organisation. [. . .]

References

Bain, A. and Barnett, L. (1986) *The Design of a Day Care System in a Nursery Setting for Children Under Five* London: Tavistock Institute of Human Relations (TIHR) Document No. 2T347.

Bowlby, J. (1993) *A Secure Base. Clinical Applications of Attachment Theory* London: Tavistock/Routledge.

Brooks-Gunn, J., Sidle-Fuligini, A. and Berlin, L.J. (2003) (Eds) *Early Child Development in the 21st Century Profiles of Current Research Initiatives* New York: Teachers College Press.

Dahlberg, G., Moss, P. and Pence, A. (1999) *Beyond Quality in Early Childhood Education and Care – Postmodern Perspectives* London: Falmer Press.

Dalli, C. (2000) Starting child care: what young children learn about relating to adults in the first weeks of starting child care. *Early Childhood Research and Practice*, 2(2), 1–32.

Department for Education and Skills (2002) *Birth to Three Matters: A Framework for Supporting Early Years Practitioners* London: DfES Publications.

Department for Education and Skills/Department for Work and Pensions (2006) *The Early Years Foundation Stage: Consultation on a Single Quality Framework for Services to Children from Birth to Five* London: DfES Publications.

Elfer, P., Goldschmied, E. and Selleck, D. (2003) *Key Persons in the Nursery: Building Relationships for Quality Provision* London: David Fulton Publishers.

Elfer, P. (2004) Observation observed, in Abbott, L. and Langston, A. (Eds) *Birth to Three Matters* Buckingham: Open University Press.

Goldschmied, E. and Jackson, S. (1994) *People Under Three. Young Children in Day Care* London: Routledge.

Leach, P. (1997) Infant care from infant's viewpoint: The views of some professionals, *Early Development and Parenting*, 6(2), 47–58.

McGurk, H., Caplan, M., Hennessy, E. and Moss, P. (1993) Controversy, theory and social context in contemporary day care research, *Journal of Child Psychology and Psychiatry*, 34(1), 3–23.

Manning-Morton, M. and Thorp, M. (2001) *Key Times: A Framework for Developing High Quality Provision for Children under Three Years Old* Camden Local Education Authority and University of North London.

Melhuish, E. (2004) *Child Benefits: The Importance of Investing in Quality Childcare: Facing the Future* Policy Papers, Day Care Trust.

Menzies-Lyth, I. (1989) *Dynamics of the Social: Selected Essays (Volume 1) 'Day Care of Children Under Five: An Action Research Study'* London: Free Association Books.

Mooney, A. and Munton, A. (1997) *Research and Policy in Early Childhood Services: Time for a New Agenda* London: Thomas Coram Research Unit, Institute of Education, University of London.

Penn, H. (1997) *Comparing Nursersies – Staff and Children in Italy, Spain and the UK* London: Paul Chapman.

Rustin, M. (1989) Observing infants: reflections on methods in Miller, L., Shuttleworth, J., Rustin, M. and Rustin, M. (Eds) *Closely Observed Infants* London: Duckworth.

Rutter, M. (1995) Clinical implications of attachment concepts: retrospect and prospect. *Journal of Child Psychology and Psychiatry*, 36(4), 549–571.

Tavistock Clinic Foundation (2002) *Observation Observed Video 1: Fundamental Aspects of the Observation Approach. Video 2: Brief Extracts from Filmed Observations on Significant Themes* London: Tavistock Clinic Foundation.

Trevarthen, C. (2004) *Making Friends with Infants* Paper Presented at Pen Green Conference 3rd July 2004.

Chapter 21

Emotional wellbeing

Marion Dowling

The importance of regard for children's feelings is the focus of this chapter. Marion Dowling explores how children's emotional wellbeing is a crucial factor in children who have the potential to be effective learners. The author highlights the significant role of adults as key players in children's emotional development and suggests ways in which they can support children through significant experiences such as transitions and loss.

In this chapter we concentrate on the importance of regard to feelings. Emotional wellbeing is prominent in the early years national frameworks for England and Wales DfES (2007a, b) and DCELLS (2007).

Laever's work is strongly echoed in the ongoing important action research project 'Accounting Early for Life-Long Learning'. Pascal and Bertram (1998) claim that emotional wellbeing is one of four factors seen in children who have potential to be effective learners.

Emotional wellbeing is also important in other curriculum documents. The New Zealand Early Childhood Curriculum document *Te Whaariki* has a section on wellbeing which states that two of the entitlements for children are: 'an expectation that the early childhood education setting is an enjoyable place to be; a place where they have fun; and to develop a trust that their emotional needs will be responded to' (New Zealand Ministry of Education 1996).

The influence of feelings on early learning

Increasingly we recognise how emotions can foster or inhibit learning. Although this applies across (and beyond) the age group, the link between feelings and early brain development is particularly critical at the very start of life. The crucial factor is the bond or attachment formed by a few very important people in the baby's life.

This bond provides a form of protection both for the early years and in their future lives and it is a basic requirement for children to establish wider social attachments as they grow up. If a baby is physically and emotionally close to one person initially (most usually his birth mother), this makes later separation from her more tolerable rather than less. From birth, every day that this significant person can be with the baby, to discover him, help him to know her, meet his needs, give him pleasure and take pleasure in him, will contribute to a fund of confidence and inner peace.

Responsive and loving adults are crucial to all aspects of infant development. Very young babies rapidly tune into a close relationship with their mother or main carer. The baby is already familiar with her mother's voice and starts to recognise her face and smell. When held by her mum or dad a baby's heart beat calms immediately. The oldest and deepest part of a brain is concerned with feelings and its development is fundamental to all other aspects of growth. From a safe and secure base the young baby will start to explore her environment and become open to new experiences. If sensory experiences are repeated often enough, connections between brain cells are strengthened. When babies are provided with familiar and consistent routines this helps them to start to make sense of what is happening to them – they begin to build up a predictable mental structure in their lives. Daily routines such as feeding, nappy changing and bath time allow babies and their carers to enjoy loving exchanges.

Maria Robinson reminds us that young babies cannot handle their feelings and are dependent on their carer to interpret their signals of distress – a hungry cry or wriggle of discomfort. Over time, if the baby's signals are recognised and responded to he begins to trust that his mum or carer is always there to 'make things better' (Robinson 2003). The most effective provision is based on 'contingent care' which is a bespoke response to the baby's actual needs rather than what the carer thinks he might need (Gerhardt 2004).

Given this optimal start the baby is helped to be calm and to start to manage his behaviour. For example, a toddler, who has been loved, respected and listened to, starts to show care and concern for others.

Babies also thrive on companionship and the important person provides this both through being physically close and through being responsive. Although mum or dad are likely to be the most significant carers, a baby may form a bond with other close family members – a sibling or grandparent in particular. However, important attachments will only be made with a small group of people who know the child well.

A young child's need for an attachment is also on-going throughout and beyond the early years phase. When she moves into a group setting and comes to separate from her parents, the essential need is to appoint a key person with whom the child can make a similar (but not identical) attachment. It is now mandatory in England for all children in the Early Years Foundation Stage to have a key person who plays a central role in making the child feel special and unique.

Experiencing and expressing emotion

Children's experiences and expressions of feelings develop tremendously during the early years of life. Most of a child's basic emotions are in place by the time he or she is two years old but the process starts long before then. Trevarthen suggests that 'every infant is born with the receptive awareness and expressive body needed to communicate fully with others. They can feel and express curiosity, intention, doubt and anxiety, and pride in admired accomplishment, shame or jealousy at being misinterpreted. Their manifest need is for expressive contact with sympathetic, joy-seeking, generous company (Gerhardt 2004). Young children also quickly develop their own means of expressing their feelings and then use them deliberately to suit the occasion.

Case study

Maggie's emotions change frequently and rapidly. She can be furious one moment when her block construction collapses, but jump for joy the next moment when her childminder announces they are going out to the shops. By contrast, Kirsty's feelings are more long lasting and even. She rarely shows excitement, but plays equably by herself for most of the time. When Kirsty is upset or angry it is difficult to cheer her up. Her angry feelings (or mood) remain with her, sometimes for a whole day.

Comment

Linda, the childminder, was aware that these two three-year-old girls had different emotional styles which required a different approach. Maggie was often easier to deal with, although unpredictable. Kirsty's feelings were less easy to 'read'.

In certain situations young children may cope with their feelings in ways which are puzzling to adults. On experiencing the death of a loved relative or a close family friend, children will show their grieving through withdrawal, anger or denial. Paula Alexander, a parent at the Pen Green Centre of Excellence, describes how her three-year-old son went back to bed-wetting at home after being told that his father had died:

> At nursery he kept taking things to the sandpit, burying them and digging them up to bring them back to life again. Then he'd say out of the blue 'My daddy's dead.' You have to pay close attention to what they are trying to express. The nursery did a lot of work with him through play.

Adults are usually very prepared to cope with a child's grief in the short term but may not recognise that the impact of bereavement is not always immediate. Woolfson, a child psychologist, suggests that while adults feel the need to recover from their grief, there is no urgency in children. You tell them the news and their immediate reaction is to go and play, but it all takes time to work through. One minute a three-year-old will say granny's dead and the next minute will ask you not to forget to set a place at table for her (Williams 1997).

It is important for adults not to have any preconceptions about how children will react to grief. However, there is likely to be a time, once children have absorbed the news, when they will want to talk about their loss and to recreate their understanding through play. Early years practitioners can play a critical role in responding to each child's needs at a time when the child's family members are likely to be distressed and vulnerable themselves.

Despite important differences in expressive style, most young children are full of raw emotion and feel acutely. The power of their emotion is heightened as their feelings are not tempered by experience. Most things are happening for the first time; as a consequence children can be desolate in their distress, pent up with fury and over-brimming with joy. They are receptive to all experiences that are offered to them. The effect of this responsiveness for those children who live turbulent lives is that they may live their lives on an emotional roller-coaster. In situations like this children can be ruled by their emotions. This is particularly noticeable with those young children who find it hard to express themselves in spoken language. It is difficult for adults to be fluent and articulate when they are angry or distressed – how much more so for a three- or four-year-old when emotions overwhelm them.

Young children's feelings, positive and negative, will initially be best reflected from actions. An early years curriculum should actively help all children to make this transition to using symbols. However, children's readiness cannot be pre-empted. Requiring all children to do things for which only some are ready will result in only some of them making any sense of what they are doing.

The effect of transition on children's feelings

A young child on familiar territory at home or in an early years setting is likely to feel secure and to be confident and competent. Any move means that a child is emotionally challenged. The initial effect on young children's confidence and independence of moving from a known setting is well known to early years practitioners. Children experience many complex and often conflicting feelings. Excitement and anticipation of the move are tempered by anxiety, distress and confusion about the unknown. In these circumstances children's emotional wellbeing is not secure; this affects their ability to learn.

We know now that a successful initial attachment helps a young child to move from dependence to independence; a child who has made a secure attachment within the family is more likely to bond happily with another significant person. Nevertheless very young children under two can experience high levels of stress when they move to a group. A Cambridge study, reported in the *Guardian*, of babies (11–20 months) who were starting nursery full-time after being cared for at home, showed double the levels of the stress hormone cortisol during the first nine days of day care. Even five months later these levels were still significantly high which alerts us to how some children can be psychologically challenged (Ward 2005).

Although children will initially show their feelings through what they do, their spoken language is important for them to learn to deal with emotions. In order to cope with such momentous experiences involved when moving from reception to Year 1 when starting school, children need to talk to express their feelings and also to make sense of what is happening to them during the school day.

An Oxfordshire project on transition encouraged reception children to say how they felt about the prospective move. Children expressed their worries about facing the big playground, not knowing where to go, fears about being bullied and having to write. Staff were able to pick up on these messages and improve their transition procedures accordingly (Oxfordshire County Council 2006). Other children in the project were very positive and relished the prospect of new challenges, doing homework and being with their friends. This re-enforces the view in the Early Years Foundation Stage that children will respond differently to a transition (DfES, 2007a, b).

The influence of the family

Young children's understandings and use of their feelings will be heavily influenced by interactions with the significant people around them, initially their parents. An important part of knowing about ourselves is to be able to recognise the different feelings that we have and that other people experience. Peter Elfer suggests that this empathetic behaviour is dependent on the child having experienced a good attachment where his own feelings have been understood (Elfer 2007). In these circumstances children under two years can be very sensitive to the feelings and needs of others and show this when playing with their toys. Dunn also reminds us that once children can talk they will show their understanding of others, for instance in the language they use with younger children or adults (Dunn 1999). By stark contrast, there is evidence of how less fortunate children learn different lessons. Goleman provides case studies of the dire emotional effects on small children who have been repeatedly physically abused (Goleman 1996). The most noticeable result is that these children who have suffered so much completely lack care and concern for others. At two and three years of age they typically ignore any distress shown by other children; often their responses may be violent. All they are doing is mirroring the behaviour that they have received themselves.

In families where feelings are not only expressed but are openly discussed, a young child is helped to recognise and accept his emotions and those of others. In these circumstances children are also more likely to talk freely about what they feel. These intimate contacts between parents and child involve shared experiences and loving attention over a period of time. Some parents lack this as a result of the busy lives they lead. While the early years setting would never claim to be able to replace these family interactions, it can play a crucial role in working with parents and sharing the task of helping children understand what they feel.

Children's emotional understandings are dependent not only on the degree of family support but also on what sex they happen to be. Different messages about emotions are given to boys and girls. In one small study, mothers talked more often to their 18-month-old daughters about feelings than they did to their sons at this age. By the time they were two years old these little girls were seen as more likely to be interested in and articulate about feelings than the boys (Dunn *et al.* 1987).

Other studies offer further evidence. When parents make up stories for their small children they use more emotion words for their daughters than their sons; when mothers play with their children they show a wider range of emotions to girls than to boys. Brody and Hall, who summarised these studies, suggest that as a result of the experiences they have, and because girls become more competent at an early age with language than do boys, this results in the girls being able to use words to explore feelings. By contrast boys are not helped so well to verbalise and so tend to be confrontational with their feelings and become less tuned in to their own and others' emotions (Brody and Hall 1993). These early experiences and consequent emotional differences can very often continue into adulthood and be seen in relationships. Goleman suggests that women are well prepared to cope with the emotional aspects of a relationship; conversely, men are more inclined to minimise emotions and are less aware of the importance of discussing and expressing feelings as a way of sustaining a partnership. He argues that this emotional imbalance between the sexes is a significant factor in the break-up of marriages (Goleman 1996).

Young children's developing understandings of emotion

Through early relationships with their important people, very young children experience their basic feelings. However they need to have experienced a range of emotions before they begin to understand them. Using puppets with children, Denham found that those who showed both positive and negative feelings in their play were more likely to recognise and comprehend what others were feeling in different situations (Denham 1986). Moreover, using puppets again, Denham suggests that children are beginning to recognise that in a given situation people may feel differently. For example, many children could understand that a puppet could be sad about going to nursery, while they would be happy (Denham and Couchard 1990).

It is much more difficult though for children to recognise that emotions can be mixed. When six-year-olds were asked to predict the feelings of a person who eventually found his lost dog, but it was injured, they typically said that the owner would feel totally happy or sad, but not a mixture of both. Children at ten years acknowledged that it was possible to feel both emotions (Harris 1983). Furthermore, although they may show complex feelings, they cannot predict them. However, it seems that social convention plays a part; from a young age children can be influenced to show feelings which are socially acceptable but are not genuine. In one study, four-year-old girls responded to social pressures by smiling when the researcher presented them with a disappointing toy, although when they examined their toy alone they showed their disappointment. (Interestingly, boys did not attempt to mask their feelings in the same way.) Questioned later, when they were able to swap their disappointing gift for a more exciting one, the little girls admitted to being disappointed, but thought that this would not have been recognised because of their polite words of thanks. These children made no reference to their smiling faces or the control of their real emotions and despite their behaviour were unaware of how their displayed emotion could beguile observers (Cole 1986). As children grow older they begin to understand that the feelings that they show to others may not be the same as their true feelings. This lesson is a necessary one as part of becoming socialised. Nevertheless, where young children are pressurised or coerced into constantly masking their true feelings and substituting socially acceptable responses, this could lead to them misunderstanding the function of emotions in life.

Seizing opportunities for emotional learning

We see and hear a great deal about how those adults with emotional problems can track them back to some difficulties in childhood. Goleman suggests that because early childhood is one of the very critical times for nurturing emotional growth, if this opportunity is missed or the nurturing becomes abuse it becomes progressively harder to compensate for this at a later date. If early years practitioners are to aim to prevent these problems in adulthood they must take advantage of the receptive nature of young children and positively help them to achieve emotional health. This means looking at a climate in the setting which helps children to feel, think and talk about feelings. They will think carefully about how to organise this climate. For example, circle time has become a common means of encouraging children to converse about things that matter to them. Sometimes, though, even where staffing ratios are good, these occasions are organised for the whole group of children. Even though the adult has very good relationships with all of the children, a large group involves a degree of formality and does not provide an atmosphere conducive to sharing intimate thoughts.

Anecdotal evidence from groups of early years practitioners who studied when children in reception classes were more likely to share personal thoughts and feelings highlighted the following occasions:

- times when the child approaches an adult individually, particularly during outdoor play or when an adult was helping a child get ready for PE;
- during easy conversations with small groups in the book area, and on the dough and drawing tables;
- when children are involved in self chosen play (such as building dens) where they have an illusion of privacy.

Less effective times were after children had had physical activity such as swimming and PE and whole group times, particularly when these were conducted on a formal question-and-answer basis. Children, like adults, are more likely to talk about things that affect them with people who show that they are genuinely interested and who are prepared to give time to listen.

Children's feelings will be stirred by sensory experiences such as listening to music, looking, and touching beautiful things, tasting and smelling. If they can talk about their reactions to these positive experiences, it will alert them to recognise similar feelings on another occasion. In the same way they need to recognise negative emotions. Anger and fury which results in loss of control can be extremely frightening for a three- or four-year-old. Sensitive adults can provide safety and reassurance and encourage children to try to see patterns in their behaviour and reasons for their strong reactions. In this way children come to accept and regulate their feelings.

Children who are emotionally vulnerable desperately need a calm and safe environment. However, occasionally the setting that emphasises calm therapy can be in danger of repressing emotions. Children have the right both to witness and to experience different feelings. Living in a calm, bland atmosphere can produce dull people. Children's feelings should also be respected (Scott 1996). It is questionable whether adults should attempt to jolly children along when they are bereft at being left in the nursery, or their friend won't play with them. This sorrow and desolation is more devastating than that experienced by an adult in a comparable situation for the simple reason that the child does not have the life experience which tells her that the cause of the distress is only temporary. A simple acknowledgement of sympathy will at least show the child that he or she is being taken seriously. As always, practitioners themselves play a very important role as models. A strong relationship between adults and children is founded on feeling. In such a setting children recognise that the adults care for them, laugh with them, share their tragedies and excitements and also become angry when boundaries of behaviour are broken. So long as the love and care are prevalent, children will flourish and grow given this healthy emotional repertoire.

Summary

We now recognise that strong attachments very early in life are fundamental to young children's learning and development. Emotional development is rapid and closely tied to other areas of development. In order to achieve emotional health, children need to experience and be able to express a range of emotions in their own way through a broad curriculum. They need to talk through negative emotions, particularly during times of stress, as when moving into school. Children's understandings about their feelings are heavily dependent on the support they receive from their families and also whether they happen to be a boy or a girl. Given support, they start to show empathy as toddlers and then learn to understand that people can feel differently from them. Early years settings can play an important role in aiding children's emotional wellbeing through their curriculum and organisation and the ways in which early educators work with children and act as role models.

References

Brody, L. R. and Hall, J. A. (1993) 'Gender and emotion', in M. Lewis and J. Haviland (eds) *Handbook of Emotions*. New York: Guilford Press.

Cole, P. M. (1986) 'Children's spontaneous control of facial expression', *Child Development* 57, 1309–21.

Denham, S. A. (1986) 'Social cognition, social behaviour, and emotion in pre-schoolers: contextual validation', *Child Development* 57, 194–201.

Denham, S. A. and Couchard, E. A. (1990) 'Young pre-schoolers' understanding of emotion', *Child Study Journal* 20, 171–92.

Department for Children, Education, Lifelong Learning and Skills (DCELLS) (2007) Foundation Phase, framework for children's learning, Welsh Assembly Government.

Department for Education and Skills (DfES) (2007a) *The Early Years Foundation Stage*, DfES. Nottingham: DfES Publications.

Department for Education and Skills (DfES) (2007b) *The Early Years Foundation Stage, Principles into Practice Cards, 2.1*. Nottingham: DfES Publications.

Dunn, J. (1999) Mindreading and Social Relationships in M. Bennett (ed.) *Developmental Psychology*, London: Taylor and Francis, 55–71.

Dunn, J., Bretherton, I. and Munn, P. (1987) 'Conversations about feeling states between mothers and their young children', *Developmental Psychology*, 23, 1–8.

Elfer, P. (2007) Life at Two, Attachments, Key People and Development (user notes). Siren Films Ltd. 5 Charlotte Square, Newcastle upon Tyne NE1 4XF. website: www.sirenfilms.co.uk

Gerhardt, S. (2004) *Why Love Matters*. Hove: Brunner-Routledge.

Goleman, D. (1996) *Emotional Intelligence*. London: Bloomsbury.

Harris, P. L. (1983) 'Children's understanding of the link between situation and emotion', *Journal of Experimental Child Psychology* 36, 490–9.

New Zealand Ministry of Education (1996) *Te Whaariki, Early Childhood Curriculum*. Wellington: Learning Media.

Oxfordshire County Council (2006) *Transition Foundation Stage to Year One*. Oxford: Oxfordshire County Council.

Pascal, C. and Bertram, T. (1998) Accounting Early for Life-Long Learning. Keynote talk at Early Years Conference, Dorchester, July.

Robinson, M. (2003) *From Birth to One. The Year of Opportunity.* Buckingham: Open University Press.

Scott, W. (1996) Choices in Learning, in C. Nutbrown (ed.) *Children's Rights and Early Education.* London: Paul Chapman.

Trevarthen, C. (2006) 'Doing' Education – to know what others know, *Early Education,* 49, 12.

Ward, L. (2005) Hidden Stress of the Nursery Age, in *The Guardian News,* 19.09.05, p. 3.

Williams, E. (1997) 'It's not bad to be sad', *TES Primary,* 12 September, 13.

Chapter 22

The physical environment

Sue Robson

The importance and potential of the physical environment – indoors and outdoors – for young children's learning and development is the focus of this chapter. Sue Robson considers how the actual environment of the early years setting can give strong messages to children about how they are respected and valued as individuals. She argues for enabling both children and adults to contribute to the way in which their space is and can be, arranged.

Introduction

'Until this matter of environment is settled no method can save us.'

(McMillan 1930: 2)

In recent years, more attention has been paid to design and architecture for young children (Cohen 2005). In England, this has, in part, been as a result of the Neighbourhood Nurseries and Children's Centres initiatives (see www.surestart.gov.uk), which have often necessitated new builds, or extensive reorganisation and development of settings. This has focused attention on the relationships between both children and adults and their environment. The nursery and school environments within which we 'live' have an effect upon us all (McLean 1991), and contribute to the formation of our identities (Zini 2005). Underlying the ways in which these spaces are organised are the philosophies and values of early years practitioners and settings, and their beliefs about children and childhood, care and learning. Many early years settings will contain much similar apparatus, and may be organised in what seem to be physically quite similar ways. Any similarities may, however, end there. The provision we make comes to life through the ways in which it is used, and it would be very wrong to equate *provision* with *curriculum*. It is what we *do*, or, more importantly, what the *children* do, with the environment which matters. Hartley describes two similar nursery buildings, each espousing broadly similar intentions for their physical organisation: 'To be structured so they (the children) can be unstructured' and 'The freedom to control themselves' (Hartley 1993: 63). In practice, their appearance, and what went on in both, was quite different. Van Liempd looks at the links between what she describes as 'pedagogical vision' (2005: 16) and the environment, in settings in the Netherlands. Different pedagogical visions, and the ways in which the physical environment reflected these, had an impact on the extent to which children made free use of the space, and the amount of their play with other children, particularly those from other groups in the setting.

The central importance of the environment is recognised in the *Statutory Framework for the Early Years Foundation Stage* (EYFS) (DCSF 2008a), where 'Enabling Environments' is identified as one of four Themes, along with 'A Unique Child', 'Positive Relationships' and 'Learning and Development'. The *Practice Guidance* document asserts that 'The environment plays a key role in supporting and extending children's development and learning' (DCSF 2008b: 5), by facilitating observation, assessment and planning, providing support for every child's learning and development, and contributing to the successful delivery of the five *Every Child Matters* (DfES 2003) outcomes. Practitioners in Reggio Emilia regard space as the 'third educator', and an active force with the capacity to support children's emotional, physical and intellectual development (Edwards *et al.* 1998). The potential exists, then, for the physical setting to have a positive impact upon the children in it. By implication the converse is also possible: the physical features of the places in which young children are expected to live and learn can lead to poorer quality for them (Stephen and Wilkinson 1995).

Undoubtedly (and unfortunately) some aspects of these environments can be beyond our power to change. Practitioners may work in purpose-built centres with sufficient indoor and outdoor space, good equipment and appropriate furnishings. On the other hand, many may find themselves in 'hand-me-down' (Rinaldi 1998) rooms converted for use with young children, with no outdoor space, toilets a long trek away, and poor equipment and furnishings. A seemingly poor environment, however, can never be an excuse for offering poor quality to the children. Here I look at the ways in which we can make the most of the spaces we do have, to provide a 'provocative environment' (Tovey 2007: 64) in which adults and children alike can live and work happily, and which has a positive impact upon each child's development. As Moss and Petrie describe it: a 'place(s) where things *happen*' (2002: 110). While you are reading, you may find it useful to think about settings with which you are familiar, looking particularly at what seem to be the underlying assumptions and beliefs about teaching, learning and the care of young children.

Why do we need to plan our environment?

The chief reason we need to consider how early years settings are physically organised is one which underpins all aspects of working with young children, that what we do should never become 'a standard practice beyond . . . reflection' (Hartley 1993: 66). This is particularly important when considering the organisation of space and resources, because the 'givens' (Wood *et al.* 1980) are so many. Opportunities to alter the physical construction of buildings are rare, and money for equipment may be very limited. All this can lead us towards focusing on limitations rather than possibilities: 'I can't do that, because . . .', rather than 'how can I do that?' This implies the importance of continued reappraisal of the environment, and its appropriateness for the children concerned and their needs and interests. For example, the needs of four-year-old children in a nursery or Reception class are different to those of one-year-old children in a nursery setting, or six-year-olds in a Key Stage 1 class, and organisation must reflect these differences. Gandini describes the ways in which settings in Reggio Emilia provide more opportunities for 'closeness and nurturing exchanges' (1998: 175) for the youngest children, while the spaces for older children may be left more open for play with blocks, toy animals and recycled materials. This should not, though, be taken to mean that children should necessarily be segregated by age, or by perceived competence. As MacNaughton and Williams point out, grouping children of 'mixed age and/or mixed ability' (2004: 20) may enhance all children's learning.

Some features of learning and young children

What must always drive this reappraisal are our aims for the children in our care, our beliefs about what will be most appropriate for them, and about the nature of learning. What, then, do we know about how young children learn? Gura describes what she calls 'the two contexts of learning', commenting that arrangements must acknowledge both the inner, or individual context, and the outer, or social context, of learning: 'They interpenetrate and together make up the human experience of learning' (Gura 1996: 149). This identifies learning as a social process (Vygotsky 1978), and suggests the need for an environment which facilitates children's efforts as social beings. Reggio Children and the Domus Academy Research Center emphasise that the environment 'must be conceived and constructed as a place of action' (1998: 119). Looked at together, these ideas imply a need to ensure that young children have opportunities to be physically and mentally active, in an environment which facilitates social interaction (MacNaughton and Williams 2004) and collaboration with others, both adults and children, as well as offering them opportunities to be alone.

Whitebread and Cottman (2008) emphasise the importance of developing skills of self-regulation, sometimes referred to as metacognition, in young children, saying that these are 'crucial to becoming an effective learner' (2008: 26). Tizard and Hughes (2002) suggest that what characterises young children is their relative ignorance and a limited conceptual framework with which to organise their experience and thought. These two ideas highlight the importance of providing a wide range of experiences which support and extend children's own interests, and of supporting their independence in exploring and organising those experiences. In so doing, it is worth bearing in mind that young children may often learn most from self-chosen play activities (Siraj-Blatchford *et al*. 2002). The *Practice Guidance for the Early Years Foundation Stage* emphasises the place of play as underpinning 'all development and learning for young children' (DCSF 2008b: 7), and identifies the crucial role of the practitioner in planning and resourcing an environment which 'extends and develops children's language and communication in their play' (2008b: 7). These points represent a consensus that the quality of opportunities young children have for both play and talk will be crucial, and that these two are the chief vehicles by which young children learn. The environment, then, must offer high-quality opportunities for children to be playful and engage in play, alone and with others, and to communicate and interact with a range of talk partners.

Alongside these cognitive aspects, the social, emotional and physical development of young children are all concerns for the professionals working with them, and will be reflected in the provision made. Vecchi cites research conducted at the Diana School in Reggio Emilia, which found that 'children incessantly seek out relationships with their peers' (1998: 130), and aims of developing children's capacity to share, and to collaborate with others, for example, will affect the organisation. Other aims may be more specific to particular centres or places. Moss and Petrie cite the Swedish pre-school curriculum which foregrounds democracy, and emphasises 'the foundation for a growing responsibility and interest on the part of children to participate actively in society' (Swedish Ministry of Education and Science 1998: 6, cited in Moss and Petrie 2002: 152).

The *EYFS* summarises the place of the environment in promoting children's 'physical, mental and emotional health and wellbeing' (DCSF 2008a: 10). Moss and Petrie go further, in asserting that 'children's spaces' should be seen as 'environments of many possibilities – cultural and social, but also economic, political, ethical, aesthetic, physical' (Moss and Petrie 2002: 9).

How do children 'read' the environment?

What of the children themselves? Arrangements of time and space, and the presence or absence of adults in particular areas, send messages to the children, telling them about what is sanctioned and prized in the setting, about relationships, and about the valuing of self and others. Dudek quotes a nursery headteacher: 'The whole site says something to the children: that we think they are important' (Dudek 2000: 23). Children's capacity to make sense of these messages and to grasp the organisational procedures of the setting will condition their access to the learning opportunities within it. Writing about a Reception class, Brooker describes how those children who were already familiar with the kinds of toys, games and tasks on offer when they started were more able to access the learning opportunities of the setting. Those children from less 'school-like' homes (Brooker 2002: 111) or with limited experience of a mainstream pre-school environment, were more at risk of being seen as 'unprepared and unready for school' (2002: 111), with potentially lasting consequences.

Settings, and the ways in which we organise them, then, have an effect on all of those within them. Pascal provides a poignant reminder that it can affect not just what children do, but, importantly, how they feel, in her record of a teacher's comment:

> I have just moved with a group of children from the nursery class to the reception class and the difference was so dramatic. Gone was the wonderful space, the large apparatus, jigsaws, construction toys . . . I felt frustrated and disappointed – can you imagine how the children felt?
> (Pascal 1990: 23)

The environment is, of course, ultimately the totality of children's experience in a setting, but in order to look closely it can be considered in particular areas, beginning with safety and security.

Safety and security

The first consideration in looking at the possibilities and constraints of the space available is to ensure children's safety and security. Outside, for example, are all exits secure? Is large climbing apparatus in good repair? Inside, are electrical sockets covered? Do radiators have guards on them? Are all floor coverings well maintained? Regular reappraisals of the space, with safety and security in mind, are vital, alongside the formal risk assessments required, at least annually, as part of the *Statutory Framework for the Early Years Foundation Stage* (DCSF 2008a). The *Practice Guidance for the Early Years Foundation Stage* (DCSF 2008b: 20–21) includes a helpful list of key areas to consider as part of a risk assessment.

However, as Tovey (2007) stresses, the word 'risk' is itself problematic, and often seen as synonymous with danger, and it may be helpful to distinguish between ideas of 'risk' and 'hazard'. Supporting children in taking risks, both physical and mental, in their play, helps them to develop vital expertise in both assessing and managing risk in everyday life, to extend their learning, and to develop the 'mastery' (Dweck 2000) associated with effective learners, as well as supporting emotional wellbeing and resilience (Tovey 2007). The consultation document, *Fair Play: A consultation on the play strategy*, stresses the importance of not trying to remove all risk from children's play, describing taking, and learning how to manage, risks, as 'an essential part of growing up' (DCSF and DCMS 2008c: 3). Helping children to develop confidence and competence in operating in their environment, and in using equipment of all kinds, is an important responsibility for adults working with them. Children's competence in handling woodwork tools, for example, often surprises those working with older children. As a message about the capabilities of young children it is hard to beat.

Appraising the environment

It will be necessary to be clear about the possibilities of the space available and to appraise the worth of equipment, relying neither on the fact that a particular resource is already there, nor on an idea that something is so 'taken for granted as essential' (Broadhead 2004: 7) that we cannot *not* have it. Goldschmied and Jackson suggest the value of a meeting for all who use a particular space, where the theme is 'What I would like to keep in this room and what I would like to get rid of' (2004: 27). Children can, and should, be part of such a meeting, and their involvement in this decision-making signals our awareness of 'the important part played by the children's own views and ideas, both in shaping practice and in supporting adults' and children's understanding' (Robson 2006: 101). Swedish pre-schools see children's participation in decision-making processes of all kinds as an important criterion for high quality (Sheridan 2007). The Mosaic Approach (Clark and Moss 2001), and subsequent work by Clark (2005), has focused on making young children's perspectives more visible, and positions children as active meaning-makers rather than passive receivers. The outcomes of this close 'listening' can be revealing, challenging adults' conceptions about what children are interested in, and the places and spaces they both actively enjoy and dislike. Rogers and Evans sum this up: 'by listening to young children and observing how they navigate through the many organisational factors that shape their play we may be in a better position to make changes to our environments' (2006: 53).

In these ways, both children and adults, including parents as recommended in the *EYFS* (DCSF 2008a), have the capacity to act upon the environment, and, in turn, for that environment to have an impact upon them (Reggio Children and Domus Academy Research Center 1998).

Arranging space

If the physical environment is to effectively support children's all-round development, we shall need to consider all types of experience. Citing evidence from neuroscience research about our perceptual and cognitive development, Zini (2005) emphasises that we need to think not just about physical positioning, but also about the ways in which the environment provides opportunities to nurture children's sight, hearing, touch, taste and smell. These 'design tools' (Reggio Children and Domus Academy Research Center 1998) are an integral part of the physical environment, and underpin the decisions we make about it.

Many settings opt for an arrangement of both indoor and outdoor space into distinct areas, for example a role play area, small and large construction, malleable materials, sand and water, and so on. Harms *et al.* (1998) refer to these as 'interest centers' (sic). What may be most important is to see the space, both inside and out, as flexible, with the potential for combination and connection across areas, as well as within each area. One feature of successful learning is the capability to transfer knowledge and understanding from one domain of knowledge to another, and the making of useful connections between ideas, deepening and extending thinking as a result (Athey 2007). If we wish to develop such competence in young children, a material provision which reflects this flexibility is vital, and too great an emphasis on particular types of play occurring in 'designated areas' (Tovey 2007: 59) may constrain the thinking and actions of both children and adults. This flexibility extends also to resources within spaces, which should provide opportunities for children to make their own meaning, and to transform elements such as blocks, fabric, and boxes in their play. Broadhead comments on the impact that provision of such 'whatever you want it to be' (2004: 73) places had on the children's collaboration and cooperation. In addition, this type of resourcing may support the development of children's theory of mind, metacognition and linguistic competence, as they negotiate with others about what such play areas will become (Robson 2006).

There are, of course, elements which are fixed – floor areas may be a combination of fixed carpet and tiling, and outdoor sand areas, for example, cannot be moved. These elements, however, are important in providing a sense of place for the children (Tovey 2007), providing familiarity within a broader structure that includes changes of physical organisation to suit the needs of the children as they develop. What may be most useful is to consider the space available as a range of different areas, some 'specialised' (Zini 2005: 23) and others generic. The space may be ordered partly according to helpful 'housekeeping' criteria (there are, after all, very good reasons for siting art areas near a sink and on an easily cleaned floor surface), and partly with a view to facilitating interesting associations and creative transformations of materials. Thus, physical proximity of areas, for example, home corners and block play areas, may enrich children's play through the combination of materials from both, but children should also feel freedom to move a whole range of materials and equipment about, to suit their purposes.

A 'transparent structure' (Hutt *et al.* 1989: 230) which encourages neither the children nor the adults involved to view spaces in rigid terms may be most desirable. Hutt and colleagues conclude that, where rigidity was a feature, children's play tended to be more stereotypical, and less innovative. The dry sand and water trays, for example, they found to be places where children could, essentially, be alone. Play was usually in parallel, and 'one can shut out some of the hustle and bustle endemic to nurseries' (Hutt *et al.* 1989: 98). There is, of course, a need for quiet niches in the nursery, where children can be alone if they so choose. However, to see an element of provision such as the dry sand as a haven of solitude may not be using it to its full potential.

Thinking about outdoors

In the early years, the indoor and outdoor environments can, and should, both be seen as one environment, with 'no firm distinction between indoors and out' (McLean 1991: 71), and, indeed, much blurring between the two, with the inclusion of 'filter' spaces such as porches and canopies, and interior courtyards (Reggio Children and Domus Academy Research Center 1998). However, outdoors also offers unique opportunities for play and activities of all kinds that are either not available indoors, such as digging, running or riding bikes, or which offer more physical and mental freedom than indoors, such as large-scale sand and water play. Swinging from a rope or climbing to the top of an outdoor climbing frame literally gives children a different perspective on the world, not available indoors. There is also much evidence to suggest that children play with materials differently, depending upon whether it is indoors or outdoors (Broadhead 2004). The *Statutory Framework for the Early Years Foundation Stage* stresses that access to an outdoor area is the 'expected norm' (DCSF 2008a: 35). In so doing, they are not only emphasising the physical, cognitive and affective benefits of outdoor play, but also acknowledging its importance for children. The DCSF and DCMS (2008c) cite research from Playday (www.playday.co.uk) which showed that 80 percent of children surveyed said that they preferred to play outside. In talking to children throughout the primary age range, Titman (1994) found that children of all ages sought a broadly similar range of opportunities from the outdoor environment: 'a place for *doing* . . . a place for *thinking* . . . a place for *feeling* . . . a place for *being*' (her emphasis) (58). She adds one other quality, too: 'In addition, and of over-riding importance perhaps, was the need for school grounds to be "a place for fun"!' (58).

Alongside the potential of outdoor spaces for young children's development, there are other reasons why opportunities for them to play outside at school may be important, more now perhaps than ever before. Increased fears about traffic and danger from strangers mean that parents are reluctant to allow their children to play outside. Three-quarters of parents feel that their children are more at risk today than they were five years ago when playing outdoors in public spaces (DCSF and DCMS 2008c). As a consequence, children are often obliged to play indoors, with sedentary activities such as watching the television and playing computer games, affording children less opportunity for physical exercise, for learning about their environment, and for social interaction. These same parental fears have led to even less independence for children, as more and more parents take them, often by car, to and from school and other activities. The consequent implications for their physical health and mental wellbeing (Tovey 2007) are clear. So, the availability of richly provisioned, challenging outdoor space in a setting is a real priority. Tovey (2007) summarises a clear rationale for the provision of outdoor play, and the unique opportunities it affords. However, as she emphasises, the quality of these opportunities is conditioned by the quality of the physical provision made. She suggests that a challenging and creative outdoor environment needs to include 'designated and connected spaces; elevated spaces; wild spaces; spaces for exploring and investigating; spaces for mystery and enchantment; natural spaces; spaces for the imagination; spaces for movement and stillness; social spaces; (and) fluid spaces' (2007: 59).

Freedom of access

Implicit in this sort of organisation is freedom of access for children, with opportunities for them to develop autonomy and a sense of control. Gura (1996) comments on the provision in nurseries in Reggio Emilia of low 'sleep nests' for babies and toddlers, containing their own belongings, into which they can crawl, by themselves, to take a nap. Older children can be helped to take responsibility for themselves, making decisions and selecting resources as they need them. So, materials, equipment and all areas of the setting, both indoor and out, need, as far as possible to be freely accessible to children at all times. Pragmatically, such an approach may minimise the number of low level demands made upon adults, to service requests for materials (McLean 1991), may support appropriate behaviour (Moyles 2007), and develop children's capacity for self-regulation (Whitebread and Coltman 2008).

In practice, staff attitudes will condition children's feelings of 'permission' to use equipment, timetables will need to ensure uninterrupted time for children to complete activities, and materials and equipment will need to be stored in such a way that children can retrieve what they need when they need it and put it back ready for someone else. Shelves and containers clearly labelled (with words and pictures), at child height can contribute to this independence. The attitudes of adults in supporting children in taking on responsibility will be crucial to the development of children's autonomy.

Organising time

Time is an important resource which needs to be considered with the same care as any other aspect of provision. Children's time in settings is often fragmented as a result of being called away to complete an adult-directed activity (Brooker 2002), but also by organisational aspects outside their, and sometimes practitioners', control. Children may not start an activity knowing, from past experience, that they will not have the chance to complete it because of the restricted time available. Gura (1992) comments on the way in which a 'hit and run' attitude developed amongst the children where lack of time prevented them from embarking on sustained play over time.

If children are to feel enabled to take on challenges, and to sustain their interest over a long period, then they will need to have the opportunity for continuous uninterrupted activity, and to know that this will be possible. This includes opportunities to carry on with an activity or project from one day to another, and the confidence of practitioners in not 'push(ing) for immediate results' (Edwards *et al.* 1998: 170). As with physical space, flexibility will be vital. While routines, and a measure of predictability, are important for children's feelings of security and understanding of events, it is important to ensure that these do not become 'routinous' (Moyles 2007: 176). Polakow (1992) points to the potential dangers of an overly-rigid approach to time: feelings of dependency on teacher authority and learned helplessness on the part of the children, and potential problems for both children and adults when there are deviations from the established routines.

Equal opportunities: access to the classroom

All professionals working with young children have an obligation to ensure equality of opportunity, access and participation for all children. One factor which will condition the ways in which such aims can be realised is the quality and type of material provision made, to ensure that all children have access to the events of the setting, and to counter stereotyping and prejudice. A wide range of resources, representing and respecting cultural diversity and not supportive of stereotypes of race, gender, class and disability is one element of this provision, but it must be complemented by the ways in which that provision is used. For example, much research (Browne and Ross 1991, Hutt *et al.* 1989) points to the attraction of different types of activities for boys and girls, with consequent effects upon practitioners' perceptions of their maturity, adjustment to school, and behaviour. Vecchi (1998) also found that boys tended to be more 'nomadic' in their play than girls. All of this has implications for the ways in which practitioners position and resource activities, and their own presence or absence in areas. MacNaughton and Williams (2004) suggest the placing and combining of materials that disrupt the 'normal' placement of materials, as well as use of images that challenge children's perceptions and understandings.

The culture of the setting will need to encompass many viewpoints and experiences if all children are to derive most benefit from it, and to feel a sense of belonging and ownership.

Conclusion

This chapter stresses the importance of the physical environment. It points out that:

- practitioners' beliefs about and aims for young children's learning and development are visible in the way the environment is organised;
- the environment can facilitate learning and development or conversely foster a 'learned helplessness';
- there is a need for versatile materials and spaces which extend children's understanding and imaginations and which can be adapted to their needs.

It concludes that only by providing a quality environment for children can we hope to ensure a quality experience for them, and thus have high quality expectations of them.

References

Athey, C. (2007) *Extending Thought in Young Children*. London: Paul Chapman.

Broadhead, P. (2004) *Early Years Play and Learning*. London: RoutledgeFalmer.

Brooker, L. (2002) *Starting School – Young Children Learning Cultures*. Buckingham: Open University Press.

Browne, N. and Ross, C. (1991) *Science and Technology in the Early Years*. Milton Keynes: Open University Press.

Clark, A. (2005) *Spaces to Play*. London: National Children's Bureau.

Clark, A. and Moss, P. (2001) *Listening to Young Children: The Mosaic Approach*. London: National Children's Bureau and Joseph Rowntree Foundation.

Cohen, B. (2005) 'Whose space is it anyway?', *Children in Europe*, 8: 2–3.

Department for Children, Schools and Families (DCSF) (2008a) *Statutory Framework for the Early Years Foundation Stage*. Nottingham: DCSF Publications.

Department for Children, Schools and Families (DCSF) (2008b) *Practice Guidance for the Early Years Foundation Stage*. Nottingham: DCSF Publications.

Department for Children, Schools and Families (DCSF) and Department for Culture, Media and Sport (DCMS) (2008c) *Fair Play. A Consultation on the Play Strategy*. Nottingham: DCSF Publications.

Department for Education and Skills (DfES) (2003) *Every Child Matters*. London: DfES.

Dudek, M. (2000) (2nd edn) *Kindergarten Architecture: Space for the Imagination*. London: E & F N Spon.

Dweck, C.S. (2000) *Self-Theories: Their Role in Motivation, Personality and Development*. Hove, East Sussex: Psychology Press.

Edwards, C., Gandini, L. and Forman, G. (eds) (1998) (2nd edn) *The Hundred Languages of Children*. Westport, Connecticut and London: Ablex.

Gandini, L. (1998) 'Educational and Caring Spaces', in C. Edwards, L. Gandini and G. Forman (eds) *The Hundred Languages of Children*. Westport, Connecticut and London: Ablex.

Goldschmied, E. and Jackson, S. (2004) (2nd edn) *People Under Three. Young Children in Daycare*. London: Routledge.

Gura, P. (ed) (1992) *Exploring Learning: Young Children and Blockplay*. London: Paul Chapman.

Gura, P. (1996) 'An entitlement curriculum for early childhood' in S. Robson and S. Smedley (eds) *Education in Early Childhood*. London: David Fulton in Association with the Roehampton Institute.

Harms, T., Clifford, R.M. and Cryer, D. (1998) *Early Childhood Environment Rating Scale*. New York: Teacher's College Press.

Hartley, D. (1993) *Understanding the Nursery School*. London: Cassell.

Hutt, J., Tyler, S., Hutt, C. and Christopherson, H. (1989) *Play, Exploration and Learning: A Natural History of the Preschool*. London: Routledge.

MacNaughton, G. and Williams, G. (2004) *Teaching Young Children. Choices in Theory and Practice*. Maidenhead: Open University Press.

McLean, S. Vianne (1991) *The Human Encounter: Teachers and Children Living Together in Preschools*. London: Falmer Press.

McMillan, M. (1930) *The Nursery School*. London: J.M. Dent.

Moss, P. and Petrie, P. (2002) *From Children's Services to Children's Spaces*. London: RoutledgeFalmer.

Moyles, J. (2007) (3rd edn) *Beginning Teaching Beginning Learning*. Maidenhead: Open University Press.

Pascal, C. (1990) *Under Fives in the Infant Classroom*. Stoke-on-Trent: Trentham Books.

Polakow, V. (1992) *The Erosion of Childhood*. Chicago: University of Chicago Press.

Reggio Children and Domus Academy Research Center (1998) *Children, Spaces, Relations*. Reggio Emilia: Reggio Children.

Rinaldi, C. (1998) 'The space of childhood', in Reggio Children and Domus Academy Research Center (1998) *Children, Spaces, Relations*. Reggio Emilia: Reggio Children, 114–120.

Robson, S. (2006) *Developing Thinking and Understanding in Young Children*. London: Routledge.

Rogers, S. and Evans, J. (2006) 'Playing the Game? Exploring Role Play from Children's Perspectives', *European Early Childhood Education Research Journal*, 14(1): 43–55.

Sheridan, S. (2007) 'Dimensions of pedagogical quality in preschool', *International Journal of Early Years Education*, 15(2): 197–217.

Siraj-Blatchford, I., Sylva, K., Muttock, S., Gilden, R. and Bell, D. (2002) *Researching Effective Pedagogy in the Early Years*. London: DfES.

Stephen, C. and Wilkinson, J.E. (1995) 'Assessing the quality of provision in community nurseries', *Early Child Development and Care,* 108: 83–98.

Titman, W. (1994) *Special Places; Special People: The Hidden Curriculum of School Grounds*. Toronto: Green Brick Road.

Tizard, B. and Hughes, M. (2002) (2nd edn) *Young Children Learning*. Oxford: Blackwell.

Tovey, H. (2007) *Playing Outdoors*. Maidenhead: Open University Press.

van Liempd, I. (2005) 'Making use of space: theory meets practice', *Children in Europe*, 8: 16–17.

Vecchi, V. (1998) 'What kind of space for living well in school?', in Reggio Children and Domus Academy Research Center, *Children, Spaces, Relations*. Reggio Emilia: Reggio Children, 128–35.

Vygotsky, L. (1978) *Mind in Society*. Cambridge, MA: Harvard University Press.

Whitebread, D. and Coltman, P. (eds) (2008) (3rd edn) *Teaching and Learning in the Early Years*. London: Routledge.

Wood, D., McMahon, L. and Cranstoun, Y. (1980) *Working with Under Fives*. London: Grant McIntyre.

Zini, M. (2005) 'See, hear, touch, taste, smell and love', *Children in Europe*, 8: 22–4.

Chapter 23

The future of childhood

Jennie Lindon

In this short chapter Jennie Lindon highlights the growing concern that children and their environments are becoming too safe for their own good. She argues that children need to be enabled to take risks within a caring environment that offers support if needed. The author identifies strategies for early years practitioners to encourage children to learn about risk-taking so that they can become competent and confident learners.

Children matter. Their emotional wellbeing is of importance to every member of society, not just their own families, because children are a vital and irreplaceable resource for everybody's future.

Children are not babies for ever, any more than they remain members of a nursery or primary school community. We need to remember that for each individual child an important point of their childhood – their own positive outcome of those years – is that they are enabled to emerge as competent and confident adults.

Let children take risks

Children's learning has to be grounded in their own personal, social and emotional development. Their ability to continue to learn rests on the development of a positive view of themselves as people who can learn, who can deal with mistakes or setbacks and draw on the support of adults who care about them as individuals. Helpful adults do not shield children from all risk, whether this is physical, emotional or intellectual. Children need to explore new experiences in order to extend their skills of problem solving, planning and reflection. They learn a great deal through play but play is definitely not their only medium for learning. Children and young people want to learn from adults who share their own skills, both in a specific practical how-to-do-this context and in more general ways, such as talking around a problem or voicing feelings.

There is a growing concern that our approach to children and young people in the UK is too much on the side of identification and avoidance of problems rather than supporting children to develop a sense of competence in the face of the normal ups and downs of life. Children cannot develop properly in an environment in which adults look only to the short term and to what could go wrong.

The Mental Health Foundation's report *Bright Futures: Promoting Children and Young People's Mental Health* (1999) addressed the need for adults to consider a positive sense of mental health and not just the absence of specific problems. The report draws on the research into *resilience* that emerged from American studies of children from disadvantaged backgrounds who overcame upromising early circumstances. The insights from these studies, as well as the ideas of children learning a *mastery* rather than a *helplessness* orientation, alert us to our adult role in helping children to learn positive skills and outlooks, rather than a focus on children as passive victims whom adults have to protect.

Children need to be enabled to take risks within a caring environment that offers support if they need it. Risks will sometimes be within the arena of physical skills, but they are just as often within emotional and intellectual learning. Children's lives are full of puzzling new ideas and the possibility of making mistakes. The children who develop resilience towards everyday adversity seem to share experience in the following areas:

- They have a secure attachment to parents and other consistent carers. So their learning can be grounded in relationships that last over time.
- Children learn step-by-step a problem-solving approach which boosts their confidence that initial difficulties with skills or in relationships can be resolved.
- They grow in their broad communication skills, enabling them to express concerns, to reflect and to share happy experiences with people whom they trust to be interested in them and not to belittle any difficulties.
- What important adults say to and do with children enables them to develop a 'can-do' approach that is realistic. Adults offer constructive feedback that helps children to work out what has gone awry. Helpful adults do not simply drench children in unconditional praise that fails to help them to address mistakes or struggles. Children gain in confidence and a sense of competence that they can, with help if they wish, face and deal with situations in which the answer is not obvious.

Learning from adults' experience

The final goal of childhood is to emerge as a competent and confident adult. Adults need to consider how best to share their grown-up skills, experience and insights with children.

Step-by-step coaching

Coaching is a way of supporting children's learning of any life skills, especially those in which there are safety implications. The idea of coaching children is positive because it locates adult expertise in specific areas rather than depending on an image of adults who always know more than the children. As children grow older, they soon have areas of expertise, knowledge and specific skills that they can share, in their turn, with adults.

The relationship of coaching, skill sharing and exchange of knowledge can become a pleasurable two-way process.

Tell-show-do

The essence of coaching, so that children can learn as well as possible, has been summed up as 'tell-show-do'.

- *Tell* children what you are doing and explain why, as and when this is appropriate. Describe your actions in words and phrases that are simple enough for these children. Be prepared to explain again or several times, if necessary.
- *Show* children clearly what you mean through demonstration. Children need to see how to do something and be able to make a clear link between what you say and do.
- Give children an opportunity to *do* it themselves, as soon as you have completed 'tell' and 'show'. Encourage them to ask for help as and when they want. Offer guidance as they wish . . .

Encouragement and constructive feedback

Children will gain in skills and satisfaction far more effectively if adults offer plenty of encouragement with constructive and accurate feedback. Encourage children with the following approaches:

- Acknowledgement of children's efforts that does not always focus on the end-product. Children learn from 'well done' for what they have managed so far, as this acknowledges the fact that they had the sense to come and ask for more help and another explanation.
- Warm words of encouragement will help a child to persevere or to try another method. You might say: 'You've done really well so far, let's see how you've got stuck here' or 'I can see you're frustrated, let's see if it will work this way.'
- Children are encouraged by appropriate compliments from adults such as: 'I'm so pleased I can trust you all to do this on your own' or 'That's worked so well: I wouldn't have thought of doing it this way.'
- Constructive feedback works alongside encouragement by providing honest and accurate information to the children. Children do not benefit from being given indiscriminate praise or actually told something is 'fine' when it is not. When children realise that things have not gone right, but an adult is still saying 'lovely', then the child loses confidence in that adult's judgement . . .

Children can learn if you 'tell-show-do' about any safety implications . . .

- Share useful tips and techniques in how to do a practical activity. Children can learn a great deal through discovery but it is unhelpful to leave them to reinvent the wheel, when there are tried and tested ways to undertake an activity.
- Good technique is also likely to be safer as well as leading to a more satisfying end-product for children. You might say, 'It works better if you do little sawing movements

like this . . .' or 'This kind of sewing goes up and down again into the material. It doesn't go over the side.'

- Take opportunities as they arise to be explicit about safety but obviously don't overdo the message. You risk losing children's attention through excessive repetition or by harping on possible dangers rather than practical approaches such as 'This will work better if we . . .' or 'I've found this is a good way to . . .'

Raising children is a long term project in which ideally children's own parents will provide the essential continuity as the years of childhood pass into adolescence. Early years practitioners of all backgrounds have an essential role to play over those months or years, when you share with parents the care and learning of their children. You have a responsibility to ensure that the children are indeed safe enough in your setting. However, you have an equally strong responsibility that children are enabled to experience and negotiate challenges appropriate to their age and ability level.

Chapter 24

Creating contexts for professional development

Angela Anning and Anne Edwards

In this chapter Angela Anning and Anne Edwards report on a project involving collaborations between higher education, local authority officers and early years practitioners in creating an informal community of practice. They consider how this project enabled professional learning for the practitioners concerned, which in turn they argue, supports children's learning.

Times of change

[. . .]
An important feature of more recent policy, in the UK and elsewhere, has been to expect practitioners to work collaboratively across professional boundaries and to encourage them to work with the family networks which support children as well as with the children themselves. These expectations are leading to new forms of practice which have at their core the wellbeing and social inclusion of children. [. . .] These new forms of practice include the following features (Edwards 2004a):

- a focus on children and as whole people i.e. not as specific 'needs';
- following the child's trajectory overtime and across services;
- an ability to talk across professional boundaries;
- an understanding of what other practitioners are able to offer the responsive package of protection or care that is built around the child or young person;
- acknowledgement of the capacity of service users and their families to help to tailor the services they are receiving;
- an understanding that changing the life trajectories of children involves not only building confidence and skills but also a reconfiguring of the opportunities available to them through systems-wide change.

[. . .]
In this chapter we look at professional learning in a changing system: the learning of

individuals; the contexts in which their learning takes place; and what this learning means for practice, training and management. We use the term 'learning' rather than 'coping' not simply because we want to avoid the rather negative tone of coping, but also because we believe that dealing with change is a matter of simply learning something new and taking a positive approach to that learning. Even better is when they can communicate this excitement about learning to the children's parents or main carers. We are therefore optimistic that an area of provision that has expertise in helping children learn will also be good at helping adults learn. [. . .]

Sound quality interactions with adults are central to the development of children's dispositions to learn. It is a truism, but nonetheless a powerful one, that children learn to love learning through being with adults who also love to learn, and are themselves in contexts that encourage their learning. This truism, therefore, means that children deserve to be supported by adults who are driven by their own intellectual curiosity to understand their practice better. Children's learning, we would argue, is supported by a system that has the learning of both children and adults as a priority.

Supporting the learning of practitioners

In our project the learning goals for practitioners, like those for the children, focused on the *who* as much as on the *what* of learning and particularly on helping participants develop a capacity to interpret and respond to the learning opportunities available for children. The goals included:

- developing the capacity to see the educational potential in experiences shared with children;
- developing the capacity to respond to the demands they have identified as they work with children;
- developing dispositions for enquiry and learning;
- developing ways of seeing and being which draw on the professional expertise of early years practitioners.

Like children, adults learn best in safe and well-supported contexts where they are able to learn through a form of *guided participation* (Rogoff 1991). Guided participation is important because we are suggesting that enhancing professional practice is a question of learning to interpret familiar events in fresh ways and developing a repertoire of responses to new interpretations. Fresh interpretations and responses usually need to be modelled or guided and can seem quite risky. Interpretations might be wrong and responses may misfire. Practitioners need support if they are to persevere in changing their practices.

Support for practitioners' learning through guided participation occurred in two ways in the project:

1. collaboration between higher education, local authority officers and the key participants in Steps 1 and 2;
2. collaboration within settings on action research in Step 3.

During these *collaborations* practitioners' learning was supported by:

- the modelling of strategies with children by more expert practitioners – for example, when Mollie worked with children on mark-making and was observed by a colleague;
- discussions for planning and reviewing;
- joint data collection and analysis;
- shared frameworks for data collection – for example, observation schedules;
- a shared focus on children's learning in numeracy and literacy.

Practitioners' learning became evident in how they used language (for example, the idea of joint involvement episodes became central to several projects); and in how the familiar materials of pre-school provision took on new educational meanings. For example, the construction area became a site for children's early mark-making in one setting and their mathematical thinking and action in another.

In the structured and non-threatening learning contexts provided by the project, practitioners were able, in their discussions, to *appropriate* the frameworks and language of early learning shared in the workshops and readings. Similarly, while they worked with these new ideas with children they were able to identify the educational potential of familiar materials – such as how blocks and play people could be used together to develop children's use of mathematical language in a fantasy play context – and respond knowledgeably.

[. . .] Participants did not identify a need for new resources as a result of an increased emphasis on curricula. Instead, [. . .] existing materials were being given new (educational) meanings by practitioners. The changes appeared to be in the way the adults were interpreting events and responding while working with children. The professional learning that occurred through well-supported participation in new forms of practice seemed considerable. The adults learnt through developing new ideas, representations, or ways of thinking about familiar occurrences in project meetings. They then took these ideas into action in their action research projects. But like children, adults can only change their ways of thinking and acting in contexts that allow these changes to occur. Learning contexts for adults, therefore, need careful management.

Current work on educational settings as learning organizations

[. . .]

We intended that the project would give key participants experiences of frameworks for evidence-based practice which would help them develop their colleagues as practitioners. Our focus was therefore as much on the adults as learners as on the pupils. We were therefore also interested, as outsiders at least, in the settings as learning communities.

Louis *et al.* (1996), in a detailed study of teachers' professional communities identified five components which they found to be significant in schools as learning communities which in turn supported children as learners. These components were:

1. a shared sense of purpose;

2. a collective focus on pupil learning;
3. collaborative activity;
4. deprivatized activity;
5. reflective dialogues.

A shared sense of purpose takes time to achieve and cannot be imposed. Quite often a sense of coherent purpose only emerges in the processes of discussion and action as colleagues clarify exactly what they mean by, for example, the community values underpinning the work of a preschool centre. Fullan (1991, 1993) points out that one sign that change is not really happening is when people demonstrate 'false clarity' – for example, the rhetoric is spoken and accepted but the implications for practice are barely explored. Parental involvement is an area where false clarity is frequently seen. False clarity is evident, for example, when parental involvement is discussed as a 'good thing' without anyone being clear about what they really think parents can do to help their children learn. In our study, [. . .] our colleagues took the time necessary to move way beyond any sense of false clarity in their work with parents and identified coherent rationales for parental involvement.

A collective focus on pupil learning allows the development of a professional dis-course which centres on the professional actions of colleagues as they create contexts and plan and evaluate actions taken to support children's learning. In our study two strong themes in the collective focus on children's learning were (i) detailed and clearly focused observations of how children were making sense of the opportunities available to them and (ii) careful consideration of how adults interacted with children while they engaged with the materials provided.

Collaborative activity is essential for the development of a professional discourse of multi-agency practice and the professional learning of practitioners. We have pro-posed that learning occurs as people take action and interpret and react to events in increasingly informed ways – i.e. as they become people who see and act differently. Knowledge, we have therefore argued, is constructed in action as well as in discussions of action. Collaborative activity was central to our study. [. . .]

Deprivatized activity links closely to both a collective focus on learning and taking action together. Compared with schools, most pre-school settings are well placed for ensuring that adults' activities are visible. What did have to be worked at was finding space for the open discussion of activities in which new practices were tried out or modelled. Key activities became the focus of frequent staff meetings in which areas for action were identified, strategies selected and the evidence gathered during the activities was discussed. Early childhood services in Reggio Emilia similarly emphasize deprivatized activity in the stress they place on documenting their work to ensure that their practices are visible to colleagues and parents (Edwards *et al*. 1993). These documents not only render expert practice visible but enable colleagues to respond more coherently to children.

Reflective dialogues, in which evidence either about the settings or action taken is discussed, encourage careful observation and analysis and the sharing of insights and information. But above all they ensure that the tacit expertise of professionals is revealed. [. . .] These conversations were the vehicles for knowledge exchange and joint knowledge construction and were carefully built into project planning in every step.

[. . .] However, there is evidence to suggest that supervisory practices which focus on professional issues, attend to the personal development of practitioners, emphasize the learning of individuals and groups and allow roles and practices to develop responsively are found in cultures usually described as developmental or learning (Hawkins and Shohet 1989). We would argue that supervisory systems for early education practitioners in many ways parallel key worker systems for children. Good quality supervision which focuses on how adults are helping children develop as learners and encourages reflective dialogue based on evidence and joint activities may prove to be one important driver of change in early years provision.

[. . .]

Working with other agencies

Let us look in a little more detail at how learning relationships were sustained through links between settings, other agencies, the community, adult education, higher education, parents, and other types of pre-school provision.

Speech therapy

Ivy's project involved her learning while working alongside speech therapists while Ivy herself guided the learning of the mothers on whom her project was focused. Ivy collaborated with speech therapists in devising a tightly focused learning programme for the mothers which aimed at developing their interaction skills with their children. [. . .] The speech therapists' specialist expertise, their experience in developing communication skills and their familiarity with the nursery were invaluable in both planning and carrying out the programme. The sessions with mothers operated as boundary zones where Ivy, therapists and mothers all focused on children and interactions with them, then mothers took those ideas back into their practices at home.

A local multicultural service

Bernie and Reza work for the multicultural services section of one of the collaborating local authorities. They were also project members who collaborated with teachers in two inner-city nurseries. Bernie's collaboration focused on number use. Working with a group of practitioners in one nursery, he was able to advise practitioners on how to make the most of the cultural strengths that the children, from up to 11 different ethnic backgrounds, brought to the nursery.

For Reza, the project allowed him to explore a long-held professional hunch: that children's musical experiences at home vary across ethnic groups and that this may have an impact on how they are able to engage with number-related learning experiences in nurseries. He collaborated with June, a nursery-based practitioner, and learnt through the interviews undertaken with parents at home about what the parents from a range of ethnic groupings thought about children's early number experiences at home and in the nursery, and how music was used within each home. Ideas from the home were brought into the school.

[. . .]

Partnership in early literacy

Meg and her staff at her children's centre on a large outer-city council estate had, for a long time, been keen to involve parents in supporting their children as learners. Meg started with an unstructured book loan scheme for the 3- and 4-year-olds which brought the parents into the centre to choose books with their children. Our advice was that Meg should work with the parents' strengths – i.e. the strong emotional links they have with their children and make sure that anything they asked parents to do was easily managed and was fun. We discussed nursery rhyme cards that we had seen in use in another project and Meg took up the idea.

Meg produced simple cards with rhymes on one side and suggestions on the reverse. These suggestions included actions to accompany the rhyme, help with finding familiar words in the rhyme, help on how to point to print and ideas for using the same sounds to make up your own rhymes. Parents shared their children's enjoyment with staff when they exchanged cards and appeared to have lost their earlier diffidence about how they might support their children as learners. It seemed that the book and card loan scheme with their realistic expectations broke a barrier between home and nursery that had been troubling Meg.

[. . .]

These brief outlines of several of the individual projects illustrate four key features found in each of them:

1. a coherent sense of purpose;
2. a strong sense of the possible;
3. an openness to new possibilities;
4. an openness to new relationships.

We would suggest that these features are essential in pre-school settings in order for them to deal with the rapidly changing contexts in which they are operating.

The project as a learning network

We designed the project with relationships very firmly in mind. New ways of thinking and acting could not be developed unless relationships across boundaries were possible and new forms of practical knowledge could be generated in joint action. We were influenced in our thinking by the idea of learning networks. We thought that networks would allow participants to bring together the best of current practice, refreshed by external insights, and develop understandings that would allow them to make informed decisions about future practice. In this section we therefore reflect how we operated as a network for learning.

We were aware that our roles as higher education-based researchers in the action research of settings-based practitioners, and in the project as a network, needed exploring. Elliott's (1994) work on teachers' knowledge and action research reminds us of the place of theory and the role of higher education in action research networks. He argues that the ideas of theorists don't threaten practitioners if these ideas can be translated into concrete curriculum proposals that can be scrutinized in action by practitioners who then decide what should be ultimately absorbed into practice.

Action research, he suggests, gives the university-based 'theorist' a role as supplier of theoretical resources for practitioners to draw on when analysing and developing practice. However, he emphasizes that the practitioner is the ultimate judge of what is useful knowledge. [. . .]

Elliott's summary of the role of university-based staff in teachers action research projects is a useful starting point. However, our project as a network did more than simply focus on how individual practitioners developed practical reasoning. Our role involved us in working at three organizational levels: the local authority, the pre-school setting and groups of practitioners. Key stakeholders in each of these levels were crucial to the success of the project and we could not have found ourselves with better collaborators. Each level in turn enabled the next. The senior local authority officers with whom we planned the project shared our vision and identified experienced and responsible stakeholders at the level of the settings and then did all they could to support the activities at settings level. The experienced settings-based staff became our research partners and, in turn, enabled the responsive activities of their colleagues as they worked with new strategies with children and with other agencies or parents.

This strong, multi-level commitment to the project then served as a sound basis for the learning network we established. Learning a new form of professional practice in the acts of practice can be highly challenging. [. . .] Part of the difficulty lies in the need to experience a destabilization of current understandings before new ones are recognized as necessary. The destabilizing can be professionally threatening when working publicly with children.

Going slowly was therefore essential. At Step 1 we gained agreement on (i) the purposes of the project and (ii) that we would work slowly from evidence gathered in the settings. During Step 1 we spent time at workshops, building relationships through sharing current understandings and concerns, and everyone visited each others' settings. We cannot overestimate the importance of the time taken to establish sound relationships across the network. At two residential meetings and workshops at Steps 2 and 3, participants provided each other with both enthusiastic interest in progress and informed support at times of glitch. Mutual support was an extremely important feature and gives us some confidence in the sustainability of the network we helped to establish.

Our roles changed over the duration of the project as the practitioners gained control of the presentation of knowledge in discussions and written texts.
[. . .]

Conceptual framings were increasingly represented in the contexts of practice by our research partners who appropriated the frameworks we shared and used them in discussions of practice. Experience sharing occurred regularly in workshops and, as we visited each setting, we carried information about developments from one setting to another and shared experiences and practical ideas we had gained elsewhere in similar projects. Help with observations came through advice on observational methods for both exploring practice and formatively assessing children Analysis of observations also occurred during our visits and in workshops. By Step 3, most settings were managing their own evaluations of their work in their own settings.

We saw the network as a set of overlapping communities of understanding, all with the interests of children as learners as a central concern. As researchers we belonged primarily to the research community. Our research partners were primarily practitioners, who themselves belonged to the communities of, for example, either care or education. The senior managers were led by the concerns of that role. We all brought a range of strengths and experiences to the project. We learnt from each other as we moved in and out of the overlapping communities, gathering information and sharing insights drawn from our particular expertise.

[. . .]

Contexts for the development of new forms of practice

An informed professional can only work responsively in a context that allows this to happen. This does not mean that professionals are victims of the systems in which they find themselves operating. Neither does it mean that an individual in isolation can change a system and what is allowed to occur within it. Early years practitioners, working together, need to see the possibilities for informed responsive action that are available to them in their settings, and use those possibilities. They need to talk about what they are doing and why they are doing it and so take responsibility for the generation of their own knowledge base.

The development of practice will depend upon the continuous development, in action, of a common store of practical knowledge that is itself constantly open to scrutiny. Such scrutiny can only occur in a professional climate that encourages the confidence to value openness and collaboration across boundaries of profession and location so that the best interests of children are served.

References

Desforges, C. (1995) How does experience affect theoretical knowledge for teaching? *Learning and Instruction*, 5 (4): 385–400.

Edwards, A. (2004) The new multi-agency working: collaborating to prevent the social exclusion of children and families, *Journal of Integrated Care*, 12 (5): 3–9.

Edwards, C., Gandini, L. and Forman, G. (eds) (1993) *The Hundred Languages of Children: The Reggio Emilia Approach to Early Childhood Education*. Norwood, NJ: Ablex Publishing Company.

Elliott, J. (1994) Research on teachers' knowledge in action research, *Educational Action Research*, 2 (1): 133–7.

Fullan, M. (1991) *The New Meaning of Educational Change*. London: Cassell.

Fullan, M. (1993) *Change Forces*. London: Falmer.

Hawkins, P. and Shohet, R. (1989) *Supervision in the Helping Professions*. Buckingham: Open University Press.

Louis, K.S., Marks, H. and Kruse, S. (1996) Teachers' professional communities in restructuring schools, *American Educational Research Journal*, 33 (4): 757–98.

Rogoff, B. (1991) Social interaction as apprenticeship in thinking: guided participation in spatial planning, in L. Resnick, J. Levine and S. Teasley (eds) *Perspectives on Socially Shared Cognition*. Washington: APA.

Index